T0302123

The Growth of Shadow Banking

The "Shadow Banking System" refers to a system of credit provision occurring outside of the official regulatory perimeter of commercial banks. Facilitated by securitization vehicles, mutual funds, hedge funds, investment banks, and mortgage companies, the function and regulation of these shadow banking institutions have come under increasing scrutiny after the subprime crisis of 2007–8. Matthias Thiemann examines how regulators came to tolerate the emergence of links between the banking and shadow banking systems. Through a comparative analysis of the United States, France, the Netherlands, and Germany, he argues that fractured domestic and global governance systems determining the regulatory approach to these links ultimately aggravated the recent financial crisis. Since 2008, shadow banking has even expanded and the incentives for banks to bend the rules have only increased with increasing regulation. Thiemann's empirical work suggests how state–finance relations could be restructured to keep the banking system under state control and mitigate, if not avoid future financial collapses.

MATTHIAS THIEMANN is Assistant Professor at the Centre d'Études Européens, Sciences Po Paris.

The Growth of Shadow Banking

A Comparative Institutional Analysis

MATTHIAS THIEMANN
Centre d'Études Européens, Sciences Po Paris

CAMBRIDGE
UNIVERSITY PRESS

CAMBRIDGE
UNIVERSITY PRESS

University Printing House, Cambridge CB2 8BS, United Kingdom

One Liberty Plaza, 20th Floor, New York, NY 10006, USA

477 Williamstown Road, Port Melbourne, VIC 3207, Australia

314-321, 3rd Floor, Plot 3, Splendor Forum, Jasola District Centre, New Delhi - 110025, India

79 Anson Road, #06-04/06, Singapore 079906

Cambridge University Press is part of the University of Cambridge.

It furthers the University's mission by disseminating knowledge in the pursuit of education, learning and research at the highest international levels of excellence.

www.cambridge.org
Information on this title: www.cambridge.org/9781107161986
DOI: 10.1017/ 9781316676837

© Matthias Thiemann 2018

This publication is in copyright. Subject to statutory exception and to the provisions of relevant collective licensing agreements, no reproduction of any part may take place without the written permission of Cambridge University Press.

First published 2018

A catalogue record for this publication is available from the British Library

ISBN 978-1-107-16198-6 Hardback
ISBN 978-1-316-61416-7 Paperback

Cambridge University Press has no responsibility for the persistence or accuracy of URLs for external or third-party internet websites referred to in this publication, and does not guarantee that any content on such websites is, or will remain, accurate or appropriate.

To Karl and Katharina

Contents

Preface

As this book goes to press, there is an eerie calm in financial markets. Ten years after the first major turbulences in Western financial markets that heralded the beginning of the Great Financial Crisis, stock indexes are at all-time highs. After the seizure of 2008/2009, and a long tepid recovery, countries in the West have finally regained a growth momentum, which allows the International Monetary Fund (IMF) concurrently to provide an optimistic assessment for the near future (IMF 2017a). Large banks have been forced to recapitalize over the course of the last ten years, almost doubling their tier 1 capital (Vojtech 2017). In general, Basel III, the new global capital accord for banking regulation, is seen to be much stricter than its predecessors. Including a simplified leverage ratio (which limits the degree of borrowing banks can undertake and limits short-term debt), it allegedly makes the system much more resilient (Financial Stability Board 2017a). As the chair of the Financial Stability Board, Mark Carney, stated in rather self-congratulatory terms, "The fault lines of the crisis have been repaired. The financial system is now better supervised and regulated ... leaving a safer, simpler, and fairer financial system" (Carney 2017).

Yet, as the IMF points out, beneath this rosy picture, risks are lurking (IMF 2017b). Growth has come at the price of a further buildup of household debt; persistently low to negative interest rates have led to a search for yield, fueling the growth of speculative bubbles in different asset classes, including property prices in global cities such as New York, London, and Paris. Investment banks, particularly in the United States, have reached new peaks of profitability riding a wave of leveraged loan buyouts financed by collateralized loan obligations, structured debt products once described as toxic (Johnson 2017). New "nonbanks" have emerged and engage in lending to riskier, high-yield borrowers – while the banks stand behind financing them (Tett 2017). Overall, financialized capitalism, fueled by asset-led rather than demand-led growth, seems to have been restored and any intrusive change to finance averted (Arestis and Karakitsos 2013).

Arguably, this trend has been nowhere more evident than in the regulatory treatment of shadow banking, the provision of credit outside of banks' balance sheets but often involving banks after the financial crisis (Financial Stability Board 2011a). In the current official discourse, shadow banking is rebranded as "market-based finance" and is to be turned into resilient market-based finance by vigilant regulators, allowing further diversification of funding sources in a financial system seen as too dependent on banks (Carney 2014). Yet, in a glaring omission, no anticyclical regulations to contain booms emanating from that sector of the financial system have been created, nor are they forthcoming.[1]

It seems fair to say that we are witnessing a cyclical upswing, driven by finance, which, if no regulatory intervention occurs, will likely lead to another crisis. But far from that, the regulatory pendulum seems to have swung in favor of finance. This impression is reinforced by a US government seeking to undo much of the regulatory burden imposed after the financial crisis. As of October 2017, there are nineteen measures in front of the US Congress to revoke or lower postcrisis regulation (AFR 2017).[2] In Europe, in the context of the initiative for a capital markets union, simple, transparent, and standardized securitization is supposed to revive the market for asset-backed securities as an alternative, nonbank financing channel for Europe, deliberately ignoring the fact that securitization always involves banks. Innovative debt contracts are seen as a way to wean Europe off from its dependency on bank credit (Langfield and Pagano, 2016). This attempt to expand nonbank finance in the EU will be further encouraged by the new Basel III Accord, which will be applied to global as well as regional and local banks. Owing to their coarse measures, they will again align European policymakers and

---

[1] Indeed, a recent study in the United States found that US banking regulators had no means at their disposal to control a financial boom emanating from the shadow banking system and driven by house price appreciation, ironically exactly the factors that led to the last crisis (Adrian et al. 2015).

[2] One of them is the risk retention tool by banks issuing asset-backed securities, which is supposed to align the interests of issuers and investors by forcing issuers to have "skin in the game," that is, to share the losses if securitized loans default.

banks in their search for loopholes, to facilitate credit provision outside of the official balance sheets of banks, albeit being continuously
linked to them.

This recurrence of the same pattern could remain indifferent to the
populace at large, were it not for both the deleterious consequences
of the last financial crisis and the state of defense for the next one.
The bailing out of banks led to a ballooning of state debt, to which
most governments in the West reacted with a regime of austerity, in
the case of the EU imposed by Germany and its allies (Blyth 2014).
This wave was used to reduce welfare state provisions and stripped
many European policymakers of policy space for policies seeking to
foster social inclusion. On the other hand, central banks, acting as
lenders of last resort, bought up much of the debt produced during
the last upswing to cushion the economic busts. With the interest rate
at zero and with central banks already having large balance sheets,
the question is: Which tools will the central banks have available to
cushion the next crisis? If it is just more of the same, more quantitative easing that has benefited the rich overproportionately by inflating
their asset wealth and more austerity-imposed welfare curtailment,
the tensions within the social fabric will become even more difficult
to bear.

In that context, looking back and understanding the reasons for the
development of shadow banking, its contribution to the last crisis, and
its mitigated regulation afterwards is a worthwhile endeavor. Shadow
banking, simply put, denotes a system of credit intermediation outside
of banks' balance sheets. As I argue in this book, it is the outcome of
a domestically and globally fractured governance system, which unites
the interests of banks and their regulators as they face the threat of
losing business to much less regulated capital market actors domestically and/or much less regulated international banks operating within
the turf of domestic banks. As a consequence, banks have decided to
merge their business models with capital market actors, and banking
regulators have all too often acquiesced to their demands, regulatory
competition playing a major role in these dynamics. That such a policy
setup does not automatically lead to a situation of laissez-faire is well
demonstrated by the case of the French regulation of shadow banking
studied in this book, which was able to channel the off-balance-sheet
activities of its banks into credit provision for domestic industry, while
avoiding the excesses of repackaging of debt encountered in most

other legislations. This stance and the actions by French regulators demonstrate that regulatory agency does matter.

But it also demonstrates that such agency requires institutional empowerment, both within the regulatory networks that determine compliance with banking regulation, but also in the general setup of the governance of domestic banking systems. Most notably, in France large domestic banks were well protected from foreign takeovers and from aggressive competition by nonbank capital market actors, enfeebling deregulatory discourses by banks. This finding questions the unambiguous embrace of competition we still too often find in the discourse of regulators. Hopefully, this book can lead to a rethinking on this issue as well as others – for instance, the myth of regulators as hapless victims of bankers who simply outsmart them. The growth of shadow banking, and the form and extent it takes, is in no way the outcome of a natural process, unpreventable in its path. Instead, it is shaped by the institutional constraints banking regulators impose on their banks and how these are adjusted to changing circumstances. This book sets out to contribute to a better understanding of when and how these institutional constraints are adjusted by regulators and which factors impinge on their action. It is at the same time a call to arms for critical academics, to spot contradictions within regulatory discourses and to support those regulators critical of the rule circumventing activities of "their" banks. Pointing them out might just be a small contribution we can provide, but not a useless one either.

This book has been a long time in the making. Initially conceived as my dissertation project at Columbia University, it has kept me busy for most of the last seven years, going through multiple iterations and amendments.[3] My gratitude goes to my thesis advisor at Columbia University, Tom DiPrete, who pushed me to pursue a comparative study to better understand the variegated impact of the financial crisis; to David Stark, for pushing me to better engage with the sociological literature on financial markets; and to Katharina Pistor, for encouraging me to confront thorny legal issues and to include Minsky in my writing.

---

[3] Parts of Chapters 2, 5, 6, and 7 have been published as articles in *Competition and Change* (Thiemann 2012), *Business and Politics* (Thiemann 2014a), the *Review of International Political Economy* (Thiemann 2014b), and the *American Journal of Sociology* (Thiemann and Lepoutre 2017).

I am also grateful to Martin Hellwig for his encouragement and helpful feedback along the way. Jan Lepoutre's inexorable demand for clarity and precision, as well as Mike Schuyler's editorial help were irreplaceable components to complete the project, as was the patience and goodwill of Phil Good, my editor at Cambridge University Press. In Frankfurt, Hans-Helmut Kotz, Andreas Noelke, Daniel Mertens, and Roman Goldbach were important conversation partners helping me clarify my argument. Len Seabrooke and Daniela Gabor were sources of inspiration as they listened and commented on parts of the work published in this book. Research assistance by Marius Birk, Vanessa Endrejat, Jan Friedrich, and Max Nagel is also gratefully acknowledged. Of course, I am deeply indebted to the more than eighty financial market practitioners, auditors, and employees of rating agencies and banking and accounting regulators as well as accounting professors who helped me gain an understanding into the obscure processes of producing off-balance-sheet finance. Without their willingness to answer my questions and thereby to help me understand the intricacies of their interaction with legal texts, much would have remained in the shadow. Last but not least, my gratitude goes to my family, without whom this work would not have been possible.

1 | *States and the Regulation of a Globalized Finance*

In September 2008, as Lehman failed and AIG neared a similar fate, three decades of relentless financial innovation and the expansion of financial markets in the Western world came to an abrupt halt. Following suit, the neoclassical regulatory utopia of self-regulating markets died as well. This utopian worldview had sought the creation of complete markets that would allow rational agents to make optimal decisions regarding their risk exposure, thereby making regulatory intervention unnecessary. Financial innovations in securitization, which facilitated the pooling of risk and its subsequent trading, held the promise of optimal risk spreading, thus making the financial system ever more resilient (Bhattacharya et al. 1998). In this idealized world of self-regulating and self-disciplining markets, what other role could regulators take on than to facilitate innovation that would allow the completion of markets and the subsequent spreading of risk in the financial system?

Permitting the creativity of bankers who would use these new securitization techniques as a means of circumventing regulatory requirements, and thus shifting the risks onto the ultimate guarantor of the financial system, the state, seemingly remains the most profound regulatory shortcoming precrisis. When the crisis hit, the world came to realize that, rather than spreading the risk, securitization had led to the concentration of risk in the banking system itself (Greenlaw et al. 2008, p. 35; Acharya et al. 2013, p. 515). The crisis revealed the close interlinkage between the banking system and a complex system of credit intermediation that had formed outside of banking regulation – the shadow banking system. The latter system, in effect, experienced a situation analogous to a bank run, which is the sudden and self-reinforcing withdrawal of funds from the system that requires fire-sale liquidation of assets (Gorton 2010). The return of impaired, "toxic" assets on the balance sheets of banks from the shadow banking system impacted them heavily, contributing to the $2.6 trillion of losses

1

concentrated in the banking sector (see IMF 2009c, p. xii). The unexpected reappearance of these assets increased uncertainty over the true risk exposure of these banks, thereby sowing distrust and contributing to the freeze in the interbanking market. This system, its emergence, its underlying practices, and the lack of regulatory intervention that allowed it to grow and to "prosper" serve as the focus of this book.

With the breakdown of financial markets in 2008, the intellectual edifice of potentially self-perfecting markets that influenced regulators' outlook on financial markets lies in shambles. This raises the questions of when and how much regulatory intervention into the evolution of financial markets is appropriate to secure financial stability (FSB 2011a; Omarova 2012; Black 2013). There is a consensus that to prevent a recurrence of events requires more comprehensive regulation as well as the inclusion of these shadow banks into the system of banking regulation (FSB 2011b). Indeed, a whole host of regulatory measures has been instituted postcrisis to disentangle banks and the shadow banking system and to transform the shadow banking system into "resilient market based financing" (FSB 2014), led by efforts of the newly empowered transnational regulatory body, the Financial Stability Board. Regulators now insist that there exists a need both to monitor and to update the frontiers of regulatory supervision continuously (FSB 2014). However, we know little about the sociopolitical context in which regulators do observe this frontier and its implication for regulatory practices. The reasons that impeded such action on the regulatory frontier precrisis are insufficiently understood.

To assess how "robust" these new regulations are and whether they "can withstand attempts at circumvention" (Stiglitz 2009, p. 12) for the banking sector in the future,[1] we need to understand why so few regulators put financial institutions in the shadow banking system under banking regulation in the first place. The financial sector exists as one of the most heavily regulated sectors of the economy (owing to its potential to produce large negative social externalities), which makes explaining this regulatory permissiveness before the crisis that

---

[1] Stiglitz rightly emphasizes that "the ingenuity of man knows no bounds, and whatever system we design, there will be those who will figure out how to circumvent the regulations and the rules put in place to protect us" (Stiglitz 2010b, p. xxv; see also Kane 1988, 2008). In response to this immutable fact, we need regulations and regulatory systems that can adapt quickly to such circumvention and, as such, will become robust in achieving their goals.

much more confounding. Without an understanding of the failures of banking regulation precrisis, we run the risk of instituting rules that, on the one hand, close current loopholes, but, on the other hand, remain incapable of dealing with the underlying dynamics from which the shadow banking sector emerges. This effectively means coming to terms with the attempts at circumventing rules by banks, where incentives to do so have only increased postcrisis (Blundell-Wignall and Atkinson 2010) and the larger institutional context within which it evolves. Given that regulatory costs have only increased as a major component of overall costs for the banking business, the innovative spirit of financial and legal engineers now even more often turns to the question of how to circumvent them (Blundell-Wignall and Atkinson 2010). By undermining regulatory constraints, however, these extra profits come at the expense of systemic stability, thus creating a threat of future calamities.

Nowhere has this tendency expressed itself more virulently than in the bank-based shadow banking system. There, banks used regulatory arbitrage and securitization techniques to engage in off-balance-sheet banking activities, that is, outside of banking regulation, booking the savings on regulatory costs as profits (Pozsar et al. 2010). The vulnerabilities stemming from the exposure to these activities, which were part of a broader trend toward market-based banking since the 1980s (Hardie et al. 2013a, b),[2] were powerfully demonstrated during the market turmoil of 2007–9. The impact of the financial crisis was greater on those national banking systems that were more exposed to the use of wholesale markets in general and of shadow banking in particular (Hardie and Howarth 2009, 2013a; Chang and Jones 2013; Howarth 2013; Royo 2013; Fligstein and Habinek 2014). Despite these events, market-based banking, the fusion of capital markets and bank business models, is here to stay. While the crisis has evoked substantial regulatory change, causing shrinkages in the field of investment banking (Helleiner 2014), regulatory change has been incremental

---

[2] Market-based banking designates the increasing exposure of banks' balance sheets on the asset and liability side to developments in financial markets, as commercial banks come to rely more on wholesale funding for their lending capacities (Hardie and Howarth 2013b, p. 24) and engage in shadow banking, "lending activity that is "wholly or partially off the banks' balance sheets" (Hardie et al. 2013a, p. 714).

(Moschella and Tsingou 2013) and no clear-cut separation between capital markets and banking conglomerates has been installed.[3]

Going forward, a central question thus remains as to how regulators should monitor the innovative activities that financial market actors, banks in particular, develop in capital markets. How can they ensure that useful innovation is not unnecessarily strangled while at the same time preventing innovations that have the sole purpose of rule evasion? This book contends that we can learn some of these lessons by looking at the differential evolution of the size and activities of a central market for shadow banking activity, the asset-backed commercial paper market in different countries. This evolution was driven by decision making of banking regulators as much as by the regulated. Studying the regulator–regulated interactions regarding this market in their sociopolitical context will provide us with insights about the conditions for regulatory action, both in terms of context as well as in terms of the institutional setup and temporal patterns of interacting between the regulators and the regulated.

Context Conditions for Regulatory Action

To appreciate properly the way in which regulators related to the shadow banking system precrisis, we need, first, to understand the ideological and institutional context within which the large international banks were operating. The massive bank failures in 2007 and 2008 clarified with astounding ferocity that, as Mervyn King, then governor of the Bank of England puts it, international banks are "global in life, but national in death" (King 2009). This statement already goes a long way toward capturing the hybridity that characterizes the institutional context for large international banks then and today. However, to understand the dynamics of diffusion of the financial crisis from the USA to the entire Western developed world via large international banks (Shin 2011), one needs to qualify Sir Mervyn's statement regarding the life of large international banks. They are also hybrids in

---

[3] In the eurozone, reforms have completely stalled, whereas in the UK, following the Vickers report, a certain bank separation regime has been installed. In the USA, the Volcker rule is supposed to differentiate market making from proprietary trading, but faces difficulties in implementation. Furthermore, President Trump is likely to scrap the rule.

life: largely global in their business activity, but subject to the national interpretation of global regulation and national regulation tout court. Every time a bank creatively employs a financial product, national regulators need to decide how to deal with that long before any international decision on the issue is taken. As Kane (1987) pointed out long ago, the reaction time of international regulation is much too long to deal with local financial innovation properly. Thus, national regulators have no choice but to react on their own.

While transnational banks are widely perceived to have escaped national regulatory control before the crisis (Christophers 2013), their engagement in the shadow banking system was very often predicated on their national regulatory frame of action. Their engagement in global markets, such as the asset-backed commercial paper market, was dependent on national regulations, and hence on national regulatory decision making. Regulatory decisions regarding these markets occurred in a larger societal context that was shaped by the hegemonic ideology regarding finance of their time and the existing global financial architecture within which national regulatory action is placed. At the base of this ideology was a perception of finance as a productive force for the evolution of economics, in which an increase in financial activity was unequivocally contributing to gross domestic product (GDP) growth (Christophers 2011; Turner 2015, critical Bezemer 2009). Financial liberalization and attendant increases in competition were seen as beneficial to economic growth, in particular by the USA, which as the hegemon of the time was unilaterally pushing for an agenda of financial liberalization (Helleiner 1994). These ideological views, undergirded by political economic interests, fostered the support by state agencies for the liberalization and growth of finance.

In the 1990s, this hegemonic ideology of finance expressed a belief in the self-regulating power of markets and the incapacity of regulators to assess market developments properly, setting the ideological basis for delegating regulation to market actors themselves. This agenda was based on a selective reading of financial economics (Turner 2012) that understood market actors as able to assess properly the risks they were taking, and financial markets as informationally efficient and capable of disciplining misbehavior by market agents. Most importantly, securitization, with its capacity to slice credit risk and to spread it to those agents in financial markets most able to bear them, was seen as a revolutionary technique that would increase the resilience of the financial systems as a whole. And this ideology seemed to be borne out by the facts of the financialized boom of the 2000s (Epstein 2005; Krippner 2011). Ever-expanding liquidity in global financial wholesale markets, growing profitability of banks, and the attendant fear of national political economies to be left behind in what seemed like a new era of prosperous finance-led capitalism (Guttmann 2016) were the context of national regulatory action at the time.

When the global banking accords were revised in 2004 and Basel II was adopted, it carried much of these ideological convictions. Thus, it has been attacked as an example of cognitive and regulatory capture (Seabrooke and Tsingou 2009; Baker 2010; Lall 2012), where the industry wrote the rules in its favor (critical Young 2012; Baud and Chiapello 2014). But this focus on global accords often causes analysts to overlook the fact that for most of the financial innovations in which banks engaged, local and national adaptation played a major role: deciding if and how they could do so. While these banks sought to carve out niches for themselves among a field of global peers, one important actor for them was their respective national regulator and these regulators' views on the merits and dangers of the financial innovations in question. So that they fit well with the innovations of structured finance – whether the international tradability of domestic mortgage-backed securities (see Wainwright 2009, 2011 for the case of the UK) or the regulation of these trades, which, as banks requested, should occur with as light a touch as possible – national regulatory regimes needed reshaping.

In this situation, the regulators are largely influenced by the way the international scene within which their respective banks must compete is set up. Financial liberalization since the 1970s led to financial turbulences not experienced in the period from 1944 to 1973, as the internationalization of banking business brought about a degree of connectedness hitherto unexperienced (Goodhart 2011). When the failure of the small German Herstatt Bank in 1974 threatened turmoil in the USA, banking regulators of the developed world started to coordinate in the Basel Committee for Banking Supervision. Seeking to control the behavior of banks, regulators were coordinating their supervision between host and home countries from 1975 onwards (Kapstein 1991). The problem of securing domestic stability while keeping domestic banks internationally competitive led to negotiations over a globally harmonized set of rules for banking regulation, which crystallized in 1988 into the Basel Rules for banking regulation.

While establishing a level playing field at this point in time, it also established inhibitions for further regulatory action by national regulators at the margins of this accord, as I will show. The global architecture installed by the Basel Accords granted banks the right to operate globally based on their domestic regulatory framework, installing competitive inequity concerns right at the heart of national regulatory decisions. Postcrisis, several amendments have been made to this fact by national regulators, especially in the USA, where foreign bank subsidiaries are often forced to incorporate domestically, thereby making them subject to US regulation (Dodd-Frank Act Section 165/166; see Fed 2014).

As Saskia Sassen (1996) and others pointed out long ago, globalization in this situation does not mean the withering away of the state; instead, globalization tends to become internalized and shapes the activities of state administrations faced with globalizing markets. By internalizing the effects of their actions in the globalized context, the respective regulatory agencies and the ministries of finance may well cede to the deregulatory demands of their primary clientele, the banks. In a situation in which regulation of banks is not yet fully global, but no longer national only, regulation tends toward leniency because of the intention of each to support its national champions in the international marketplace. As the literature on the evolution of global regulatory standards for banking points out, regulators need to weigh the competing goals of financial stability and the competitiveness of their industry with respect to foreign banks, seeking to avoid squashing profitable activities by too stringent regulation (cf. Singer 2007).

In addition to international competitiveness concerns, regulators also needed to weigh the emerging threats to their commercial banks that stemmed from evolving business models of nonbanks. Based on abundant money market funding, these became active competitors for the business of credit intermediation, a fact that was most pronounced in the USA. Prior accounts of the shift toward shadow banking activities have focused on bankers' agency in this context of increasing competition (Acharya and Schnabl 2010; Hardie et al. 2013b, p. 1; Bell and Hindmoor 2015), largely ignoring regulatory agency.[4] However,

---

[4] Bell and Hindmoor's (2015a) empirical analysis of the Australian and Canadian cases shows the role of regulators rather well. However, in their theorization of their four cases, this crucial role of regulators and regulation remains underemphasized.

shadow banking activities, such as securitization, require favorable regulatory environments to flourish as they are quite sensitive to regulatory costs. As shadow banking activities generate only very low margins (Claessens and Ratnovski 2014, p. 5), including them in costly banking regulation would thwart their growth. Regulatory agency is thus an important factor in constraining or facilitating these activities.

Research on the shift to shadow banking activities in banking systems has acknowledged this structuring role, but it has not properly focused on the factors driving regulatory agency.

As Hardie et al. put it, "Clearly, institutional factors shape bankers' business choices: *banking regulation and banking supervision ... and protectionism in the banking sector*" (2013a, p. 697, emphasis mine). Researchers to date, however, have emphasized the agency of bankers within these regulatory constraints (Acharya and Schnabel 2010; Hardie and Howarth 2013b, p. 51; Hardie et al. 2013a, p. 697; Hardie et al. 2013b, p. 1), but have neglected regulators' agency that shaped these constraints as well as the institutional constraints within which it itself evolves.[5] This is problematic, as the shift to shadow banking was more than bankers "acting out institutional change" prepared by the (de-)regulatory efforts of rule makers (O'Sullivan 2007). Instead, banks actively circumvented the rules, and a crucial question regarding the profitability of these activities was whether regulators updated regulation to include them or not.

To overcome the bank-centric focus in current explanations, this book focuses on those regulatory decisions that hindered or facilitated these activities and places all of this in the context of global and European financial market integration,[6] providing a more complete account for the differential exposure of national banking systems to shadow banking activities. The shift to shadow banking can then be analyzed as the endogenous outcome of the interaction of rule takers and rule makers (Streeck and Thelen 2005, pp. 13–14) within a larger and changing institutional context, where rule takers seek to circumvent regulation and rule makers either do or do not expand regulation to capture these activities (Kane 1988).

---

[5] But see the contributions by Gabor (2016) and Gabor and Ban (2015), which show the active intervention by the European Central Bank for the case of the European repo market.

[6] Deeg (2010, pp. 426ff) similarly suggests theories of European financial market integration as mid-range theories to explain financial system change.

The Dialectical Unity of Regulators and the Regulated

This book argues that to understand the evolution of this regulatory framework properly, we need to employ a dialectical understanding of the relationship between regulators and more broadly conceived state agencies as well as the regulated. Regulators and regulated together form a dialectical unity of opposing and shared interests and together determine the evolution of financial systems, as both actors depend on each other. Absent state regulation and state support, banking systems are too unstable to exist (Ingham 2004). Collective action problems and the danger of the overextension of individual banks, which can lead to the demise of the entire system, cannot be overcome through self-regulation, despite the arguments of extreme liberals to the contrary (see Dowd 1992 for the argument for regulation; see Calomiris and Gorton 1991 for the liberal argument). Conversely, nation-states have depended on stable banking systems for their projection of power and their developmental projects at large.[7] This dependence is even more evident with respect to regulators, whose existence, without a prospering domestically owned banking sector, would become largely redundant. In the context of financial liberalization, which permitted the acquisition of domestic by foreign banks, such a scenario became a distinct possibility.

United in their mutual dependence, these actors also carry opposing interests. Whereas individual banks will seek to maximize returns within existing regulatory constraints and to evade those constraints, which they see as unnecessarily burdensome, regulators seek to maintain the stability of the sector, concerned about financial stability as a public good, while taking the competitiveness of their banks into account (Singer 2007). Hence, conflict evolves around what is perceived as privately rational action by banks that endangers the public good as understood by the regulators. The outcome of this regulatory dialectic (Kane 1988) determines the regulatory framework as a dynamic synthesis of these opposing interests, which determines the evolution of the system. In this evolution, the system might veer toward excessive risk taking on the one hand, as banks escape regulatory control, which ends in financial crisis and reregulation. On the

---

[7] This state finance nexus was forged at the latest with the founding of the Bank of England in 1694 (Ingham 2004), a public–private partnership that sought to mobilize private resources to finance war capacities of the state.

other hand, however, risk taking can be subdued by excessive regulatory constraints, which lead to a crisis of profitability and threaten the
existence of banks, as nonbanks unburdened by regulatory constraints
challenge them. This crisis, in turn, will lead to a process of deregulation, one brought forth by both regulators and the regulated to protect
the banks.

Using this dialectical view and its explicit temporal dimension, we
can better appreciate that the agency of one actor in this pas de deux
can constitute an important part of the structural constraints within
which the other must act. That is to say that the regulators and the
regulated "collectively and interactively shape the environment that
they confront" (Muegge 2010, p. 7). If we consider structure and
agency from the point of view of both the regulator and the regulated,
we gain the notion of an evolving ecosystem, in which timing is of
crucial importance. As the regulated circumvent the regulation, how
quickly do regulators understand and react to these innovations? As
Funk and Hirschman (2014) point out regarding the case of the regulation of swaps before the crisis, at a certain point the sheer size of
such markets limits the capacity for regulatory intervention as market
segments become quasi-irreversible. Regulatory intervention then can
act only at the margins, without questioning these markets themselves. Conversely, once regulation has undergone negotiation and
implementation, there is only little that the regulated can do to change
these structures directly. Instead, creative actors will seek to circumvent these regulations through new financial products, which achieve
similar results in economic substance but are sufficiently different in
legal form.

But a crucial point is that the agency of both is driven also by their
dialectical unity, by an attempt to secure the survival of the domestic
banking system in the face of competitive challenges, be they internal
or from abroad. Changing and increasing competition both from foreign banks and from domestic nonbank actors who exert their agency
in the face of changing forms of financial intermediation require
responses by this contradictory unit of banks and regulators. Adapting
to a changing competitive landscape that involved the (re-)ascendance
of capital markets as new sources of financing as well as threats from
foreign banks, banks sought to integrate the provision of services to
capital markets into their business models (Hardie et al. 2013a, b).
The decisive question then was how regulators would react to this

integration of capital market activities into banks' business models. The competitive threats, emerging from financial liberalization on the one hand and an ideology that saw the growth of finance as unequivocally positive (Christophers 2013; Turner 2015), on the other hand, were important in shaping this reaction.

At the same time, evaluation of these financial innovations would emerge from local supervisors on the ground, and the way their input would be processed into decision making in the regulatory agencies was also of crucial importance. As it turned out, these decisions would largely affect how the crisis would impact national banking systems. If regulators did not impose regulatory charges on the financial innovations that bank holding companies engaged in to enter into capital market activities, banks from these countries faced no constraints to fully engage in what later came to be known as the "shadow banking system," the epicenter of the financial crisis. In their decision making, national regulators could and often did take inspiration from different regulatory proposals of how to deal with these innovations that stemmed from fellow national regulators and transnational bodies such as the Basel Committee for Banking Supervision (BCBS). They were also (sometimes) attentive to the work of adjacent regulatory bodies, such as the International Accounting Standards Board. Nevertheless, in the end, the tasks of weaving together the rag rug of regulatory proposals and aligning the various transnational and international regulatory regimes covering these financial innovations into a coherent set of regulations fell squarely on the shoulders of national state agencies.

The National Level: Regulatory Dialogues on Financial Innovations

For us to gain a better understanding of precrisis regulatory failures, we need to study how national administrative agencies came to understand and act on financial innovations, many of which sought to evade regulation. Such regulatory evasion often occurs at the fractures of different regulatory regimes (such as accounting and banking regulation), thus necessitating a truly synthetic view that promotes understanding of the legal engineers' work and puts an end to the most blatant attempts. This work, then, is as much national as it is interior transnational, as the different state authorities must unite the different and fracturing national, global, and transnational regulatory proposals. Weaving them together serves as the regulators' task. Focusing on this fractured context of regulatory action (Muegge and Perry 2014) allows us to appreciate the institutional structures that both regulators and the regulated face when acting in the regulatory dialectic of rules, rule evasion, and reregulation and to appreciate in how far the agency of both actors is shaped by these structures.

In this context of structural inhibition for regulation, we must appreciate the deregulatory faith of the 1990s and 2000s, for doing so will allow us to overcome simplistic interpretations of regulatory action precrisis, the kind of interpretations that focus on regulatory capture via industry ties. These views stipulate that owing to the prevailing incentive structures, regulators will end up captured by the very industry that they supposedly regulate. These theories focus their attention on the relations public regulators entertain with the private sector, pointing to the dangers of revolving doors (Seabrooke and Tsingou 2009; Barth et al. 2012). Although such effects cannot be denied, an overly strong negative focus on industry–regulator relationships can prove rather unhelpful, as regulators do need to interact with the regulated in their day-to-day work. In her work on Japanese regulators, Anneliese Riles (2011) describes perhaps the starkest example of the negative effect of this concept. Influenced by the very concept discussed earlier and coming under public pressure because of dinners that regulators used to attend to exchange information, Japanese regulators decided to withdraw from contacts and the direct exchange and regulation of the market, instead seeking to structure self-governing mechanisms. This preemptive "unwinding" (Riles 2011, p. 147) of the old system of state interference, enacted to avoid temptation as well as to increase the legitimacy of the regulator, meant that regulators became detached from the industry's most recent developments and reactions of the financial community toward its regulatory interventions. By effectively choosing to blind themselves, they ostensibly denied themselves a deeper understanding of financial market developments.

In a dynamic and evolving business landscape such as financial markets, however, regulators do need interaction with market participants so that they can understand how the market evolves. Furthermore, there is an information asymmetry between the regulators and the regulated about the interpretation and, thus, application of laws and regulation, which makes contact between these groups necessary for effective financial market regulation (Black 2013). With the acceptance of these realities, the questions become, first, which pattern and structure of ties with the regulated can help to assuage the problem of information asymmetry and rule circumvention without falling into the traps of regulatory capture? Second, with whom and how should regulators interact to overcome the asymmetry between compliance officers applying rules and regulators setting them? By inquiring into the interactions between regulators and the banking industry that allowed for or hindered the exponential growth of the shadow banking sector before the crisis, this book seeks to provide answers to these questions. As such, it asks, did the dangers of these organizational innovations remain unknown to regulators? Furthermore, were they all duped by "the smartest men in the room," financial engineers who were simply hiding the risks, that is, which capabilities do states need to detect regulatory circumvention and to limit it? And, once such recognition has occurred, how does the international context influence national regulatory action?

State–Society Relations and the Supervision of Finance

The questions raised in the previous section point to the centrality of state–society relations in solving the regulatory problem of dealing with financial innovations, based on information asymmetries on the one hand and international competitiveness concerns on the other. Borrowing from Evans' work on the developmental state, but shifting his focus from development to regulation, we can say that for us to find answers, we need to look at the covariation of state structure, state–society relationships, and regulatory outcomes in a comparative fashion (Evans 1995, p. 42). The financial crisis has not only raised the importance of these questions, but it has also provided strategic research sites that allow constructing empirically grounded answers to them. Not all banking regulators were equally permissive, and the shadow banking sector did not reach the same proportions in all developed countries. To inquire into the conditions that facilitated the growth of the shadow banking sector, then, means to focus on the institutional framework of exchange between regulators and the regulated that permitted or hindered the timely recognition of regulatory arbitrage by national regulators and their capacity to act on their knowledge. Recognition and intervention were shaped by the domestic regulatory culture, the regulatory institutional setup, and competencies as well as the national legal framework, enabling or inhibiting regulatory action. It was also shaped by the larger political economy, which enabled or prevented banks from acting as veto players and inserting their competitiveness concerns into the policy process.

Focusing on the point of recognition of rule circumvention, we need to appreciate the socially constructed nature of the data on which regulators act. The problems involved in capturing rule circumventions is most pronounced with respect to the banking conglomerate where boundaries are not clearly defined before the process of observation by auditors (Chiapello 2009; Robe 2011), as boundaries are set in the process of observation only with the help of accounting rules. Owing to pressure from the auditors' clients, namely, the audited conglomerates, biases occur in this process to create the most beneficial picture of the conglomerate's size and vulnerability to risk. The fractured nature of the regulatory process that produces and processes these data, one that often separates accounting from banking regulation, leads to the danger that rule circumvention, specifically, exploitation of the malleability of accounting rules, goes potentially unnoticed by the banking regulator for too long a period (see also Muegge and Perry 2014). The functional differentiation of accounting and banking regulation that goes together with the increasing transnational setting of accounting rules by the International Accounting Standards Board further aggravates the problem. Allowing these tendencies toward institutional separation to proceed causes banking regulators to become cut off from the process of production of the data on which they operate, which, in turn, makes the comprehensive oversight of industry developments by banking regulators significantly more difficult.

I argue that to limit this (self-)destructive potential of the industry and to do justice to the problem of the social construction of the data on which regulators operate, we need to envision new ways of public–private interaction regarding the creation and the interpretation of financial regulation (in a similar but more general vein, see Block 2010). Chances of limiting regulatory arbitrage from within the system of private agents seem misplaced to me. The capacity to secure extra profits in legal gray zones that prevent the criminal conviction of legal engineers or their clients will likely prove too tempting to resist.

In addition, even if the power of ethics convinces certain segments of the market to abstain, should their results fall below those of their respective peer groups, the inexorable comparison of profitability by investors will eventually force them to adopt these practices. For this reason, the hopes placed on ethics seem utterly misguided. Instead, the industry requires a system of public–private interaction permitting early detection and intervention concerning acts of regulatory arbitrage. This involves a paradox, once one considers the discourses about regulatory capture that have been promulgated since the crisis. This book argues that instead of sealing off regulators from the regulated because of the fear of capture, in order to control the tendency of market participants to destroy the regulatory infrastructure on which their market is based, regulators need to draw on private expertise more than ever.[8] They need to appreciate the diversity and the complexity of the chains of production involved in producing regulatory arbitrage, co-opting crucial knowledgeable actors in these chains, who by their function as gatekeepers can be drawn into the regulatory dialogues necessary to understand changes in market practice.

To appreciate the modus of observation and intervention of regulators into these market practices, we need to acknowledge the fact that cognition is socially distributed in markets (Hutchins 1995). With respect to rules, this means that specific knowledge of how to interact and to deal with those rules is distributed among compliance officers (Edelman and Shauhin 2011), gatekeepers (Coffee 2006), and banking regulators in an institutionally shaped way.

The role that service intermediaries, such as the Big Four auditing companies[9] and international lawyers, play in generating regulatory arbitrage (Coffee 2006) needs to be appreciated in order to draw on these agents to limit regulatory arbitrage's destructive potential. As much as internal compliance officers of banks, these agents need to serve as the addressees of regulatory intervention and dialogue by regulators, as regulators are seeking to draw upon their

---

[8] In contrast to Rajan and Zingales (2003), this saving of capitalism from capitalists involves the direct interaction of market participants with the rules seeking to constrain their behavior, rather than their attempts to influence the rule making itself.

[9] The big four auditing companies are the globally operating auditing companies Ernst and Young, KPMG, Deloitte and PwC, each employing about 200,000 employees.

expertise to generate an understanding of unfolding processes and to overcome the information asymmetries inherent in supervision. With respect to bankers themselves, a different style of dialogue is necessary, one which allows regulators to learn while not forgetting the reason why they are learning. A simple approach to these issues, asking the basic questions that cut across the mathematical elegance of models, perceived precrisis as a stigma in a culture of highly mathematized financial engineering, needs to be encouraged. Regulators needn't understand all the mathematics and every mathematical nuance; instead, they need to focus on simple questions regarding the functions of innovations and their potentially detrimental effects.

The Empirical Content of the Book

Such requests, with their abstract language, read beautifully but are hardly convincing. How, one may ask, can this work? How can one get these individuals to participate for the sake of the greater good, especially if their own motivations and incentives exist in opposition to this greater good? A two-part answer exists to this question: first, not all individuals will be accessible to collaborate with regulators, so that focusing on specific professional groups in the financial services seems necessary; second, these agents must get something out of this, also. Whether social status, recognition as important members of the community, or influence on rule making and interpretation, these agents need an incentive to collaborate. As such, I suggest focusing on compliance officers rather than on business partners in banks and service intermediaries alike, as not only do they have an interest in collaborating with regulators to keep their banks/financial intermediaries compliant, but they also stand to lose less than business partners in case a certain legal construction is not allowed to operate. They will, thus, cooperate more willingly and let reasoning – over partial interest – win.

These claims, although inspired by theoretical works, such as those by Julia Black, on regulatory dialogues (1997, 2001, 2003, 2008, 2012, 2013) have not emerged deductively themselves. Instead, they have resulted from an inductive empirical study that sought to understand why, in certain countries, parts of the shadow banking system were not allowed to flourish (such as in France and Canada), whereas in other countries (such as the USA, UK, Germany, and the Netherlands), they grew rather uninhibited. To keep the comparative study tractable and to maintain the comparability of cases, I decided to focus on one segment of the shadow banking system that had particularly lethal implications during the financial crisis (the ABCP market) and to focus on the USA, where this market originated and three eurozone countries with remarkably different engagement in this market traceable to regulatory differences. The analysis of the USA is important because it is there that the new configuration of banks and capital market actors (the bank–nonbank nexus) was first created, forming the backbone of shadow banking. It is also in the USA that the ABCP market was institutionalized in 1983 and where regulators first faced the task of developing a regulatory framework, operating as an important foil for foreign regulators concerning their interventions. The European cases, conversely, help us to understand how the crisis came to impact the EU in such a surprisingly strong manner and also why that impact differed between countries.

American banks had a strong presence in both the segments used for regulatory arbitrage and the one used to provide real economic benefits to clients. In Europe, the situation was more divergent. Starting their engagements in the ABCP market at the same time (the early 1990s), banks from these countries would take up very different roles. Whereas French banks had only a subdued engagement in the market and particularly abstained from the segment most characterized by regulatory arbitrage, the banks from the two neighboring countries, Germany and the Netherlands, remained extremely active in this segment, such that banks from these countries became, respectively, the second and fourth largest national players in this market. These three countries are inside of the eurozone and, thus, bound by the same European legislation, which evoked the comparative question of why this segment characterized by regulatory arbitrage flourished in the latter two countries and not in France. Did the national regulators play a role, and, if so, what capabilities and resources allowed the French regulators to limit this activity? And, how can we explain the different evolution in the USA?

To answer these questions, I first set out to reconstruct the complexities involved in the rule evasion by banks. Then I focused on the interaction between regulators and regulated, to understand the national evolution of the regulation of this market better. Lastly, I sought to understand the dynamics of the regulation of this market internationally and how it related to the national regulation for my four cases, seeking to understand the interaction between the two levels of regulation better. The US regulator observed market developments attentively and was aware of the rule-bending activities of its banks, both in its supervisory role and its regulatory role. However, in a context of entrenched business lobbying power and of an ideology that deferred to market discipline and the capacity of ratings to predict future losses, it left regulation largely to markets themselves. In contrast, the French regulator intervened from 1999 onwards in a recalcitrant manner to close the regulatory loopholes that allowed banks to engage in risk-taking activity without building up buffers to deal with the realizations of these risks. In contrast, in the German and Dutch cases, regulatory action was late or not forthcoming at all. Instead, regulators contented themselves with regulatory action on the international level, which came into force only in January 2008. This different stance posed a puzzle that I was seeking to answer by engaging in eighty-five semistructured expert interviews with agents involved in the national and international regulation of this market, on the side of accounting as well as on the side of banking regulation. I interviewed officials engaged in regulation, market participants as well as employees of the Big Four auditing companies to understand when regulators were sensitized to the acts of rule circumvention and what limited or facilitated their intervention in this market.

Methodological Considerations

While this study, as suggested earlier, is seeking to provide an explanation for the differential growth of the ABCP markets in the USA and Europe before 2007 and their specific national character, it seeks to extend beyond the idiographic goal of explaining the impact of this single dynamic and to distill the international regulatory context that explain its growth and the regulatory styles and capabilities that facilitated the prudent regulation of this segment of shadow banking. In this respect, it seeks to explain the different accommodation of a financial innovation based on regulatory circumvention in different jurisdictions by evoking sufficient versus insufficient regulatory capabilities and different regulatory styles. While comparative in nature, the study pays attention at the same time to the transnational context of regulatory action, characterized by financial liberalization (strongest for the EU countries), which acts as a common factor hindering more stringent financial regulation in all cases.

To show the influence of these different factors, I employ congruence analysis and process tracing to ascertain which actors prevailed in regulatory struggles and how they did so. To do so, I collected eighty-five interviews between 2010 and 2016[10] and multiple independent observations from journalistic sources, public documents, and background interviews that I used to verify statements encountered in the interviews. The triangulation of this evidence provides me with a higher degree of confidence in the reliability of my interview data.[11] The reader should note that process tracing and the comparative method cannot provide us with certainty about the degree of impact a specific variable has on an outcome, knowledge that is produced by large *n* statistics. At the end, by using this method, a researcher will be able to present a causal model for how the different configurations in the cases explain different outcomes, but he will not be able to specify which of the variables had exactly which kind of effect. In this respect, case studies are much better in identifying the scope conditions under which a causal mechanism holds, not the degree of impact single variables have (George and Bennett 2005, p. 25).

Anticipated Conclusions

What I found was a mixture of concerns over the competitiveness of domestic banks, simple regulatory capture, as well as a structural separation of regulators from the action, which limited regulators' understanding and capacity for corrective action. These issues were accentuated, not diminished, for the problem of shadow banking by global banking regulation. Indeed, one may argue that the growth of shadow banking owes much to the way in which global regulation is currently set up. These matters are traditionally negotiated in the field of international and comparative political economy of regulation

---

[10] Most interviews were undertaken in 2010 and 2011, with several follow-up interviews in 2015. But for two interviews in 2012, interviews in the USA were all undertaken in 2016.

[11] More information on interview data can be found in Appendix 1.

(Helleiner 1994; Helleiner and Pagliari 2011). This literature does provide us with an understanding of national regulators' scope of action in the transnational field of banking regulation and the impending concerns coming with it.

What it does not provide us with, however, is an understanding of the practices that structure regulatory arbitrage as well as the interaction of the regulators with the regulated. To elucidate my findings on these matters, I will draw on the social studies of finance as well as the literature on experimental governance and regulatory dialogues (Black 1997, 2003; Ford 2010; Black et al. 2013). Both of these fields help us to understand better the dynamics facing regulators and how the embeddedness of regulators in "communities of interpretation" can help to control these activities. At the same time, these two streams of literature stand to benefit from political economy considerations, considerations that allow a better understanding of the evolution of finance and its governance.

This study then brings together the transnational and the national levels of action, focusing on regulators and the private–public interaction involved in crafting techniques of regulatory arbitrage as well as the limitation of these techniques. Observing the evolution of this market characterized by regulatory arbitrage and the individual regulator's involvement with it, I developed an understanding of the evolution of this phenomena as not one-sided but rather seeking to combine political reasons (who has power and why) with questions of information flow (who knows what and why). Only by answering these two jointly can we understand the unfolding of the regulatory arbitrage that serves as the structural reason for the evolution of shadow banking.

In particular, the comparison will reveal that the timing of intervention remains the most important aspect of the governance of these activities. Once banks have engaged on a massive scale in activities, which depend for their profitability on regulatory loopholes, closing these loopholes will become all the more difficult for the authorities. Their resistance, and with them the political elite to which they are connected, will grow with the size of the market and its profitability (Funk and Hirschman 2014). Expertise has been gained and legal infrastructure built up, investments that would be devalued through the closure of these loopholes. Thus, early intervention is key, and the comparison of the different regulatory infrastructures in the four cases will allow me to pinpoint some structural features such infrastructures should have in order to facilitate said intervention.

So, investigating the growth of the ABCP market, this book also sheds light on how and why shadow banking as a whole came to flourish. It is structured in the following way. In Chapter 2, the particular market of the shadow banking system that is at the center of this study, the asset-backed commercial paper market, is presented. Particular attention is paid to the loopholes legal engineers used to establish it and its role in the crisis. A comparison of the different size of the market in different countries and of the regulation of the market is provided, showing the general broad-based trend of regulatory exemption as well as the correlation of regulation and size of the market. Questions are raised regarding the timing and severity of intervention in different cases, thus establishing the comparative difference in market evolution that is to be explained. In Chapter 3, I review the strength and shortcomings of theories of regulatory and cognitive capture to explain regulatory failure precrisis. Subsequently, I propose to expand them within a comparative analytical framework in order to capture the socio-institutional context as well as the particular historical conjuncture that explain the regulatory exemptions at the heart of shadow banking.

In Chapter 4, the emergence of the ABCP market is recounted in the context of changes in the US financial system and placed into the financial dynamics from the 1970s to today. The regulation of the market is traced from the early days up until the crisis, pointing to the administrative battles within the Fed as a main decisive factor for its regulation. This battle played out within the international context of the negotiation of the first and second Basel Accords, where the faction within the Fed critical of the ABCP market used the international negotiations to upload its preferences onto the international level in 1999, then to download it into US regulation in 2004 in the context of pending accounting rule changes.

Chapter 5 pursues the theme of the national regulation of the ABCP market at the fringes of the global Basel Accord, which put national regulators into the difficult position of regulating a global market. In a broad-based comparison, it shows the large degree of regulatory exemption these market activities experienced globally. It then hones in on the European context, pointing to the competition of national banking systems that shaped the attitude of national banking regulators toward permitting or hindering the evolution of the ABCP market.

In Chapter 6, I analyze the transformation of the regulatory governance architecture caused by transnational pressures in the realm of accounting and its impact on shadow banking regulation. In particular, I show how the separation of accounting and banking regulation that occurred in all three EU countries considered, although in different ways, influenced the convergence of national accounting rules with the transnational accounting rule SIC 12 capable of forcing the consolidation of ABCP conduits on the balance sheets of banks. It shows that the effective convergence to this transnational rule required a pro-challenge alliance, which included the banking regulatory body. Hence, only where the banking regulator was directly involved do we see such convergence. Paradoxically, the transnational body that issued this rule delegitimized banking regulators as members of accounting–standard-setting bodies, making convergence to its standards less likely.

Chapter 7 comparatively analyzes the differential embeddedness of banking regulators in the construction process of the ABCP market and in the communication circuits in general, completing the account as to why the French banking regulator was capable of detecting the regulatory arbitrage inherent in the ABCP market and inhibiting its growth, whereas the Dutch and German regulators failed. Chapter 8 analyzes the fate of the ABCP market as well as the Money Market Mutual Fund industry postcrisis. It shows how decisive regulatory action was applied to the former, but not the latter, leaving large parts of the shadow banking system largely untouched.

The conclusion begins by arguing that the same conditions that fed the ABCP market precrisis remain in place. A fragmented international governance system, which is based on both different accounting frameworks and different national definitions of banking activity, is placed into the context of a liberalized financial market, in which banks from different countries continue to compete based on national regulatory costs. The conclusion summarizes why and how the French were capable of limiting the growth of the ABCP market and applies these lessons to the current reform agenda and activities of the Financial Stability Board, the European Union, and the USA.

2 | The ABCP Market at the Heart of Shadow Banking and the Financial Crisis

When HSBC announced losses on its US housing portfolio in spring 2007, deteriorating default rates of subprime mortgages finally started to cause reverberations in financial markets. Given the small size of the subprime mortgage market in relation to the overall debt markets in the USA, observers in those days expected a correction and some losses, but nothing of the magnitude that was to characterize the next two years (Bernanke 2007). As the size of the subprime mortgage market suggests, residential mortgage backed securities (RMBSs) were the trigger, but not the cause, of what were to be twenty-four truly historical months in US and global financial markets. The multiplication of losses and the almost complete standstill of global finance can be understood only by appreciating the complex system of credit intermediation that had formed outside of banking regulation, which, in effect, experienced the analogy of a bank run (Gorton 2010). In the following, I will outline how, as a paradigmatic example of the interlinkage between shadow banks and banks, this system interacted with the banks initially to produce the freeze in the interbank market that set off the crisis, then to focus on the asset-backed commercial paper market. Subsequently, I trace the development of this market in the USA and European countries and show how it correlates with the impact that the crisis had on these financial systems.

Shadow Banking and the Financial Crisis

In July 2007, the IKB, a mid-sized bank in Germany known for lending to the German Mittelstand, the small and medium-sized enterprises that form the backbone of the German economy, had to be rescued by the German government. It was the first bank to face bankruptcy in the course of events that would, in the next twenty-four months, lead to a global financial crisis and the Great Recession. Unbeknown to the public at large, the bank, by sponsoring a company that bought these papers and refinanced them through short-term asset-backed commercial papers, had, at the same time, engaged in the American market for structured products. While officially off the balance sheet, the bank was fully exposed to the liquidity risks of that entity. The bank had refinanced long-term structured assets, such as RMBSs with paper of an average length of forty days. A few weeks later, another relatively small German bank, the Sachsen LB, suffered the same fate, its losses being absorbed by the Land Saxony and itself being taken over by the Landesbank Badenwuertemberg on August 8th, 2007. Tensions escalated further when BNP Paribas announced the trading of papers issued by three of its funds on August 9, 2007, due to the illiquidity in markets that made an evaluation of the value of the assets these three funds held impossible, in turn making it impossible for investors to know the true value of their shares in these funds.[1] In effect, BNP was then shouldering the refinancing needs of these funds through its own access to markets.

That day, the interest rate for short-term refinancing spiked upward and increased above the rate at the Federal Reserve Bank by several dozens of basis points. Although spreads would fall back in the next weeks, this event marked the beginning of the collapse of the interbank market, central to the business model of banks that had come to rely on wholesale finance, rather than deposits to refinance their assets. It was not only the unexpected increase in default rates that led to market jitters. Instead, the fact that banks assumed risks deemed supposedly outside of banks' responsibilities led to an increasing distrust between banks regarding their true risk exposure to structured assets. The unexpected breakdown of the two German banks mentioned previously and the fact that these problems extended to truly global banks such as BNP made markets nervous. Further revelations about the large off-balance-sheet exposure of Citibank in fall 2007, amounting to more than $80 billion in off-balance-sheet structured investment vehicles and conduits, worsened these concerns over the true risk exposure of banks. A result of the uncertainty regarding the true risk exposure of banks, the lack of trust is crucial to an understanding of the crisis (Swedberg 2010).

These problems of distrust would only aggravate in the coming twelve months. In essence, what was witnessed was the collapse of

[1] Woll (2014, p. 18).

an entire system of credit intermediation outside of banking regulation that became known as the shadow banking system and the devastating effect it had on the banking system itself (Gorton 2010; Pozsar et al. 2010). This link between the shadow banking system and the banking system itself was maybe the greatest surprise to outside observers (Bernanke 2013). As postcrisis research has clarified, this shadow banking system was a network of activities engaged in credit intermediation outside of banking regulation, where the banks were centrally involved. It was based on a symbiosis between banks, broker-dealers, asset managers, and little capitalized off-balance-sheet entities that had formed over the course of the last thirty years, beginning in the USA (see Chapter 3). This network was highly dependent on liquid wholesale funding and global debt markets and was the outcome of the adaptation of banks to the competitive challenges they faced from investment banks, money market mutual funds, and the easier capital market access for many of its clients. Rather than merely fighting their new competitors, banks sought to adjust their business models to integrate capital markets and these new rivals for deposits, such as money market mutual funds, into their own activities. They facilitated access to capital markets for their clients and tailored products to the new large institutional investors (such as pension funds, asset managers, and money market mutual funds). They did so through an elaborate network of financial intermediaries, often off balance sheet, that were refinancing themselves in wholesale markets. These shadow banking activities of banks would usually produce only low margins for the banks involved, thereby increasing the need to trade in high volumes (Claessens and Ratnovski 2014).

A first elaborate analytical treatment of the shadow banking system was provided by a Moody's employee who had worked on rating the products produced by that system before the crisis, drawing a map of the interlinkages of different financial institutions involved in shadow banking and their link to the banking system (Pozsar 2008). What became clear was that instead of a single banks' balance sheet undertaking credit, liquidity, and maturity transformation, there now was a chain of financial institutions doing a bank's work. Later, in a remarkable report by the Federal Reserve of New York, the development and functioning of the system was explained (Pozsar et al. 2010). There, shadow banking was divided into an internal and an external component, but the main reason for its existence was seen to be savings on regulatory costs, or in other words, regulatory arbitrage around the costs of banking regulation. In what follows, I will draw on this report to clarify the structure of the shadow banking system.

The Role of Banks in Securitization

Central to this arbitrage activity was securitization, which initially hailed as the mechanism to distribute risk more evenly in the financial system, but in practice concentrated risk in the banking system. The organizational infrastructure of securitization requires the installment of special-purpose entities (SPE). These were part of an array of new nonfinancial institutions, commonly called the "shadow banking system," which together were engaged in credit intermediation. What previously involved only one organization, the bank that was engaged in maturity, liquidity, and credit transformation, was divided in the shadow banking system between different financial institutions. Shadow banking "essentially amounts to the vertical slicing" of traditional banks' credit intermediation process and include loan origination, loan warehousing, abs issuance, abs warehousing, Abs cdo issuance, abs intermediation and wholesale funding" (Poszar et al. 2010, p. 12). This is done in a strict sequential order and with a specific type of shadow bank engaged with a specific funding technique (Poszar et al. 2010). Such restructuring of the production of credit was largely aimed at circumventing banking regulation, by slicing the different functions of credit, liquidity, and maturity transformation, such that no single entity involved would be characterized as a bank, whereas the network of linked organizations together fulfilled the same function as a banking system. As Pozsar et al. put it,

The shadow credit intermediation process binds shadow banks into a network (s. exhibit 3), which forms the backbone of the shadow banking system and conducts an economic role that is analogous to the credit intermediation process performed by banks … In essence the shadow banking system decomposes the simple process of deposit-funded, hold-to-maturity lending conducted by banks into a more complex, whole-sale funded, securitization based lending process that involves a range of shadow banks. (Poszar et al. 2010, p. 13)

These networks can be further divided into an internal shadow banking system that was directly linked to the banks[2] and an external shadow bank system that was constituted by broker-dealers and other institutions that were not regulated by banking regulators.

The internal shadow banking system has been motivated mostly by regulatory and tax arbitrage concerns, driven by financial holding companies (FHCs) exploiting the legal frameworks to undertake their activities in the most beneficial space in terms of tax and regulatory requirements for credit transformation (Poszar et al. 2010, p. 25[3]; see Hansmann and Matthei 1998; Gorton and Souleles 2007; BCBS 2009b[4]; Ehrlich et al. 2009; Gorton 2010). FHCs were increasing their return on equity via reducing capital requirements for their lending activities (see Poszar et al. 2010, p. 26).[5]

Later, this perspective on the shadow banking system was enhanced by showing the underlying drivers of these activities, which was the increased demand of financial market investors (in particular money market mutual funds) for safe, private assets that would yield a little more than Treasury bills (Pozsar 2011, 2015). Banks set out to service these demands by engineering assets that had the exact characteristics investors were looking for: short-term, safe, but with a slight uptick over Treasury bills, using the techniques of securitization to tailor the risk profile demanded. To achieve this transformation of assets, banks often employed SPEs, robot companies controlled by autopilot contracts (Figure 2.1).

---

[2] This means that the activities of these shadow banks acted with indirect official enhancement of depository institutions, such as lines of credit to special-purpose entities. In this internal system, the goal was to transform risky long-term loans into seemingly risk-free short-term money market instruments (see Poszar et al. 2010, p. 14) and to earn the spread between the underlying loans and the interest to be paid to investors in the money market as fee income.

[3] "Whereby each of these functions and activities were conducted from those on- or off-balance sheet corners of an FHC and in a manner that required the least amount of capital to be held against them" (Poszar et al. 2010, p. 25).

[4] In a survey by the Basel Committee in 2008, some large institutions reported having more than 2,000 affiliated SPEs, "regulatory capital optimization" being a central motive (BCBS 2009b, p. 35).

[5] As we now know, before the crisis the entire financial system was based on the symbiosis among banks, broker-dealers, asset managers, and shadow banks, which generated a fee-based high return on equity for FHCs. This business model is highly dependent on liquid wholesale funding and global debt markets; if that is not given, the business model of FHCs breaks down.

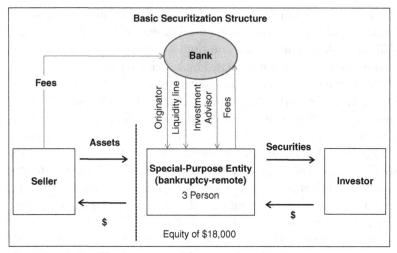

Figure 2.1 Role of banks in securitization.
(*Source*: BCBS 2009a, enlarged by some common features of support from banks for SPEs, based on a typical Dutch SPE; see Brinkhuis and van Eldonk 2008, p. 216)

The Infrastructure of Shadow Banking: SPEs and Bank Conglomerates

De facto controlled by banks, these SPEs were independent in legal form, thereby keeping the assets inside of these SPEs outside of the balance sheet of the FHC. These shell companies and their links to the banking conglomerate will be explained shortly in the text that follows.

As shown earlier, banks as originators and sponsors of an SPE[6] were central to the functioning of the shell companies. The contractual structure among the investors, the SPE, and the sponsoring bank guaranteed that the sponsor would absorb much of the revenue emanating from the credits held in the SPE, but also most of the risks. They gained fees from the companies that refinanced their credits in financial markets via the SPEs; they acted as investment advisors to the SPE; they often handled all the paperwork for the SPE; and they provided

---

[6] The originator is the corporation that sets up an SPE, the sponsor, the one that supports its day-to-day operation. Over the course of the lifetime of an SPE, the sponsorship may change in case an FHC wants to divest itself from this business.

the SPE with a liquidity line in case there should be a problem with the refinancing. Such dependence on refinancing the debt was particularly pronounced for SPEs refinancing their debt in the money market – that is, SPEs issuing asset-backed commercial paper, where the average duration of a commercial paper was forty days.[7] In effect, such SPEs could not exist without liquidity facility of their banking sponsor, as any short-term incapacity to refinance through short-term paper would mean an immediate closure of the SPE.

At the same time, the relationship between SPEs and banking conglomerates was structured in such a way as to avoid the possibility of consolidation on the balance sheet of the bank, transforming the SPE into an "orphan company" (see PwC 2005, p. 36). Ensuring that the SPE was not consolidated as a subsidiary of the bank required the structuring of the relationship between banks and SPEs in contraposition to the accounting standards for consolidation of subsidiaries in banking conglomerates.[8] In the 1980s, when SPEs for securitization were developed, this meant avoiding any capital link or daily interference with the SPE by the bank. Avoiding indicators of control in legal form while simultaneously maintaining control in economic substance required a shift of control into the contractual realm, where with the help of contracts all relevant actions by the SPE were prespecified, putting the SPE on a contractual "autopilot."[9] Furthermore, banks could not hold shares in the SPEs or provide any other capital for them, as this would have required them to place these SPEs on their balance sheet. This legal engineering led to very specific organizational structure for SPEs, described as "robot firms that have no employees, make no substantive economic decisions, have no physical location, and cannot go bankrupt" (Gorton and Souleles 2007, p. 550).

The most evident relationship of regulatory circumvention of sponsoring banks for SPEs in the internal shadow banking system was for

---

[7] Without a liquidity line, any incapacity to refinance through short-term paper would mean an immediate closure of the SPE.

[8] In the USA and Europe before 1998, the rules for consolidation in accounting terms maintained that a company needs to consolidate a subsidiary company in which it holds the majority of shares and/or controls its business strategy. Accounting norms stated that the control of the business had to be visible in the daily operation of the firm.

[9] These "autopilot mechanisms" specified that SPEs could not sell or buy assets on their own but that the investment advisor (the bank) made the investment decision (these are called service-level agreements).

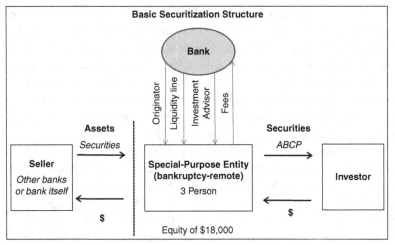

Figure 2.2 Securities arbitrage conduits.
(*Source*: BCBS 2009a, enlarged by some common features of support from banks for SPEs, based on a typical Dutch SPE; see Brinkhuis and van Eldonk 2008, p. 216)

securities arbitrage conduits, which served the function of off-balance-sheet proprietary trading of banks. For these conduits, the seller to the SPE became the banks themselves or other banks selling long-term asset-backed securities to the SPE, which were then refinanced via short-term asset-backed commercial papers, transferring the spread as fee income to the bank (see Figure 2.2).

These structures were invented in 1988 by two Citibank bankers in conjunction with British and American lawyers as a mode of regulatory arbitrage, in order to comply with Basel 1 capital requirements, without having to shrink the actual size of the bank's assets (see Ehrlich et al. 2009, p. 30). Given the minuscule amount of equity these entities held,[10] these robot companies had no capacity whatsoever to deal with a deterioration of the assets parked inside of them. In the market for medium- and long-term securities, where SPEs issued securities with at least one-year maturity to refinance their assets, the credit risk was

---

[10] A typical Dutch special-purpose entity, for example, is holding 18,000 euros (see Brinkhuis and van Eldonk 2008, p. 216) given that such SPEs might issue asset-backed commercial paper of 500 million euros or more in the money market. Such an SPE was effectively dealing with a leverage of 1 to 27,777, it was in the language of the accounting rule FAS 46R not viable without subordinated financial support.

transferred to investors. In the case of short-term asset-backed commercial papers, papers with a maturity of less than one year and usually less than ninety days, the credit risk was legally transferred to investors only through a contractual fire sale function.[11] In economic substance, however, the risk of credit deterioration remained with the sponsoring bank, as the bank had swapped exposure to the assets with an exposure to the SPE (Gorton and Souleles 2007). Given that asset-backed commercial paper had such a short maturity, beginning problems of credit deterioration, which did not yet trigger the fire sale, would lead to a refusal of investors to buy ABCP from this conduit, essentially forcing the bank to step in, as it had granted a liquidity facility to the SPE. In the following, Acharya and Schnabl (2009, p. 2) provide a good explanation of the business model of these off-balance-sheet entities:

banks use off-balance sheet vehicles to purchase long-term and medium-term assets financed with short-term debt. However, contrary to other forms of securitization, such as mortgage-backed securities or collateralized debt obligations, banks effectively keep the credit risk associated with the conduit assets. Hence, as long as banks are solvent, conduits are risk-free for outside investors but can generate significant risks for banks. In exchange for bearing these risks, banks have access to low-cost funding via the asset-backed commercial paper market.

Further, Acharya et al. (2013) call this financing technique "securitization without credit-risk transfer" and Gorton and Souleles (2007) speak of a collusion of investors and banks against the regulators to generate a risk-free asset.

The orphaning of credits and their risks into the balance sheets of special-purpose entities meant that credit risk was building up in the system to a much larger degree than preventive measures were being taken to deal with the possibility of the actualization of these risks. Instead of distributing the risks into financial markets, this form of securitization concentrated risks off the balance sheets of banks, returning on the balance sheets of banks in case the assets deteriorated. If they could avoid consolidation, banking conglomerates did not need

---

[11] If the credits in the balance sheet of the SPE deteriorated to a certain degree, all assets were to be sold and the remaining money distributed to investors.

to account for these risks via capital charges. At the same time, the risk exposure that was transformed into fee income improved their financial ratios and their evaluation in financial markets. In effect, banks, rather than engaging in risk transfer to private clients, were engaging in risk shifting: by maintaining most of the risks associated with these securitized loans and without increasing core capital requirements, banks were essentially shifting the risks of these assets onto the final guarantors of their solvency, that is to say, nation-states.

When the Music Stopped: The Run on the Shadow Banking System

It was at this point of the chain, the point where long-term complex products were refinanced by short-term papers, that the "music" stopped in 2007, and where the liquidity freeze in the interbanking market began. The dramatic impact of the crisis on the volume of asset-backed commercial papers outstanding in the USA, a market in which, owing to its liquidity many European banks were also active, can be seen in Figure 2.3.

The figure depicts the sudden fall of the market during the financial crisis, a fall occurring in two steps: the first starting in August 2007 and the second after the Lehman default in September 2008. This initial fall has been identified by many observers as the beginning of the financial crisis. The asset-backed commercial paper market, which had emerged in 1983 in the USA and experienced strong growth during the 1990s and 2000s, thus became the first in a series of markets related to the shadow banking system to collapse, having grown from $2 billion in 1983 to about $1.2 trillion in July 2007, when its growth came to a sudden end. By then, there were 296 ABCP conduits, 75 percent of which were sponsored by banks (Acharya and Schnabl 2009, p. 40).

These commercial papers, however, had come to finance a remarkably different mix of assets than what had been the case in the early 1990s. Whereas, back then, multiseller conduits were clearly the predominant organization that issued commercial paper to refinance self-liquidating short-term debt, conduits now would be used to warehouse mortgages and mortgage-backed securities before constructing further securities from them. They were also increasingly used to place assets with longer maturity off balance sheets and profit from the arbitrage generated by financing them with short-term loans. Outstanding

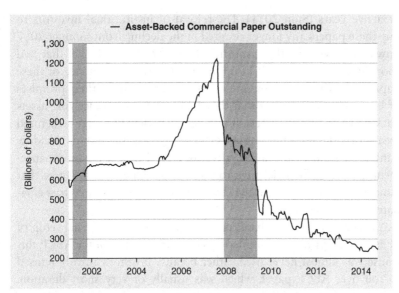

Figure 2.3 Volume of US asset-backed commercial paper market. Shaded areas indicate US recessions – 2014 research.stlouisfed.org
(*Source*: Board of Governors of the Federal Reserve System)

ABCPs climbed to unprecedented levels in 2005. Analyzing the upswing, Moody's points to "the ramping up of mortgage warehouse conduits, an increase in short-term tranches of CDOs, the growth of SIVs, the emergence of 'repo' conduits, and a continued increase in funding through multiseller conduits" (Moody's 2005, p. 2) to explain this growth. By mid-2007, hundreds of billions out of the $ 1.2 trillion US ABCP market were backed by mortgage-related assets, including some with subprime exposure. Collateralized debt obligations with a maturity of more than four years would also be refinanced by commercial paper for thirty days, with liquidity facilities provided by large American banks, such as Bank of America (FCIC 2011, p. 238f) or Citibank. Through these vehicles, the ABCP market became an important ingredient in the machinery that bought and packaged mortgages into MBSs and then, by placing them off balance sheets, sought to profit from them (Fligstein and Goldstein 2010, 2012).

In the next five months, the ABCP market fell by 36 percent, to $833 billion (Acharya et al. 2013, p. 516), by about 50 percent in the next two years (Standard and Poor's 2010, p. 5), and by 75 percent in the next five years (Shin 2011). The refusal of institutional investors to buy these papers any longer resulted in the decline from summer 2007 onwards. Owing to the institutional linkages of the banks that had sponsored the financial institutions involved in the issuance of these papers, banking conglomerates were forced to fulfill their promises of liquidity, which meant that they had to take the underlying assets back on their balance sheets. In fact, the way the SPEs were structured meant that the liquidity promises of the banks to the internal shadow banking system in the financial crisis turned into a credit enhancement, shielding financial investors from losses to such a degree that almost no triggers were drawn and almost no losses to investors emanated from this sector.

Although there was a bankruptcy clause in the contractual setup of SPEs, ensuring the distribution of losses to the holders of the ABCP, this clause was almost never used, either because investors already refused to roll over ABCP paper, which was usually of very short duration, or because banks either were contractually forced or had voluntarily decided to shield their clients from losses due to reputation risks. In this way, the strong shrinkage of the money market in asset-backed commercial papers (between almost 100 percent for structured investment vehicles to 66 percent for securities arbitrage conduits and more than 50 percent for multiseller conduits; see S&P 2010, p. 5f) led to a reappearance of the assets placed into these SPEs on the balance sheets of banks (see Acharya and Schnabl 2009, 2010). In the view of Poszar et al. (2010, p. 50), "Ultimately, it was the embedded rollover risks inherent in funding long term assets through short term securitization sold into money markets that triggered the run on the shadow banking system."

As in the nineteenth-century bank runs, the fact that the assets of investors were not insured against the breakdown of the system led to the breakdown of the system itself through a complete freeze in liquidity. The run on the shadow banking sector could be stopped only once public credit puts were enacted, as the Federal Reserve has done repeatedly starting in 2007.[12] The private system that had provided

---

[12] The most dramatic intervention with respect to the ABCP market was the commercial paper facility installed by the FED in October 2008 in the vein of the Lehman failure, when the entire commercial paper market came to a halt. It lasted until 2010 and at its peak in January 2009 acquired ABCP to the value of about $120 billion, making up about one-third of the total volume (Adrian et al. 2010, p. 27).

such credit puts had come to create severe doubts over its ability to pay for them. Of all the SPEs involved in the internal shadow banking system, the SPEs issuing asset-backed commercial paper are the only ones that undertake all three functions of banks (credit, liquidity, and maturity transformation) at the same time (Poszar et al. 2010, p. 18), making them the most bank-like. However, in almost no legislation – not in Europe or in the USA – were these SPEs even deemed to be financial institutions, let alone credit institutions. They frequently remained off balance sheet, and the liquidity lines granted to them by banks were often excluded from regulatory capital charges. In those countries where they actually were regulated, their growth before the crisis as well as their negative impact during the crisis was smaller, as will be shown in the text that follows.

The Impact of the Fallout of the ABCP Markets on the USA and European Nations

The different impacts of the financial crisis on the national financial systems of different countries have been linked to the extent the banking conglomerates of these countries were engaged in the shadow banking system in general, and in the asset-backed commercial paper market in particular (in the following ABCP market, see Acharya and Schnabl 2009; Acharya et al. 2009; Diamond and Rajan 2009; Hardie and Howarth 2009, 2013; Jablecki and Machaj 2009, p. 302). In general, European countries compared with all other regions, but the USA has been disproportionately affected by the US subprime crisis. One reason was the strong engagement of European banks in the ABCP market (Shin 2011), as can be seen in Figure 2.4.

Up until 2001, the USA and continental Europe were at the same level, but then a massive divergence set in, leading the exposure of European continental banks to become almost double that of US banks. The breakdown in the ABCP market affected US and eurozone banks massively, but eurozone banks at a much larger scale, with the latter, from 2002 onwards, persistently sponsoring the majority of assets in ABCP conduits (Arteta et al. 2013, p. 43), making up 45 percentage points of global volume in January 2007 (Shin 2011, p. 21; see Figure 2.4).

Analyzing the differences in the impact of the crisis around the globe, the committee on global financial systems, a subgroup of the

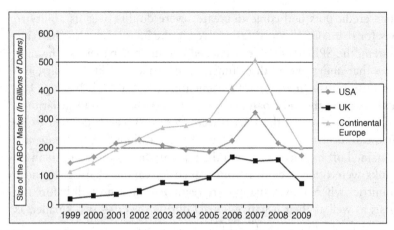

Figure 2.4 Engagement of banks from the USA, UK, and the eurozone in the ABCP market.
(*Source*: Moody's Index Program)

Basel Committee, comes to the conclusion: "it might be that the regulatory structure in respect to off-balance sheet vehicles is the determining feature for security of different banking sectors" (CGFS 2009, p. 6). In line with this observation, some countries have escaped the first phase of the crisis rather unscathed, such as Spain[13] or France, where ABCP conduits were negligible and regulated, while others such as Germany and the Netherlands have severely suffered because of the large-scale engagement of their banks. Figure 2.5 shows the exposure of banks from the US and eurozone countries for all countries that had such an exposure.[14]

The figure shows that both absolute exposure and the temporal development of the market are by no means uniform. Table 2.1 provides further numeric information on the evolution of the engagement of banks in that market, showing both the absolute and relative

---

[13] This statement refers to the financial crisis that started in 2007; it does not refer to the subsequent eurozone crisis that has deeply engulfed Spain and has threatened to engulf France.

[14] Finland, Portugal, and Luxembourg, the other continental "western" European banking systems, are excluded from the comparison, as none of their banks ever engaged in the ABCP market, making a regulatory update unnecessary. Portugal's update stemmed from an institutional linkage to decisions of the Bank of Spain (Acharya and Schnabl 2010).

Table 2.1 *Asset Volume of ABCP Conduits by Nationality of Sponsoring Bank and Evolution between 1999, 2007, and 2009*

	Asset Volume of ABCP Conduits in 2007 (in billions of $)	As Percentage of Size of Banking System	Growth from 1999 to 2007 (%)	Asset Volume of ABCP Conduits in 2009 (in billions of $)	Decline 2007/ 2009 (%)
USA	256,863	1,855	75	173.245	46.5
Germany	204.009	3.15	397	60.558	73.5
UK	153.941	2.203	662	73.784	52.1
Netherlands	153.850	4.64	200	54.980	64.3
France	60,599	1.055	183	62.136	−2.5
Belgium	35.975	2.88	1014	15.715	56.4

Sources: Moody's Program Index, OECD Banking Database, author's calculations.

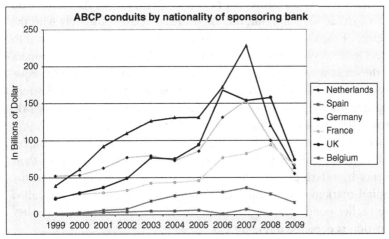

Figure 2.5 Differential exposures of different continental European countries to the ABCP market.
(*Source*: Moody's Index Program)

exposures in relation to the overall size of the banking system. It also depicts growth of the market from 1999 to 2007 and the decline from 2007 to 2009.

Table 2.1 again shows the different growth dynamics, with European banking systems exposure growing much more extensively from 1999 to 2007. Reviewing the table, we see that after the USA, German banks were those with the largest exposure to the asset-backed commercial paper market in 2007 ($256.863 billion in June 2007), with British and Dutch banks closely following ($154 billion); French banks at a distant fifth, had $60,599 billion in June 2007; Belgian banks are sixth ($36 billion). All of these European markets exhibit a rather continuous growth up until 2007, whereas the US market reaches a first peak in 2001, to be reached again only in 2006, showing a spike in 2007 (see Figure 2.5).

Once a reader puts the size of the ABCP conduits sponsored by national banks in relation to the size of the banking system, the differential exposure of these national banking systems in 2007 can be better appreciated. The numbers in Table 2.1 document the pronounced exposure of Dutch and Belgian banks, which are at least as exposed as Germany (see also Hardie and Howarth 2013, p. 44). As Hardie and Howarth (2013) point out, this exposure correlates positively with the impact of the crisis, with those countries more exposed also forced to inject more capital and to provide more credit guarantees. The impact of the crisis was worse for banks from those countries that were especially active in the securities arbitrage segment of this market, an engagement that was heavily influenced by the regulatory framework, as will be explained in the text that follows.

At the inception of the ABCP market, securitization techniques had been used by banks to facilitate the capital market access of their clients by offering to buy their credits and to refinance them in the capital markets. The entities facilitating these transactions are called multiseller conduits and dominate the global market. The way they function is depicted in Figure 2.6.

As can be seen, companies sell receivables and loans (such as outstanding credit card payments) to the ABCP conduit, which, in turn, refinances it with ABCP. The bank provides services and liquidity as well as credit enhancements for which it receives service fees.

From 1999 onwards, another type of conduit gained prominence, the securities arbitrage conduit, which grew in value from $56 billion in 1999 to $241 billion in 2006 (Moody's Program Index). These

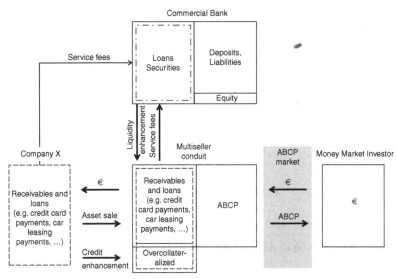

Figure 2.6 The structure of a multiseller conduit.

conduits no longer served clients or securitized loans the bank itself had originated. Instead, the bank directed the ABCP to buy highly rated securitized products from other issuing SPEs, thereby becoming the final stage in the long chain of off-balance-sheet credit extension and maturity transformation, later known as the internal shadow banking system (Pozsar et al. 2010).[15] Securities arbitrage conduits were a way for banks to engage in simple arbitrage activities in capital markets by buying long-term assets and refinancing them with short-term paper without having to withhold core capital for it. Other market segments were structured investment vehicles, hybrid conduits, and single-sellers, which are positioned between those two conduit forms. Single-seller conduits are vehicles where the bank sells assets directly from its loan books to the conduits in order to warehouse them before they can be sold off as asset-backed securities. Here, the main purpose is to generate further liquidity for the bank, but banks can also use these structures for regulatory arbitrage. The category hybrid conduit represents conduits where multiseller and securities arbitrage business are combined. Structured investment vehicles (SIVs)

---

[15] A graphical representation of such a securities arbitrage conduit can be found in Appendix 2.

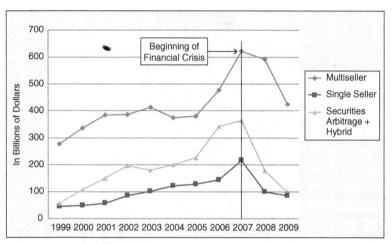

Figure 2.7 Evolution of different ABCP market segments pre- and postcrisis. (*Sources*: Moody's Program Index, author's calculations)

are a form of securities arbitrage conduits; however, they can also issue longer term notes and have more active portfolio management (see Ehrlich et al. 2009). Figure 2.7 depicts the way these different segments of the market developed from 1999 onwards.

Figure 2.7 shows that the multiseller segment dominated the market but that from 1999 to 2007, its dominance is reduced. Making up 75 percent of the market in 1999, its volume represented half of the market in 2007. Still, though, the segment of securities arbitrage and hybrid conduits, conduits that involved some degree of rule circumvention and regulatory arbitrage, would grow almost ninefold in those eight years. Making up $50 billion in 1999, they would grow to almost $400 billion, representing one-third of the market. Single-seller conduits, often used by banks to warehouse structured products before they could be sold, would also reach about $200 billion, or one-sixth of the market, in 2007. Since the onset of the crisis in 2007 up until 2009, the ABCP market experienced a decline of about 50 percent in two years (S&P 2010), structured investment vehicles declined by 100 percent, securities arbitrage conduits declined by 74 percent, while multiseller conduits declined only by 38 percent.[16] While multisellers

---

[16] This difference clarifies that while using the same construct, securities arbitrage conduits were disguised proprietary trading in complex securities, while multiseller conduits served client needs.

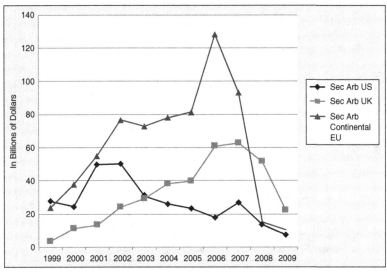

Figure 2.8 Volume of securities arbitrage conduits sponsored by US, UK, and continental European banks.
(*Data source*: Moody's Program Index)

were unaffected by the initial liquidity crunch in 2007 and fell only from 2008 onwards, securities arbitrage and hybrid conduits were directly affected and dropped by more than 50 percent over the course of one year, with similar developments for single-sellers (see Figure 2.7).

What is peculiar about the market is that European continental banks, which arrived rather late (starting in the early 1990s, but really becoming engaged after the transformation of the market in 1998, see Moody's 1998, 2002,) sponsored more than 50 percent of the volume of securities arbitrage conduits from 2002 onwards, reaching 62 percent in 2006 and 70 percent in 2007 (Figure 2.8) (see also Pozsar et al. 2010, p. 32f).

Figure 2.8 portrays the tremendous fall of the volume of securities arbitrage conduits sponsored by European banks from 2006 onward, but most importantly from 2008 when it fell by more than $70 billion in one year – in other words, about 80 percent. The exposure in the securities arbitrage market hence proved to be a huge source of loss for the banks in continental Europe sponsoring these conduits, as securitized loans returned to their balance sheets. Yet, in the segment of SIVs, a more sophisticated version of securities arbitrage conduits that

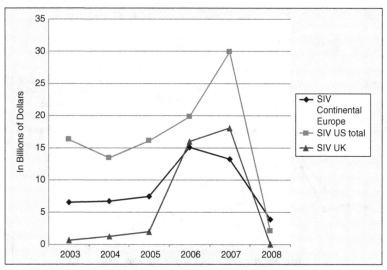

Figure 2.9 Structured investment vehicles sponsored by US and EU banks.
Note: Moody's only differentiates SIVs from securities arbitrage conduits from 2003
onward.
(*Data source*: Moody's Program Index 2003–2010)

was less reliant on short-term ABCP and, instead, depended more on
market-based liquidity management, the engagement of banks from
the EU was much more muted with respect to their US or UK peers, as
illustrated by Figure 2.9. This was an expression of a certain lack of
sophistication on the part of continental European banks.

However, as I will detail in the text that follows, this was also the
expression of a different regulatory environment, where from 2004
onward a 10 percent credit conversion factor was imposed on liquidity
lines by the Federal Reserve, which made SIVs much more attractive to
US banks. Most European banks, on the other hand, faced no capital
charges on securities arbitrage conduits, which is why they preferred
this simpler version.

Owing to very weak margins, these market segments where regulatory arbitrage was rampant were particularly sensitive to regulation, as
regulatory costs could wipe out any gains to be had from this business
(Hellwig 2010, p. 27). The large engagement of European banks in these
segments, then, was an outcome of lacking regulatory adaptation and
points to different regulatory stances. Table 2.2 depicts the differential
exposure in the Western countries most engaged in this market.

Table 2.2 *Exposure to the Different Segments of the Market by Banks from the Five Countries in 2007*

	Multiseller Conduits (%)	Single-Seller Conduits (%)	Hybrid Conduits (%)	Securities Arbitrage Conduits (%)	Structured Investment Vehicles (%)	Others (%)
Global	43.8	16	13.2	13.8	9.3	4
Germany	38.5	1	26.5	22	6.7	5,3
Netherlands	29	37	8	21	2.3	2.7
Belgium	0	0	78.9	8	0	13
France	93	1	0	0	1.2	4.8
USA	55.3	11.8	10.5	4.9	12.6	4.9

Source: Moody's Program Index 2007.

As is evident from the table, Germany has an exposure to hybrid conduits and securities arbitrage conduits that is much higher than the global average, whereas in the Netherlands, it is the exposure to single-sellers and securities arbitrage that is equally above average. The Belgian market features only conduits that, at least to some degree, engage in regulatory arbitrage. In complete contrast, France's exposure to the multiseller segment, which served client needs with 93 percent, is exceptionally high. Lastly, the US exposure is largely in line with global averages, with a slightly lower exposure to the securities arbitrage segment, but with a higher exposure to SIVs.

In line with these different exposures, the impact of the initial phase of the crisis (summer of 2007 to summer of 2008) in these five countries has been very different. In the USA, off-balance-sheet exposure forced several banks into write-downs and downgrading, even before Lehman Brothers failed in September 2008. No other American bank was more affected by the fallout of the ABCP market than Citibank, the bank that had started the entire market in the early 1980s by setting up two large multiseller conduits and in 2003 would still sponsor 9 percent of it.[17] In 2007, Citibank had more than $80 billion financed off balance

---

[17] Already in 1988, it had set up the first SIV, seeking to comply with the new core capital requirements creatively (Ehrlich et al. 2009). It would set up six further SIVs, together refinancing about $96 billion of assets (mostly asset-backed securities) in summer 2007. It had furthermore extended liquidity

sheet in ABCP conduits. This and its pronounced exposure to SIVs led to severe financial problems to be resolved only through several injections of public money in 2008, totaling more than $45 billion as well as state guarantees.[18]

The Dutch, Belgian, and German financial systems stand out as those continental European systems whose large and complex banks have incurred the highest losses and precipitated many billions of credit lines and credit injections by the respective governments in the early crisis phase (Chang and Jones 2013; Hardie and Howarth 2013b).[19] In contrast, the French banking system incurred smaller losses and more limited government interventions (see IMF 2009a). In July 2009, the IMF enumerated total write-downs of German banks to constitute 9 percent of the total, while French banks only accounted for 3 percent (see Hardie and Howarth 2009, p. 1017; Howarth 2013). A remarkable fact about the distribution of loss-making banks is that in August 2008, two-thirds of the write-downs in Germany were taken by public banks or banks with indirect public ownership.[20] The IMF consultation paper on Germany states, "As of end-September 2008, Germany accounted for about a quarter of European bank write downs. Of these, about two thirds have been in public or quasi-public sector banks" (IMF 2009b, p. 12). Onaran (2008) estimates the losses of German banks in August 2008 at $54.1 billion, while French banks had lost $23.3 billion and Dutch banks $9.8 billion.

The Regulatory Impact on the Sponsoring of ABCP Conduits by Banks

The differential exposure of US and European Banks to ABCP conduits in general and conduits used for regulatory arbitrage in particular

---

facilities worth $25 billion to ensure the sale of commercial paper refinancing CDOs. Seeing it as an opportunity to gain fee income for a quasi-riskless activity, it held only $200 million against that risk. Citibank would see its assumptions radically questioned by the events of 2007 (FCIC 2011, p. 138f), requiring it to come up with $25 billion in cash as well as more capital to satisfy bank regulators.

[18] See www.wsj.com/articles/SB122747680752551447

[19] While these are the countries with the biggest government intervention on the continent, Great Britain has been required to intervene the most in the EU, with £656.5 billion (see Richerchi e studi 2009b, p. 9).

[20] IKB Deutsche Industriebank, which lost $15.5 billion, is counted among them, as it was 38 percent owned by the public Kreditanstalt fuer Wiederaufbau.

can be largely traced to different regulatory capital charges for conduit activities. Regulatory capital charges, which define the equity that banks have to own in order to be able to deal with the potential risks of banking business without going bankrupt, were central in the dynamics of the market. These charges seek especially to address unexpected credit losses from assets which are deemed part of the banking group.[21] Regulatory capital requirements are costly to banks in the sense that they reduce their capacity for leverage (that is, banks can use less borrowed money for their actions, limiting their profitability) and that equity, in contrast to debt, commands a higher price. Given the small margins that were earned in engaging in the ABCP business and, in particular, in the business of securities arbitrage conduits, banking regulators could discourage banks from operating in this market by applying capital charges to their activities. This could happen either by forcing banks to consolidate these SPEs on their respective balance sheets or by applying capital charges to the liquidity lines that the banks had pledged to their SPEs (Bens and Moynihan 2008; Acharya and Schnabel 2010).

These core capital costs that may ensue if a bank has to consolidate an SPE on the balance sheet of the banking group or for the liquidity lines provided can have a decisive impact on the decision of the bank to establish the SPE in the first place (Interview, senior managers in a German bank, July 12, 2011). If placed off balance sheet, ABCP conduits impacted favorably on profitability and required capital reserves. First, the bank could reduce the regulatory capital reserves, which it needed to hold as it needed only to account for the core capital charges for the liquidity line, if there was one. Second, banking groups that engaged in SPEs kept most of the revenues generated by the SPEs by making them pay fees for services to the sponsoring bank. These services included the selection of assets to be bought by the SPE, the collection of revenue from the assets held by the SPE, and the payout of interest to investors of the commercial papers. Thus, the entire business activity of the SPE was outsourced to the bank. Third, and as a consequence of these two effects, the return on equity for banks improved (in some cases such as IKB Deutsche Industriebank AG, markedly) as a consequence of this off-balance-sheet activity. For these reasons, off-balance-sheet securities arbitrage conduits were

---

[21] The amount of capital to be withheld is calculated according to the perceived risk of the assets.

extremely attractive for banks, especially for those with poor returns on equity (Bannier and Haensel 2006; Haensel and Krahnen 2007; Arteta et al. 2013, p. 54).[22]

The margins for this form of "proprietary trading outside of the banks' balance sheet" (Interview, German banker, June 14, 2011) are, however, not very high (see Acharya et al. 2009; Hellwig 2010). While exact margins are not known, they are estimated at between ten and thirty basis points[23] (Hellwig 2010, p. 27), which creates the need to trade in large sums. An effect of this low profitability is that if banks are forced to employ their own capital to cover the unexpected losses of the assets placed into these conduits, these entities become unprofitable because of the opportunity costs of regulatory capital (see Hellwig 2010, p. 26). The off-balance-sheet status of SPEs and the assets placed into them were crucial to manipulate earnings and regulatory capital requirements. At the same time that banks were structuring their relationship to keep these SPEs and their assets legally off balance sheet, they sought to maintain control over the assets that they transferred to the SPEs. This required an exercise in law-abiding regulatory circumvention in the field of accounting and legal engineering. The sensitivity of the ABCP market to regulatory circumstances is well captured in Figure 2.10.

Having reached a global size of $600 billion in June 2000, the growth of the ABCP market would come to a halt when Enron collapsed in the USA. The regulatory uncertainty regarding the rules for off-balance-sheet accounting in the USA in the aftermath of Enron's downfall led to a global standstill in volume over the next three years (2002–2005). This standstill was caused by a decline in issuance in the USA from 2001 up until 2006, while the exposure from banks from EU countries continued to grow (see Figure 2.5), suggesting very different regulatory dynamics.

The extent to which banking regulators could interfere with these rule-circumventing practices was limited by the degree to which core capital charges were based on national accounting rules and their capacity to force banking conglomerates to record these conduits on their balance sheets. In many countries, regulatory capital charges are calculated using the accounting numbers provided by national

---

[22] Arteta et al. (2013) find that lower returns on assets increases the probability for European banks to sponsor a securities arbitrage vehicle at a 5 percent level of statistical significance.

[23] Which is a 0.1 to 0.3 percentage point margin.

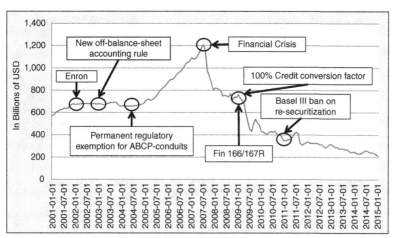

Figure 2.10 Volume of global asset-backed commercial paper market, January 2001–January 2015 (monthly average), denominated in $.
(*Source*: Reproduced from Acharya and Schnabl 2009, p. 40)

accounting rules. If securitization special-purpose entities (SSPEs) were excluded from the consolidated financial statements of FHCs, they, subsequently, are automatically excluded from the prudential scope of consolidation, if the prudential scope is a subset of the financial scope of consolidation. To force banks to account for the risks they were taking in that market, then, one option was the intervention by the banking regulator in the realm of accounting rules. If banks were deemed to control another entity (such as an ABCP conduit), the assets of that entity appear on the balance sheet of the banking group and the banking group can then be forced to account for the "riskiness" of those assets by being asked to build up additional capital reserves. Alternatively, regulators could intervene if they had the regulatory discretion to impose core capital charges if they deemed them to be appropriate on SPEs and the liquidity lines extended to them by the bank. Figure 2.11 depicts these three entry points for regulation by pointing, in the first place, to the classification of the SPE; in the second place, to the frontier of the banking conglomerate; and, finally, to the liquidity line and the capital charge that might be applied to it.

The first entry point for regulation is centered around the questions of whether and how both to regulate and to supervise the ABCP conduits themselves, as these are active agents in financial markets, emitting commercial papers into financial markets and buying up debt.

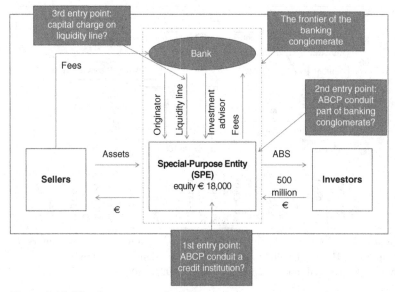

Figure 2.11 The three entry points for regulation.

This dimension is largely relegated to lawmakers.[24] The second one regards the question of whether the ABCP conduit should be deemed a subsidiary of the banking conglomerate that is sponsoring it in prudential terms. This status would imply the application of core capital requirements to the assets inside of the SPE. The third access point pertains to the liquidity lines granted by the banking conglomerates to their ABCP conduits. These last two points were directly related to supervisory work; hence, they involved banking regulators directly. At these three points, regulators and legislators could have interfered in the construction of these tools for circumventing banking regulation. In most jurisdictions, however, ABCP conduits remained completely exempted from core capital charges up until 2008 – that is to say, ABCP conduits were treated as neither credit nor financial institutions; they were not included as subsidiaries as part of the banking conglomerate; nor were core capital charges applied to the liquidity line. This book asks why this was the case and how we can understand the variations observed in this general trend toward regulatory exemption.

[24] This will be treated extensively in Chapter 5.

The Impact of Regulatory Interventions in My Four Cases

The treatment of ABCP conduits, their regulation of the off-balance-sheet criteria in prudential accounting for special-purpose entities, and their linkages with the banking conglomerate in terms of liquidity facilities represented the interaction of banking regulators with recent financial innovations from Anglo-Saxon countries made a difference to the impact of the financial crisis in the USA and the EU.[25] If regulators forced their banks to account for the risks that they took instead of allowing them to place the set off balance sheet, the extent of that activity remained small because of the lack of profitability of the activity. How far banking regulators intervened in the activities of their banking conglomerates when these set up off-balance-sheet vehicles and how they treated their linkages to the banks in the form of liquidity facilities are important aspects of regulatory capacity of states investigated in this book.[26] Figure 2.12 shows the exposure of the banks from the four countries selected for comparison to the different segments of the market. It also documents the regulatory interventions that occurred in this time frame with respect to the second and third of these three entry points.[27]

As Figure 2.12 documents, the volume of these segments of the market started at almost the same level in 1999 but developed very differently. German and Dutch banks would develop a very high engagement in this rule evading segment (in particular when taking into account the size of their banking systems as well as the overall involvement in the ABCP market; see Table 2.2). From 2001 onward, the US evolution was more moderate than in Germany or the Netherlands,

---

[25] A further difference of French banks, as noted by Xiao (2009, p. 6), is that the regulatory capital adequacy of French banks was stronger than that of their European peers before the crisis. In 2006, the Tier I ratio of French banks was about 100 basis points above that of their peers. Related to this peculiarity is the extent of assets and liabilities which French banks held at fair value (mark to market valuation), thus increasing the risk exposure and, therefore, the risk provisioning of banks.

[26] The interesting paradox that the accounting norms for off-balance-sheet financing on the EU level since 2005 were more stringent than in the USA, but securities arbitrage conduits were still growing in the EU will be treated in Chapter 6.

[27] The regulation of the first entry point, that is, the regulatory treatment of securitization SPEs as credit or financial institutions, will be analyzed at length in Chapter 5.

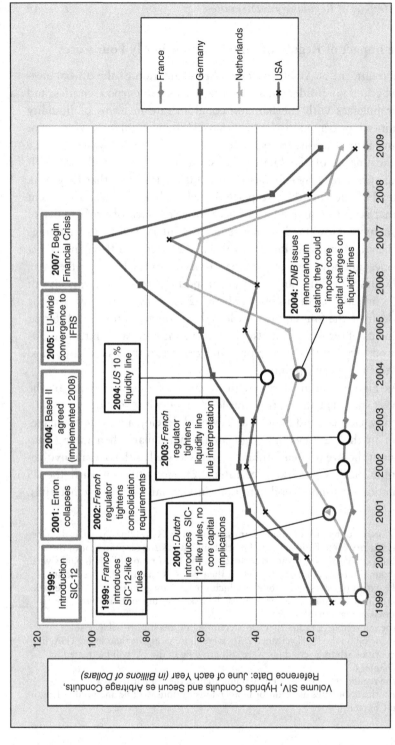

Figure 2.12 Volume of SIV, Hybrid Conduits, and Securities Arbitrage Conduits in France, Germany, the Netherlands, and the USA.
(*Source:* Moody's Program Index, author's calculations)

an outcome of the regulatory uncertainty following Enron's demise in 2001 and the imposition of core capital charges for liquidity lines in 2004.[28] In contrast to the other three cases, the volume in France in this segment actually decreased from 1999 onward to 0 in 2006, stopping before the crisis.

As Figure 2.12 indicates and the following chapters will seek to document, these developments were by no means arbitrary but were the direct consequence of conscious regulatory action. In the USA, regulatory changes occurred in 2004 as an outcome of the interaction between banking and accounting rules. It was the Enron scandal and the ensuing accounting changes that exemplified permitting a faction in the Federal Reserve critical of the largely unregulated engagement of banks in the ABCP market to push through an increase in the core capital requirements for liquidity lines for banks. Unable to push through an increase in those core capital requirements domestically and/or the consolidation of ABCP conduits on their sponsors' balance sheet in the 1990s, the regulator inserted an increase in the core capital requirements for liquidity facilities to 20 percentage points in the negotiations for the Basel II framework. Being able to point to the agreement reached on this initiative, it could in the 2000s insert an increase to 10 percent, partially explaining the move of US banks from securities arbitrage conduits to SIVs in the 2000s.

The starkest case of regulatory intervention is presented by the French banking regulator, which intervened both in the realm of accounting and banking regulation. In 1999, the banking regulator was actively involved in introducing a rule that was modeled after the International Accounting Standards published in 1998, the only standard capable of forcing conduits on the balance sheet (PwC 2006; this transition is explained in Chapter 6). In 2000, the French banking regulator issued a law transforming the accounting numbers into core capital charges. When it realized in 2002 that the standard did not have the desired consequences, it issued a recommendation that tightened the interpretation of the accounting rule and forced banks to consolidate their conduits. As a consequence, the advantages of core capital arbitrage vanished for the banks (Interview, French banker, March 25, 2011).

---

[28] The rise in the US segment in 2007 crucially involves a move toward SIVs from 2003 onward.

In contrast, the introduction of a similar rule in 2001 in the Netherlands did not have an impact on the development of the market. As I will show in Chapter 7, this difference stems from the fact that the banking regulator there had no involvement in the implementation and enforcement of these rules, leading to a lack in consolidation of conduits until 2005. Furthermore, the detachment of the banking regulator from the formulation, monitoring, and enforcement of these rules and the lack in contact with the auditors of their bank meant that they were cut off from the activities of regulatory arbitrage of their banks. This made them open to the presentation of their banks regarding the advantages this market activity posed, a stance that has been described as cognitive capture in the literature (see Chapter 3). In the German case, the banking regulator is also detached from the actual accounting decisions of the regulator's banks. It plays no direct role in the formulation or enforcement of the rules. In 2002 it even opposed the convergence with the more modern accounting rules, owing to concerns over the implication of this rule for the core capital requirements of its banks (BaKred 2002). As I will show, this stance comes closest to what the literature has described as regulatory capture (Chapter 3), but can be understood only by the particular competitive position German banks held in the European space (Chapter 5).

3 | How to Explain the Absence of Regulatory Action on Shadow Banking: Situating Regulators in Their Socioeconomic Context

There were very few (regulators) who had realized that, and really a few, Spain, they just forbid it, and Italy in big parts, the question is why do some forbid it and others don't and that is where the reflection starts regarding the question, under which pressures are regulators and who influences their way of seeing the world.

(Interview, former board member Bundesbank August 2010)

Many authors have noted the lack of regulation of securitization activities of banks in the ABCP market precrisis (cf. Acharya and Schnabl 2009, pp. 20–25, who review the lack of regulation in several countries; Adrian and Shin 2009; Adrian and Ashcraft 2012b), but a dearth of explanations for this widespread regulatory exemption exists. Research on the increasing interlinkages of banking systems with shadow banking in general has acknowledged the structuring role of regulation for the engagement of banks in this sector (cf. Hardie et al. 2013a, p. 697). However, in their research to date, authors have emphasized the agency of bankers within these regulatory constraints (Acharya and Schnabel 2010; Bell and Hindmoor 2015a, b) but have neglected regulators' agency and the institutional constraints within which that agency evolved. When it comes to explaining the regulatory exemptions, most often the concept of cognitive capture is evoked.

But as I will show in the text that follows, the argument of cognitive capture (as a particular form of regulatory capture), which has become a prominent explanation for regulatory leniency before the crisis (e.g., Buiter 2008; Baker 2010; Turner 2011) cannot account for the almost uniform global lack of regulation. Instead, I argue, we have to take into account the structural constraints that national regulators were facing with respect to the securitization activities of their domestic banks, constraints that were partially shaped by the Basel Accords and the way the European financial integration was set up.[1] Additionally, I argue the theory of cognitive capture cannot account for those instances in which cognitive capture has not occurred, as it does not have a positive theory of regulatory action. After elaborating on this account, showing its merits and shortcomings, I will thus set out to construct a positive theory of regulatory action, one that is able to contextualize regulatory action and its need for interaction with the regulated. Doing so, I will draw, on the one hand, on sociolegal studies of regulation and the social studies of finance, and on the other hand, on theories of structural constraints in international political economy.

Regulatory and Cognitive Capture

Models of regulatory capture have become a powerful metaphor for thinking about regulation in current society, so much so that they are commonly used to explain regulatory failures in general and the financial crisis in particular (Carpenter and Moss 2013, p. 2). A fundamental assumption in this private interest view of regulation is that regulatory authorities do not maximize social welfare, but are actually rather self-interested. This applies to politicians who are vying for (re-) election and also to the bureaucrats charged with regulating the sector, vying for better-paid jobs in the private sector (Stigler 1971). The regulated sector itself is seen at an advantage with respect to the public at large in its struggle for advantageous regulation, as its smaller size and common interests allow more effective mobilization (Stigler 1971, 1974; Peltzman 1976; Becker 1983; for a concise summary of this work see Harnay and Scialom 2016). This mobilization advantage is even more pronounced in technical fields such as financial regulation, which seem arcane to the public at large and require expertise to participate. In these fields, as Culpepper (2011) has shown, business power to wield regulation in one's favor is particularly strong. So, at the core of this theory stands the belief that, over time, regulation will

---

[1] This is not to deny that the ideologies prevalent in these times, emphasizing the capacity for financial markets undistorted by too much financial regulation, could act as efficient markets, if only incentives were set accordingly. However, it is to place these ideological convictions in their place, as a force to be reckoned with but that evidently was not omnipotent. This stance is driven mostly by the fact that ascribing such powers could lead to leniency once such an ideology is replaced by a different one.

come to serve the interests of the industry involved (e.g., Peltzman et al. 1989). This applies not only to regulation itself but also to financial supervision, which will be lax and low cost in accordance with the interest of the financial industry (Heinemann and Schüler 2004).

One cannot reject the immediate plausibility of this theory with respect to certain precrisis developments. For example, the light-touch regulation of the Financial Services Authority (FSA) in the UK can be seen as an outcome of too close links between the regulators and the regulated, which in conjunction with the importance of the financial sector for the UK might have well underlain the by now notorious style of the FSA (e.g., Morgan 2012). But as Carpenter and Moss (2013) have argued, theories of regulatory capture suffer from a lack of rigor in terms of evidence and the dangers of tautology, as regulation and regulatory failure are by definition redistributive, which means that there will always be winners and losers. The analyst, thus, is in danger of operating by deductive reasoning, assuming that those who benefited were the ones who captured the regulator. Therefore, rather than providing us with hard facts about the channels of influence and the ways by which the regulated captured the regulator, these accounts often are based on stipulations (Carpenter and Moss 2013).

Furthermore, regulatory capture as an explanation is dangerous, as when led to its logical conclusion, it almost inevitably leads to calls for enlightened self-regulation (critical Jasanoff 2012, 12).

As regulators will by definition be subject to capture, they cannot be entrusted with looking after the public good. In this view, proximity of regulators and regulated is seen as a problem, and transparency in these encounters is prescribed. In its most sophisticated versions, theorists suggest to introduce third parties who have the public interest in mind in order to supervise the supervisors (Ayres and Braithwaite 1992; Barth et al. 2012). However, such strategies pose practical problems, for example, how to treat confidential data and related problems with the accountability of the supervisors of the supervisor, threatening an infinite negative regress (Ayres and Braithwaite 1992). Therefore, theories of regulatory capture cannot really provide a blueprint for regulatory reform, as they cannot bridge the necessary information exchange between the regulator and the regulated on the one hand and the necessary distance between them on the other hand.

This problematic is put center stage by a particular subset of regulatory capture theories that emphasizes how regulators in their outlook were unduly influenced by the ways in which the regulated were seeing the world precrisis. The reasons for this influence are located in the dominating neoliberal view on banking and the role of regulation before the crisis. This theory postulated a fundamental asymmetry of information and expertise between regulators and the regulated and emphasized the incapacity of regulators to keep up with local practical knowledge (Hayek 1945). As such, it was enhancing the legitimacy of the delegation of regulation and supervision to the regulated (Tsingou 2004; Seabrooke and Tsingou 2009). Rather than imposing arbitrary limits to business activity, regulators were seeking to set up a market context in which rational individuals would act responsibly (Riles 2011, p. 149; Baud and Chiapello 2014). This view of regulation, then, recommended delegating the actual regulatory tasks to the regulated themselves.

What empowered this view was the fast pace of financial innovation based on the techniques that allowed credit risk transfer through derivatives and the pricing of such risks by the financial intermediaries. Seeking a competitive advantage, banks were heavily invested in these metrics, producing risk measurement devices such as Value at Risk, which suggested that market risks could be controlled (Lockwood 2015). Given that regulators were as not incentivized as the banks to produce these measurements and based on the assumption that the regulated were acting in their own best interests, regulators acted deferentially toward these new measures. As Goodhart notes, "The regulatory community became 'cognitively captured' in the sense that it was not only prepared, but actually keen, to use techniques and methods for risk assessment developed by the industry for regulatory purposes" (2016, pp. 4–5; see also Tsingou 2008).

Cognitive capture theory is often used as a complementary (Baker 2010) or alternative explanation for the regulatory failure before the financial crisis. As Kwak (2013, p. 93) puts it, "Although several signs of traditional capture were present – notably a well-oiled revolving door between regulatory agencies and industry – the argument for capture in the strict sense is weakened by a plausible alternative explanation: that agency officials were genuinely persuaded by the argument that free financial markets were good for the public." Theories of cognitive capture point to the neoliberal spirit of the late 1990s that favored self-regulation, a view held, for example, at the helm of the Federal Reserve Board (e.g., Greenspan 1998; Baud 2013). As Buiter (2012) has pointed out,

Regulatory capture can be direct or cognitive. In this crisis *blind faith in the self-regulating properties of financial markets* played a major role, with Alan Greenspan as the prophet of socially beneficial self-regulation and Ben Bernanke and many others providing the scholarly underpinnings. (Buiter 2012, p. 5, highlighting in original; see also Eichengreen 2003; Bhidé 2011, p. 105)

Leading US regulators at that time believed in the self-regulatory powers of markets, where market discipline exerted by rational, informed market agents was judged superior to regulators' arbitrary risk assessments (see Jones 2000, p. 49f). Regulators were inevitably seen as behind the curve of the more correct perception of risks by market agents. In this view, regulatory arbitrage by market agents was regarded as a means to correct for the mistakes of regulators, as correcting for arbitrary and, thus, often unnecessarily expensive capital requirements with respect to securitization. A general prohibition of these activities was deemed "counterproductive" (Jones 2000, p. 49; Major 2012). The belief in the superiority of private agents' assessments of new financial products and services led regulators, so the argument goes, to evaluate the risks of securitization based on the same concepts and numbers bankers used (see Baker 2010, p. 653f; Turner 2010).

Probably the strongest evidence for theories of regulatory and cognitive capture is the revision of the global banking accord in the 1990s and the early 2000s that resulted in Basel II (2004) as an example of disproportionate influence of international banks on regulation (Claessens and Underhill 2010; Young 2012). As Tsingou writes,

The revised Accord, Basel II, is being developed through a lengthy consultation process with strong private sector involvement ... Pillar 1 is indicative of the trend of public-private interaction and has been negotiated with financial institutions; it includes provisions for the use of internal risk-assessment methods for the most sophisticated private players. (Tsingou 2004, p. 5)

These changes are seen as the outcome of the ascending power of finance to shape its own regulation, which increasingly also applies to supervision, where "the private sector is writing its own script, increasingly influencing not just the function of regulation but also that of supervision" (Tsingou 2004, p. 11).

The close collaboration of public actors with private actors, such as the G30, which were influential in starting the negotiation process of Basel II (Seabrooke and Tsingou. 2009, p. 20), is seen as proof for the undue influence by the private sector (see esp. Griffith-Jones and Persaud 2004; Tsingou 2004, 2008). In this narrative, "revolving doors," a phenomenon whereby actors perform regulatory duties for a certain time, for them to enter (or return) to employment in the financial sector is an important mechanism used to explain regulatory and cognitive capture (Seabrooke and Tsingou 2009[2]; Zingales 2013). This practice was supposed to solve the problem of information asymmetry regarding financial innovations, which were produced at an increasing pace since the 1980s but is nevertheless seen by these authors as a major mechanism for legitimating private knowledge in public regulation, thereby laying the foundations for cognitive capture. Although there is some evidence of undue influence in the creation of Basel II, qualified by changes in the regulatory framework that contradicted private interests (Young 2012; Baud and Chiapello 2014), the problem with Basel II as evidence of regulatory failure before the crisis is that it explains only a small portion of the evolving regulation of shadow banking (Bhidé 2011).

Shadow banking was most often a result of finding ways around global banking regulation, thus falling into the realm of national regulation. Securitization activities of banks had to be fitted with the national frameworks in order to avoid costs, a demanding task (for the case of UK, see Wainwright 2009). Whereas the implementation of Basel I and the stepwise implementation of Basel II in Europe may have led to a convergence on market-based supervision and discipline, shadow banking activities were, for the most part, outside of the scope of these regulations. Therefore, the globalized Banking Accords can serve neither as an explanation for the largely homogeneous regulatory exclusion of shadow banking pre-crisis nor for the exceptional cases where regulation was imposed. This becomes clear when one realizes that Basel II came into force for the large and sophisticated European banks only by 2008 and in the USA even much later (Tarullo 2008), thus after the crisis had already started. Furthermore, it does contain some regulatory measures, even if limited, intended to contain the regulatory arbitrage in the shadow banking system, signaling the awareness of problems in this sector in the international community.

---

[2] Seabrooke and Tsingou (2009) point in particular to the placement of the private risk-regulation mechanism at the heart of public regulation as evidence.

Lastly, the qualitative style of supervision it encouraged was much more adequate to deal with the acts of regulatory arbitrage than the legal form approach that prevailed before in several EU countries.

To understand regulatory failure before the crisis, there is a need for a more detailed national analysis of the treatment of shadow banking, rather than one that focuses only on the international level. Insofar as they do focus on the national level, theories of cognitive capture, however, focus mostly on the Anglo-Saxon sphere, in particular, on the USA and the UK (Baker 2010). They cannot account for the largely homogeneous failure to regulate securitization activities of banks on the global level.[3] It seems hardly convincing that regulators in all of the countries faced with the regulation of this sector of the shadow banking system were cognitively captured.[4] Thus, it is a theory that seems to apply to the cases of deregulation in the US and UK cases, and while this is an important strength of this theory, as these are the financial centers of the world, even there, as we will see, it does not capture the political economic conflicts surrounding regulation. Furthermore, such theories of cognitive capture cannot be simply transferred to the entire Western world without a deeper investigation.

There were, of course, fundamental similarities between the USA and Western Europe in the two decades before 2008. For example, there was a common hegemonic ideological discourse regarding finance that perceived the growth of finance as invariably positive (Turner 2015). Extrapolating from the experiences of industrialization, economic research unequivocally equated financial deepening with higher GDP growth (Rousseau and Sylla 2003; critical Turner 2015). This outlook was buttressed by the way banking services were accounted for in national accounting systems. The intermediation services of financial intermediaries had been assigned a positive role in national accounting systems postwar, first in 1947 in the USA and spreading from there to Western Europe, in a process completed by the 1970s (Christophers 2013). Although not directly measurable, national accountants imputed economic value to the risk taking of financial intermediaries, thereby equating the growth of finance with the growth of national economies. The unintended consequence of this change, as Christophers suggests, was to make politicians embrace the

---

[3] See Tables 5.1, 5.2, and 5.3 in Chapter 5.
[4] Or, for that matter, captured by material incentives.

growth of banking as a means to generate GDP growth (Christophers 2011). A second aspect of this hegemonic ideology, as advanced by financial academics, was that more markets and more trading would improve the allocation of credit in the economy, leading, in turn, to higher growth (De Goede 2004). This conviction was driven by the belief that an expansion of financial markets would allow for a better pricing of risks and for the system to distribute risks within it optimally (Nesvetailova 2010).

In their quest for market completion, mainstream financial economists were convinced that increased liquidity, concomitant with increased trading activity, would permit better price discovery and allow better capital allocation for the real economy (Turner 2015, pp. 28ff). The ideology of efficient markets, market completion, and the beneficial role of market liquidity was a welcome ideational support for the finance industry arguing for its own expansion. In and of itself, it had arisen from an alliance between rising pension funds and other financial market actors in the 1960s in need of both guidance for their investment activities as well as legitimacy in front of judges as to their fiduciary duties (Whitley 1986; Montagne 2011). The efficient market hypothesis (EMH), one developed as a fruit of this interaction between academia and financial investors, which provided both data and funding for the research, was admittedly not initially very helpful in guiding financial practices (Whitley 1986), but it did provide important ideological support for the expansion and limited regulation of a market understood as a perfect information processing machine. As a nonfalsifiable theorem (Whitley 1986), the EMH, in conjunction with the idea of the potential of markets to enter into a general equilibrium that has come to dominate American financial economics from the 1950s onward (Arrow and Debreu 1954), formed a powerful bulwark in order to justify market expansion. The idea of the general equilibrium fundamentally rests on market completion, which requires markets that permit agents to buy insurance against any possible future states of the world to spread risks. Hence, economics fully embraced the idea of the expansion of markets for risk transfer that would allow markets to self-equilibrate.

This view, coupled with the idea that more credit is invariably better and that increased financial market activity would only improve the allocation of credit, seemed borne out by the success of the US and British economies precrisis, which generated higher economic growth than other Western European economies. This, in turn, was an important influence in continental European countries (Interview, German bank manager and SPD member, November 23, 2010). Deregulation and attendant credit growth seemed to corroborate these benign views on finance. Increased credit growth, in particular to finance real estate acquisitions in these countries, overcame the problems of the lack of aggregate demand growth that otherwise was suppressed by stagnating wages (Crouch 2009). Undoubtedly, these developments formed the intellectual context that national politicians as well as regulators had to grapple with as they were deciding how to react to the financial innovations in which banks engaged.

However, questions about transferability of a simple cognitive capture thesis emerge once one looks at the mechanisms seen as responsible for the spread of cognitive capture. Baker (2010), for example, links cognitive capture to postgraduate education in economics in Anglo-Saxon universities. But regulatory agencies in non-Anglo-Saxon countries are not staffed for the most part by economists trained in such universities, and until recently, regulators and supervisors were not predominantly schooled in economics. Instead, regulators are often schooled domestically, sometimes in special universities directly linked to the central bank where practical matters of regulation as well as abstract economic models are taught.[5] Whereas abstract economic models might have converged due to the transnationalization of economics driven by the USA (Fourcade 2006), it is questionable why practical matters of regulation should do the same. Regulatory styles, while changing over time, still show a certain degree of path dependency, as certain institutionalized scripts of how to do the work of an agency persist.[6]

The aforementioned focus on Basel II as a global regulatory mechanism and on Anglo-Saxon countries and the USA in particular as the

---

[5] This is the case for France's banking regulator and for the central bank in Germany. In line with this argument, the stance of the French regulator discussed in the text that follows can be analyzed as the direct opposite of cognitive capture. Nevertheless, final regulation in France is less strict than regulators there desired, suggesting other mechanisms than cognitive capture at work.

[6] For instance, the light touch regulation of the Financial Services Authority in the UK can be seen as a continuation of the gentlemen's club style of regulation of the Bank of England.

hegemon of our time has led to the fact that the theory of cognitive capture cannot provide convincing arguments for how cognitive capture could be avoided, as, in these accounts, an alternative, successful case of regulation is missing. Proponents of cognitive capture theory are subsequently left with the logical normative request that regulators should view markets from a different viewpoint than the regulated without any empirical guidance of how this may actually be achieved. In short, theories of cognitive capture suffer from a lacking specification of mechanisms, which permit or prevent regulators from seeing financial markets in the same way the regulated do. Questions, such as what are the institutional foundations that allow regulators to avoid cognitive capture and which are the mechanisms that can account for it go unanswered. Furthermore, the theory does not do justice to the context of regulatory action, where regulators do not only have to take into account their views on specific financial innovations but also the impact their regulations might have on the competitiveness of their industries (cf. Singer 2007). These shortcomings stem from the fact that a comparative institutional analysis of the growth of shadow banking is missing. To remedy these shortcomings of the current explanations, I propose to conceptualize the nonregulation of shadow banking as a phenomenon influenced by two sets of factors: on the one hand, the ignorance or lack thereof of the regulators about the actual processes of rule evasion of their banks (that is to say, their distance from these processes) and, on the other hand, the structural constraints of national regulatory action, including the competitive situation of national incumbents.

Rather than simply blaming regulators for being too close to the regulated, I suggest taking a closer look at the form the regulators–regulated interaction takes and the way the two of them are bound together in a globalizing world of competing banking systems. By doing so, we can appreciate the need for interaction of regulators with the regulated in the daily business of regulation (Black 1997, 2002, 2013) and overcome the dichotomy of equating intense exchange of the regulated with the regulator as cognitive capture and its absence as cognitive independence (Riles 2011). Instead, we can differentiate between helpful and damaging forms of interaction. Situating regulators on the one hand within their financial systems, investigating the channels of information they entertain with compliance officers of banks and "gatekeepers" (Coffee 2006) and, on the other hand, within the context of competing national banking systems, formed jointly by regulators and regulated incumbent banks will allow us to gain a more fine-grained understanding of the context of regulatory action and to go beyond simple theories of regulatory or cognitive capture. Instead of a simple "did not know better," this will enable us to envision a temporal evolution of regulatory knowledge that moves from "did not know" to "did not want to know better" or "chose to see it differently, partially also due to structural constraints."

Ignorance, State Capacity, and Structural Constraints of Regulators

Regulatory and cognitive capture are certainly part of the factors that help us to account for the lack of regulation, but expecting these factors to explain the absence of regulation in almost all developed Western countries, as will be shown in Chapter 5, is clearly stretching their explanatory power. Instead, they can be analyzed as proximate causes of the lack of regulation, an outcome of the agency of bankers and regulators within the regulatory context of their time (see Kahler and Lake 2003, p. 28). Explaining the lack of regulation in such a cross-nationally persistent manner begs for deeper inquiry into the remote causal factors, "the socio-institutional context, and the particular historical conjuncture in which actors find themselves" (Young 2012, p. 669), and a focus on "the interactive interdependence … between the properties of the given regulatory structure and the properties of the policy field concerned" (Mayntz 2010, p. 3). Poszar et al. (2010, p. 29) come close to such a structural explanation when they point to the "fractured nature of the global financial regulatory framework" and "a collection of one-off, uncoordinated decisions by accounting and regulatory bodies regarding the accounting and regulatory capital treatment of certain exposures" as the source of arbitrage opportunities that underlay the growth of the bank-based, "internal shadow banking system" Poszar et al. (2010, p. 29).

I argue that we need to link these two aspects and suggest that these uncoordinated decisions by national accounting and regulatory bodies were structured, on the one hand, by the differential institutional embeddedness of banking regulators in the processes of financial innovation and the financial accounting their banks engaged in and, on the other hand, by the common situation of a fractured transnational field of regulation all regulators were facing. This common situation was created, in part, by the attempts of the transnational regulatory community to level the playing field through the global Basel Accords, thereby creating essentially a global market for banking services. This movement found its strongest expression in the project of the creation of a European financial market – one that transformed the legally nonbinding global Basel Accords into European directives – to be transformed into national banking regulation in all of the EU.

In the EU, the ascendance of the transnational governance in accounting further meant that the national accounting standard setter in the EU started to focus on the International Accounting Standards Board in London, and, in turn, often moved away from their contacts with the setter's national banking regulator, which in many countries was an important stakeholder.

This fractured field of transnational regulation created a situation in which national banking regulatory bodies were asked to regulate a financial innovation that evaded global regulation, while their banks were competing in a newly created global market based on national regulatory costs. This fact operated as a structural constraint (Andrews 1994, p. 193) for the prudent regulation of this global market. Furthermore, the ascendance of the transnational regulation of accounting challenged the intervention of national banking regulators in national accounting regimes.

I will tackle these two analytical levels sequentially, building my argument from the bottom up. First, I will inquire into the socio-institutional context and explain the nature of regulatory arbitrage and how regulatory dialogues may help in their detection. Second, I will inquire into the structural reasons for the resistance against regulation expressed not only by banks, but also by ministries of finance and even actors within the regulatory bodies, thus paying attention to capabilities and context. The shifting context of these capabilities in accounting will then be elaborated on. To grasp properly which capabilities are needed to detect regulatory arbitrage, it is first important to understand exactly how regulatory arbitrage works.

Regulatory Arbitrage, Information Asymmetries, and Regulatory Dialogues

As a perfectly legal technique, regulatory arbitrage "exploits the gap between the economic substance of a transaction and its legal or regulatory treatment, taking advantage of the legal system's intrinsically limited ability to attach formal labels that track the economics of transactions with sufficient precisions" (Fleischer 2010, p. 3.) Exploiting this difference of economic substance and legal form, market actors, often with the help of lawyers and regulatory advisors, set out to optimize the structure and framing of their actions in such a way that they achieve the same economic result yet circumvent the regulation. Thus, they create a spread between the valuations of two different legal forms of the same economic activity, hence an arbitrage opportunity between them, arbitraging regulatory costs that can then be divided between buyer and seller (Fleischer 2010, p. 12). So, in regulatory arbitrage, the process of reflexive interaction with measures of classification and commensuration, which has been documented by sociologists and regulators alike (Borio and Tsatsaronis 2005; Espeland and Sauder 2007) do not apply to the demand side of goods, when buyers seek arbitrage profits but, rather, on their supply side (also Awrey 2013), when sellers seek the optimal regulatory classification for their goods. This form of reactivity of private agents to evaluations (Espeland and Sauder 2007) proves profitable for sellers and buyers, but it is detrimental from a societal perspective as it achieves to reexternalize the social costs.

To grasp fully how regulatory arbitrage as an activity structures the actions of financial market agents, we need to shift from a perspective that treats law as an exogenous resource for actors, where laws and regulations (such as accounting rules) are seen as the external constraints of market exchange, based on which buyers and sellers enter into contractual negotiations.

Instead, we need to understand the way legal texts are interpreted and strategically responded to by those whose behavior they are supposed to regulate, as emphasized by scholars working in the law-and-society approach (Black 2002; Stryker 2003; Edelman and Stryker 2005; Edelman and Talesh 2011). To grasp this problem fully, we should reconceptualize normal business transactions as a tripartite transaction – those involving the seller, the buyer, and the government (Fleischer 2010, p. 12), as depicted in Figure 3.1.

Whereas buyers and sellers are engaging in a private transaction, the government "imposes regulatory costs on transactions in the form of taxes, securities law disclosure requirements, antitrust constraints, environmental compliance obligations, and so on" (Fleischer 2010,

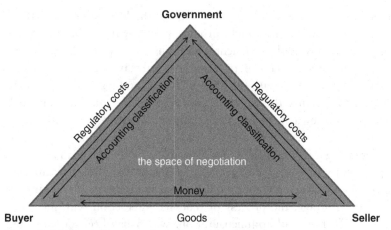

Figure 3.1 The triadic view of market transactions.

p. 12). Faced with these costs, buyers and sellers are tempted to reshape the legal structure of their transactions in such a way as to switch from an expensive legal framework to one that carries less regulatory costs. In their attempts, buyers and sellers are abetted by the fact that the government usually "has no actual *seat at the negotiating table*. Rather, the government is normally bound to specific courses of action based on the language of the statutes, regulations, and administrative rulings and how it has treated previous transactions with similar formal structures" (Fleischer 2010, p. 12, italics mine).

So, the phenomenon of regulatory arbitrage then exemplifies the work of adaptation, translation, and transformation of general, abstract laws and regulations into organizational practice, which scholars in the law and society approach emphasize (Edelman and Stryker 2005; see also Mahoney and Thelen 2010 for a similar emphasis within historical institutionalism). Organizations exploit the ambiguity and obscurity of the law in order to transform it in their favor. They do so in organizational fields, by employing professionals of compliance who actively shape the interpretation of these rules (Black 2002). The locus of this *managerialization* of the law resides in the daily application of the law in organizations and in the common interpretations in an organizational field about a law's implicit intention, what Edelman (2011, p. 92) calls the "endogeneity of law" (also Edelman et al. 2011, p. 888). Compliance professionals who are responsible for the correct enactment of these rules (Edelman 1990, 2011, p. 90f) are crucial to how they will be enacted: prior research in this stream suggests that these actors will seek to bend these rules in favor of the managers and their own professional interests. The malleability of law is central to the acts of regulatory arbitrage, and it is based on the general properties of rules, their over- or underinclusiveness (Black 1997, p. 10; see also MacKenzie 2008, 2009), which opens up spaces for creative compliance.

As with contracts, legal rules can never envision all possible states of the future, thus explaining their indeterminacy in that certain situations will only partially fit the fact pattern described in the rules. They are formulated with a certain intent (what is often called the spirit of the law), but the concrete formulation of the law (what is called the letter of the law) can lead to the application of the rule to circumstances not envisioned (overinclusiveness) or can miss important circumstances that according to the intent of the rule should be included (underinclusiveness). Owing to these facts and the ambivalence inherent in the meaning of words, these rules are subject to interpretation, which the regulated push in their favor. To do so, they employ regulatory advisors as well as in-house expertise.

According to Julia Black, "the opportunistic use of rules is prevalent in financial and business regulation, and supports a large contingent of professional advisers" (Black 2002, p. 243; see also p. 247). These consultants optimize the taxation and regulatory treatment of their corporate clients by, for example, steering the classificatory decisions in these numerical records that precede regulation into more favorable terrain (see Fooks 2003; Sikka and Willmott 2009).[7] This task is made easier for regulatory advisors, as what is being regulated "are artificial, legal and financial constructs" (Black 1997, p. 243).

In practice, such optimization often involves the structuring of business transactions where they end up in a gray zone owing to the invention of new legal constructs which are structured such that they "possess only some of the features of the paradigm case or cases but not others" (Black 1997, p. 11). Regulatory advisors reverse-engineer deals in such a way as to avoid those markers requiring the classification

---

[7] The most famous example of such balance sheet "window dressing" has been the use of repurchasing agreements by the large Wall Street investment banks to lower the size of their balance sheet exactly before the date at which they had to hand it in to the SEC, only to augment it again a few weeks later (see Ekkenga 2011).

of business activities in a costly regulatory registrar, while generating the same cash flows. Avoiding those registrars is thereby creating value added for corporations, as they can optimize regulatory costs or taxation. Deals in economic substance then are similar, but their legal treatment is different. Of course such attempts at circumvention via financial engineering are costly, as lawyers, auditors, and regulatory advisors need to be paid. But, as long as the final margins created by savings on regulatory costs are positive, creative compliance is rational for financial market actors.

Used in securitization by banks, off-balance-sheet special-purpose entities (SPEs) are a clear outgrowth of such consulting activities that optimized the classification of assets, helping banks to move them legally off their balance sheets in order to minimize the regulatory capital charges they face while maintaining maximum economic exposure to these assets. That is to say, while in legal form, these assets are no longer part of the bank, for the bank remains exposed to their risks and rewards in economic substance. Reaching this zone outside of existing regulation is abetted by rules, which clearly set out the criteria based on which the regulatory decision will be taken. Such rules allow constructing business transactions, which are similar to all those on which regulations are imposed, but that lack a certain criterion defined in the rule as necessary to be characterized as such. Given these *bright lines* in the criteria of definition, engineers just need to make sure that new constructs stay on the desired side of the distinction.

This problem is particularly pronounced in the realm of financial accounting, which forms the basis of much of financial market regulation. The demand in accounting advice by the regulated stems from the fact that regulators most often impose their regulations on the data provided by compliance officers; that is, regulators engage in "monitoring via numerical records" (Vollmer 2007, p. 578) provided to them by the compliance offices of financial agents, often additionally verified by auditors who act as gatekeepers.

As such, accounting is the basis for governance at a distance through numbers (Robson 1992; Rose and Miller 1992), as the regulated have to classify their activities according to regulation and to provide these numbers to the regulators, demonstrating that they are, indeed, in compliance with stipulated regulations. Situations of classification, however, are characterized by their indeterminacy, as accounting scholars have repeatedly pointed out (Hines 1988; MacKenzie 2008, 2009; Gill 2009). This points to a dilemma of governance at a distance with the help of accounting numbers. As Hatherly et al. (2008, p. 154) put it, "governing by numbers" (Miller 2001) requires that those "who generate the numbers are themselves governable, but ... there is a sense in which their discretion is in principle ineliminable" (Hatherly et al. 2008, p. 154). In addition, auditing companies that act as gatekeepers in verifying compliance decisions have in recent decades switched their business model to advising businesses on compliance (Coffee 2006). So, auditing companies have a strong conflict of interest in their compliance monitoring, a conflict of interest that regulation per se can hardly solve.

This malleability of laws and accounting rules, coupled with the self-interest of the regulated makes the positioning of state agencies within these processes of compliance so central. The openness of the meaning of rules leads to the need for dialogue between those writing the rules and those interpreting them in the process of application. These dialogues have been the focus of sociolegal studies of regulation as inspired by the path-breaking work of Black (1997, 2002, 2003; see also Ford 2008, 2010). Focusing on the interaction between the regulated and the regulators they have pointed to the need to establish communities of interpretation between regulators and regulated in order to establish unequivocal interpretations. Regulators thus need not only to generate and to impose good regulation on the financial system, but they also need to make sure that the numbers on which these regulations are imposed reflect an accurate picture of the business transactions, and hence, the risks the regulated are exposed to (see also Mügge and Perry 2014). As such, these problems of compliance with rules directly stem from the way value is added to corporations through the way assets and risks are accounted for (Borio and Tsatsaronis 2005).

The question, then, becomes how regulators could limit this creative, self-interested interpretation of rules. As we will see, while the under- or overinclusiveness of rules is at the basis of regulatory arbitrage, such ambiguity can also increase the power of the regulator in shaping the interpretation of regulation if the institutional framework is set up to deal with the ambiguity. In this respect, principles-based rules that do not offer clear guidelines around which to structure instruments of regulatory arbitrage do offer advantages to regulators (see also Black 2008). Such rules refuse to specify unambiguously the calculative procedures to comply with regulation, instead granting the final say to the professional judgment of the auditor and/or the regulator.[8] In order to deal with the "endogeneity of value" (Borio and Tsatsaronis 2005, p. 15), the negotiating situation between the complying and the one ensuring compliance is kept open and quite undefined. Rather than developing unambiguous calculative guidelines, these rules seek to limit the strategies of manipulation by the regulated through maintaining uncertainty over the practices of judgment of the gatekeepers and regulators. Such principles-based standards, in other words, create a gray zone of debate, where before clear criteria prevented it.

Standard setters and regulators install such rules in order to disconnect the reflexive relationship between regulation and the financial services being "produced" that resides in the malleability of financial "products" and is exploited by regulatory advisors and financial and legal engineers.[9] While regulators necessarily are a step behind in terms of compliance, principles-based rules allow them to keep rules and their interpretation in flux, forcing the regulated into a dialogue over compliance. As the later chapters will show, if these dialogues are properly structured and if regulators have the mandate and expertise to pose challenging questions, regulators can thereby also gain the necessary knowledge about attempts of rule circumvention in an effort to keep regulatory arbitrage at bay. This focus on regulatory arbitrage means to shift from the mere formulation of rules, which is the predominant focus of theories of regulatory and cognitive capture toward the creative interaction of the regulated with these rules, which includes their interested interpretation.

Hence, regulators and regulated interact with each other to determine what is allowed and what is not. These decisions can have large political economic consequences for those who have to be in compliance with them, which is why this interaction can be fierce. In the case of acts of compliance, such as accounting for conglomerates, questions of political economy not only are represented in communication, but

[8] He has to consider the situation in its entirety and weigh the distribution of risks and benefits emanating from an SPE. If he finds that one conglomerate bears the majority of risks and rewards from that SPE, the SPE should be consolidated on the balance sheet of that conglomerate. See the interpretation SIC 12.

[9] In contrast to civil engineers who have to take the physical environment into account, financial engineers start from scratch when they design these products, Therefore, they have much more degrees of freedom in the way they can structure the final product in order to serve the needs of the customer (background interview with Rating Agency New York, March 10, 2011).

also communication is the level at which they are fought out. Studying these acts and the rules that govern them, we need to move from theories of regulatory capture and cognitive capture that remain at the level of the formulation of rules to a study of regulatory practice that embeds the rule making in the negotiations regarding their application. The involvement of the banking regulator regarding the compliance of banks with accounting rules that provide the data on which banking regulation is based is a crucial variable regarding the cognitive capture of banking regulators. Once a regulator accepts the numerical display of the risks a bank has entered into, he or she is somewhat automatically forced to see the world with the eyes of the regulated. However, when the regulators are directly involved in the negotiations over what it means to be compliant, rather than simply accepting the submitted data, they can gain a quicker understanding of how banks massage the data and seek to impose their point of view.

These negotiations, however, are not free from structural considerations and constraints. The compliance of banks with national accounting rules most often have an immediate impact on the core capital requirements banks need to fulfill. However, high core capital requirements in certain fields of business, such as securitization, could represent a competitive disadvantage for domestic banks with respect to foreign banks that were free to operate in the host country according to their domestic rules. Compliance was, thus, challenged by level playing field concerns created by the Basel Accords. Furthermore, the transnational governance formation in the field of accounting meant that intervention by banking regulators in the acts of compliance of their banks was increasingly delegitimized. These structural constraints of regulatory action may have played as much of a role as the cognitive capture of regulators, but, to date, they have been largely ignored. This is a dangerous shortcoming of the analysis because even if cognitive capture can be avoided through a proper setup of national regulatory dialogues, these structural constraints will remain, tilting the actual interpretation of rules in favor of the regulated.

The Context of National Regulatory Action: Transnational Governance Formation and Level Playing Field Concerns

As shadow banking was consciously designed to evade global regulation, the only way of regaining control over bank activity was national regulation. National regulation, however, meant to impose additional regulatory costs where foreign competitors had none. The idea that the increasing cross-border integration of financial markets undermines national policy solutions remains a common one. Global governance mechanisms are seen as a possible way to mitigate these effects (inter alia Kapstein 1991, p. 24; Slaughter 2003, p. 11). But, what if global governance mechanisms themselves undermine the capacity of national banking regulators to deal with the regulatory capital arbitrage activities of their banks? In the case of bank-based shadow banking, the global Basel Accords caused and cemented this mismatch between the national and the global. Although global Basel standards for core capital requirements arose to level the competitive playing field between American, European, and Japanese banks, the undefined reach of these rules led to the national reappearance of concerns over competitive disadvantages. This multilevel dynamic in banking regulation shifted the problem of competitive disadvantages from the center of banking regulation to the margins, the shadow banking sector. In the shadow banking system, regulatory arbitrage of banks to circumvent costly capital requirements coincided with unresolved frictions between national and international banking regulation, which led to inaction by national regulators.

This facet of financial regulation and supervision stems from the fact that these two are "imposing a set of 'taxes' and 'subsidies' on the operations of financial firms" (Story and Walter, 1997, p. 129) and the "regulatory burden" imposed on domestic banks can be a decisive competitive factor, especially in fields with low margins, such as shadow banking. This situation generated a trend toward regulatory exemptions for the bank-based shadow banking sector, despite regulatory concerns at the national level. Prior work in international political economy on the regulation of global financial markets in the absence of global governance has shown that the lack of international agreement generates the forces that prevent the effective regulation of international markets domestically, even if the regulators prefer it (see inter alia Underhill 1997b, p. 18; Mosley and Singer 2009, p. 422). The regulation of such "international markets" that sit at "the nexus between national and international affairs" (Farrell and Newman 2010, p. 630; 2014; see also Mosley 2010; critical Drezner 2010) are heavily influenced by how other nations regulate these markets. National decisions in the absence of international agreements are often characterized by concerns over an even playing field for domestic actors and regulatory competition, where domestic agencies are removing regulatory restrictions or oversight to permit domestic market players to gain a greater market share (Underhill 1997a, p. 6). Regulators of such markets face a delicate task as "no regulator wants to be held responsible for crushing an industry under the weight of onerous regulation. Regulators therefore must walk a fine line between stability and competitiveness" (Singer 2007, p. 23).

The literature has pointed out that such a situation of regulatory competition does not necessarily lead to a race to the regulatory bottom (Murphy 2004; Singer 2007), especially if a hegemon can threaten to limit market access (Simmons 2004). However, the setup of global regulation (Basel I) made such threats unworkable. In the case of securitization activities of banks, then, the Basel Accords as the global governance mechanism played a crucial role both in generating the global ABCP market, one created to evade Basel regulations, and in preventing its effective regulation, as national regulators could not regulate the access conditions for the market. This shift in the balance of power in favor of banks clamoring for regulatory leniency was most aggravated in the EU. In the process of creating a common market for financial services, the Europeans had enshrined Basel I into European law, making it binding for all nations. Furthermore, the full liberalization of banking services had removed any capacity to impose market access restrictions for nation states or any other officially legitimate way of protecting the national banking industry from foreign takeovers. Both the strategies of incumbent banks and banking regulators were strongly influenced by European liberalization policies and the possibilities of national regulators for containing the threat it posed to their incumbents. This structural condition for national regulatory action is a major reason for the pronounced engagement of large European banks in shadow banking activities in general and the ABCP market in particular (Acharya and Schnabl 2010; Shin 2011; Hardie et al. 2013a).

The regulatory stance of national regulators in Europe toward shadow banking activities was shaped, I argue, on the one hand by the opportunities national incumbent banks had in gaining a European incumbent status and on the other hand by regulators' capacity to protect their national incumbents from foreign takeover attempts. If they had limited capacity for growth on the European level and if the regulator had limited capacity to protect them from foreign take-over, regulation of the ABCP market was likely to be weak. This argu-ment directly relates to a debate in financial economics concerning the impact of increasing competition on banking systems' stability. In this debate, one side emphasizes the destabilizing impact of increasing com-petition on the risk taking of banks (Allen and Gale 2000), whereas the other side emphasizes the benign effect of competition on sta-bility (Edwards and Mishkin 1995; Carletti 2008, p. 473). The crucial assumption in this latter view is that regulators do adjust regulation to changing circumstances to mitigate the risk taking of banks. This adjustment, I argue, is inhibited in those banking systems that fare badly in the process of the expansion of bank system competition, as it is not only banks, but entire banking systems, including regulators, that are competing. In this situation, regulators favor the formation of national champions and covert protectionism to favor national incumbents (Clift and Woll 2013). If these two mechanisms are insuf-ficient to protect national incumbents, the lenient regulation of risk taking is another means to increase the profitability and thereby help their capacity to persist in the competition, as is argued in this book.

Concerns over competitive inequity, however, were not the only structural factor in the setup of global financial governance that inhibited the stringent regulation of shadow banking. Transnational governance formation in the field of accounting further curtailed the capacities of banking regulators. The emergence of the International Accounting Standards Board (IASB) as the predominant standard setter in the field of accounting destabilized national institutional configurations in the governance of that sector. The ensuing reconfig-uration of domestic governance architectures had a decisive impact on the linkage of banking regulators as to how banks comply with accounting regulation, for it threatened to deinstitutionalize the stan-dard setting and enforcement role of the banking regulator. The institu-tional template developed at the transnational level, once implemented nationally, thus created an actor-mismatch between those formulating and those implementing the rules, thereby weakening the position of the banking regulator. As Halliday and Carruthers (2007) have shown, actor mismatch between global law and national implementation increases the probability of dysfunctional local regulations (Halliday and Carruthers 2007, p. 1152; see also Mügge and Perry 2014). In particular, by pushing the banking regulator outside of the governance of accounting, it weakened the coalition for rule change regarding the off-balance-sheet activities of banks.

But, before we come to analyze these dynamics initiated by the processes of globalization, we should focus on the political economic situation in the USA, the place from where the ABCP market emerged. There, the domestic threat of disintermediation from nonbanks aligned the interests of banks and the Federal Reserve as the most important banking regulator, pushing the latter to permit its banks to cross regulatory boundaries and to engage in capital market activities. This crossing was accompanied by regulatory scrutiny and unease about the expanding liquidity commitments of banks on the level of banking supervision. This unease, however, for a long time remained blocked due to the embrace of a light touch regulatory agenda at the top of the Fed, embracing market discipline and self-regulation. Only astute maneuvering between the global and the national level would allow those internal critics to bring about tighter regulation of the ABCP markets in the 2000s.

4 | The Transformation of US Financial Markets since the 1960s and the Emergence and Growth of the ABCP Market

In this chapter, I embed the emergence of the ABCP market in 1983 in the transformation of the US financial system from the 1960s onward as part of the evolution of a larger parallel banking system (D'Arista 1994). These developments brought about the engagement of banks with capital market actors, establishing the bank–nonbank nexus (Pozsar and Singh 2011) that would form the backbone of the shadow banking system. These developments can be characterized as a continuous evolution of competition and cooperation between entities in the capital markets (nonbanks) and banks, where financial innovation by nonbanks would put banks under competitive pressure. Banks, in turn, would seek to integrate capital market activities into their own business model, often collaborating with these nonbank entities (such as investment banks).

Banking regulators were to play an important role in this dynamic, as they permitted the boundary crossing of banks into capital markets. This permissiveness must be placed into the context of this rising competition for banks from nonbanks and foreign banks. Not only banks but regulators, too, increasingly worried about the fate of their commercial banks and sought to relieve them from the cumbersome burden structural regulations dating from the 1930s imposed on them (Tarullo 2015, p. 7). Furthermore, inflation that began to rise in the 1960s, itself partially an outcome of deregulation, aggravated the dysfunctionalities of the system of banking regulation installed in 1933 (Sylla 2002). In the context of this changing macroeconomic and competitive landscape, the financial system of the USA underwent a transformation that would begin in the 1950s and lead to the abolishment of structural regulations by the end of the 1990s. It is in this context of inflation and the attending deregulation that the birth and growth of the ABCP market must be understood. Before we turn to its evolution and the regulatory dialogues that shaped it, a look at the

New Deal regulation and the reasons for its slow demise is necessary in order to understand the larger context of regulatory intervention.

The Challenge to Commercial Banks on the Asset and Liability Side

Following the disastrous experience of the Great Depression, commercial banks in the United States were separated from broker-dealer activities in financial markets in 1933 by the Banking Act (known as the Glass–Steagall Act, after the two senators developing the bill).[1] While regional and local banks as well as investment banks benefited from this structural and functional regulation, money center banks would be severely constrained in their capacity to grow and to open up new profitable lines of business (Sylla 2002). Initially, in the context of war financing and the postwar boom, the business lines of money center banks were profitable and promised growing future returns. While banks sought to overcome regulatory constraints since the 1950s, regulation such as the Bank Holding Company Act of 1956 limited their capacity to engage in nonbank activity or to operate outside of their home state. Starting in the 1950s as commercial banks came under increasing competitive pressure both on their assets and liability side, this situation of rather peaceful coexistence between investment banks and commercial banks would change once constrained by the structural regulations of 1933. These pressures were largely caused by regulatory restrictions imposed on banks, but not on nonbank financial institutions, favoring the latter's expansion (D'Arista 1994).

The prosperous period of the 1950s in the USA led to the emergence of new players in the financial system, such as pension funds, investment companies, or retirement programs of companies that began to accumulate funds, seeking outlets in capital markets (Reinicke 1995, p. 30). As capital markets grew in the USA from the 1950s onward, large corporations began migrating from banks to capital markets for

---

[1] This separation was the outcome of contentious investigations into the activities of money center banks in New York City precrisis, which showed a wide range of abusive practices on the part of banks and bank affiliates in their stock market activities. National Citibank, later to become Citicorp, then Citibank, was at the center of these allegations.

long-term bond issuance and into the commercial paper market to finance short-term outstanding loans (D'Arista 1994; Gart 1994, p. 3). This development put increasing pressure on banks on their asset side, as it was difficult for them to compete with capital markets on the terms of the loans to these corporate clients. Banks were threatened by disintermediation, the secular loss of banks' highly profitable business with high-quality corporate customers to public credit markets, primarily commercial paper and junk bonds (Gart 1994, p. 4). Still, on the liability side, Regulation Q forbade banks to pay interests on demand deposits and limited the interest rates they could pay on other accounts, such as saving accounts. In an era of accelerating inflation, starting in the mid-1960s, such restrictions meant that structurally equivalent means to deposit money safely were capable to react quicker and to offer more attractive rates to customers. As such, banks were facing sudden liability shortages. Banks were thus threatened to be bypassed on both the asset and the liability side by actors in capital markets.

In reaction to the constraining domestic regulatory burden and the rising competition, money center banks in New York were seeking to expand their activities and, they developed two strategic responses (Sylla 2002, p. 53).[2] At once, they would seek to expand their international activities from the 1950s onward (Battilossi and Cassis 2002; Sylla 2002; Christophers 2013), and they would seek to tap into growing capital markets, first abroad and then domestically. Abroad, US commercial banks enjoyed a lack of regulatory constraints, successfully engaging in the business of underwriting securities.[3] To expand their activities, they relied on the growing eurodollar market, an active market in dollar-denominated bonds that had developed outside of the control of the Federal Reserve (Konings 2008). The Fed did not only know about these markets; instead, it was permissive of these engagements, seeking to compensate its banks for what was perceived as overly harsh regulation at home (Helleiner 1994; Battilossi 2002, p. 16).

Domestically, the money center banks reacted to the rising shortage of deposits in the 1950s, a shortage caused by legal restrictions on interest payments, with financial innovations such as the certificate of

---

[2] First National City Bank of New York, later to become Citibank, was to be at the forefront of both these innovations.
[3] This was in particular the case in the UK, the main destiny of foreign operations.

deposit.[4] In other words, banks began to borrow short term in money markets, tapping the new sources of liquidity in capital markets which emerged from the 1950s onwards. The use of these markets by the large money center banks was the beginning of an active management of the liability side of their balance sheet, refinancing their activities in the wholesale money market. This first step in the integration of capital markets and banking business, which would accelerate in the coming years, was to become a fundamental pillar of the survival strategy of banks, as capital markets became more attractive for their clients owing to the growing amount of funds seeking outlets in capital markets.

As a response to the latter challenge, in the 1960s, banks began aggressively pushing to expand their activities in capital markets. As a large part of their client base was moving away from them and into capital markets, banks were seeking new ways to generate income. Making up for the loss of the *Fortune 500* firms, which were increasingly refinancing themselves in capital markets, banks sought to engage in additional off-balance-sheet business, seeking wherever legally possible to support the capital market activities of their former clients, such as standby letters of credit, commercial loan sales, and syndications (Gart 1994, p. 17). In the words of Richard Sylla (2002, p. 61), "rather than being beaten by the money markets, they decided to join it" To do so, banks were exploiting the legal loopholes they found in the evolving legal form of the bank holding company (BHC).

The Bank Holding Company Act of 1956 originally sought to cement the interstate restrictions on branching and to limit the capacity of BHCs to acquire banks in other states by giving states the capacity to prevent these purchases. It permitted BHCs to purchase banks in different states, subject to the permission of the Federal Reserve, which

---

[4] The financial innovation that first and foremost would help money center banks to deal with this shortage was the negotiable Certificate of Deposits (CD). While CDs existed previously, First National City Bank paid a broker-dealer to install a viable secondary market for these CDs, allowing customers to sell their time deposits whenever they needed liquidity (D'Arista 1994). Hence, the CD became an instrument that was providing both interest payments to the customer and the possibility for an immediate withdrawal. This market would expand during the 1960s, reaching $15 billion in 1966, allowing commercial banks to ease the funding shortage they had experienced since the 1950s (Konings 2011, p. 109). As Sylla (2002, p. 61) points out, almost all of the financial innovations of that era stem from the response to regulatory restrictions.

through the Act became the primary regulator for BHCs. However, the regulation was aimed at multibank holding companies, leaving bank holding companies that owned only one bank and sought to expand into nonbank business largely untouched (D'Arista 1994, p. 69f). Subsequent regulation in 1966 would continue to leave one-bank holding companies untouched, encouraging First National City Bank and subsequently other large banks to restructure into that particular legal form. This would allow them to move into profitable nonbanking business, such as leasing or credit card operations. In the short period from 1966 to 1969, one-bank holding companies would move from making up 4 percent of bank deposits to 35 percent (D'Arista 1994). One of the profitable fields of action was their increasing engagement in the commercial paper market, a market that had steadily grown since World War II, but was about to reach a watershed moment in 1966.

The Rise of the Commercial Paper Market

One of the markets to experience a steady increase during the 1950s and 1960s was the short-term commercial paper market, based both on the increasing amount of funds that were seeking investment in capital markets and the companies that it attracted. The commercial paper market had enjoyed steady growth post–World War II, nearly reaching the peak of the 1920s in 1951 (Abken 1981, p. 13). Finance companies largely used it to refinance the credit they extended. The growth of the market would accelerate with the credit crunch of 1966 and even further with the credit crunch of 1969 (Burger 1969, p. 13; Abken 1981). In both of these episodes, the Fed refused to raise the ceiling of the interest rate banks could pay for savings accounts (Regulation Q), thereby leading to an outflow of funds by corporate and private customers into capital markets. Doing so, the Fed was seeking to constrain the provision of credit by the commercial banks, acting on its growing concern about inflation.

While largely unsuccessful in quelling inflation,[5] these events brought about a decisive shift in the refinancing practices of corporations.

---

[5] CDs as well as the eurodollar market allowed banks to circumvent the constraints by the Fed. In that moment, the Fed had to realize that, while the secondary market for CDs severely constrained its capacity to control the issuance of credit, it was too late to shut it down. Doing so would have caused a major crisis in the banking system (Konings 2011, p. 115).

During these episodes, banks encouraged their strongest customers to use the commercial paper market as a reliable source of financing, providing them with backup lines of credit (Abken 1981, p. 14). As a consequence, many corporations formerly relying exclusively on bank credit now turned to the commercial paper market, thereby accelerating the issuance of commercial paper in the late 1960s and early 1970s. As a consequence, in 1970, the commercial paper market was twenty times as large as in 1953 and twice as large as in 1966 (Schadrack and Breimyer 1970, p. 281).

This dynamic expansion of nonbank credit came to an abrupt halt when in 1970, Penn Central Transportation Company, the sixth largest nonfinancial corporation in the USA, filed for bankruptcy, and reneged on $200 million worth of outstanding commercial paper. Previously deemed a rather secure asset by investors, this default led to a run on the commercial paper market, with investors withdrawing their money rapidly (Minsky 1986, p. 102f). As commercial paper had become a major means of refinancing for commercial banks, the Fed saw itself forced to intervene and provided $600 million in emergency loans, much like it would during the previous financial crisis (FCIC 2011, p. 30). This action exceeded its normal mandate but was justified on the grounds of maintaining financial stability (Brimmer 1989). As during the financial crisis, it also facilitated the formation of commercial bank syndicates that were to refinance the organization affected by the run, in turn opening the discount window to these banks (Minsky 1986, p. 102).

In the aftermath of this crisis, investors demanded further assurances that their investments were safe. Commercial banks provided one institutional answer to that need for safety. They would henceforth offer standby lines of credit to issuers of commercial paper, so that in case of crises and market disruption, the latter programs could turn to banks for refinancing. This, in turn, would allow investors to be paid and leave the banks with the exposure to the credit risks inherent in the commercial papers. This arrangement, which, in essence, linked the issuers of commercial paper to the Fed's discount window meant nothing else but an expansion of the financial safety net to the commercial paper market. In the words of Hyman Minsky, through these credit lines, commercial paper had been transformed into a "covert liability" of commercial banks (Minsky 1986, p. 103). Conversely, it meant that an important refinancing market for banks would be stabilized and that a fee income to commercial banks would be generated in this way.

This development found the approval of the Federal Reserve, which in the same year (1970), coincidentally, had gained complete regulatory control over the activities of BHCs. Being worried about the formation of Japanese style conglomerates, Congress had passed the 1970 Amendment to the Bank Holding Company Act to limit the subsidiaries BJCs could hold to bank related activities. However, motivated by the fear of large conglomerates combining industry and banking, there was no political compromise as to what "bank-related activity" was. Instead, Congress was granting regulatory discretion to the Federal Reserve Board (D'Arista 1994, p. 70).[6] This discretion would prove crucial in the evolving engagement of BHCs, such as First National City in the commercial paper market, as the institutional innovation was approved by the Federal Reserve as bank-related activity. This allowed commercial banks to benefit from the continuous growth of the commercial paper market.

This involvement of banks in the money markets was an important stepping-stone in the increasing hybridization of the business model of commercial banks starting in the 1970s, which was a necessity given the continuous loss of business to capital markets. During the 1970s and 1980s, banks' most lucrative clients, the corporations, continued to migrate into capital markets.[7] Investment banks, themselves under competitive pressure because of the loss of fixed stockbroker fees in 1975 (Gart 1994), aggressively expanded their capital market business to support these activities of corporate America, cutting into the profits of commercial banks.

A possible shortage on their liabilities side was added to this predicament. As inflation was further accelerating in the 1970s,[8] banks

---

[6] In line with their permissive stance, the Federal Reserve, as the main regulator of large BHCs would gradually increase the amount of investment bank activity large BHCs would be allowed to undertake, starting with 5 percent and reaching 25 percent by 1996 (Sherman 2009, p. 2).

[7] This trend accelerated over the coming decades. While in 1980 domestic business borrowing was evenly split between bank loans and securities, in 1990 commercial bank loans were down to 10 percent of the total. In addition, the percentage of short-term loans to clients dropped from 83 percent to 60 percent from 1960 to 1981 (Reinicke 1995, p. 57). Yet, corporate bonds (with the notable innovation of junk bonds) and commercial paper had posted the biggest gains (Reinicke 1995, p. 44).

[8] Ironically, it is the financial innovations adopted by the banks and permitted by the Fed that severely limited the capacity of the Fed to constrain inflation (Konings 2008).

continued to suffer from the rigid New Deal system of regulated interest rates (Regulation Q). In that period of rising inflation and limited room for manoeuver for commercial banks to increase interest rates, a financial innovation called money market mutual funds (MMMFs) was to offer small bank clients access to much higher money market rates, thereby attracting many of the banks' customers. First created in 1971 under the Investment Act of 1940, these investment funds emerged as a serious challenger to bank deposits in the context of high and rising inflation (Adams 1982; Macey 2011). Replicating many of the characteristics of a bank deposit, this financial innovation was not subject to banking regulation. Regulatory framework thus carried much lower regulatory costs, providing a competitive advantage (Sissoko 2016). At the same time, shares in MMMFs, unlike deposits, were not insured by the Federal Deposit Insurance Corporation. This was part of the competitive advantage of MMMFs, which did not have to pay insurance to the FDIC, but it also meant that the likelihood of runs, largely banned for banks due to deposit insurance, still persisted for MMMFs.

Initially a niche market, MMMFs would become increasingly attractive to both institutional and retail investors. Permitting retail investors the access to much higher capital market rates and companies an improved means of cash management, MMMFs grew from $4 billion in 1975 to $232 billion in 1982. The emergence of MMMFs as a competitor for banks on the liability side, in conjunction with the increasing competition that banks faced from investment banks on the asset side, further added pressure to the profitability of commercial banks. This dual challenge emerged jointly in the 1970s. Investment banks, in order to finance their expanding activities, became crucial players in the MMMF industry. In 1976, Merrill Lynch introduced a money market mutual fund account against which customers could write checks, further increasing the institutional similarities between these funds and deposit accounts of banks. Its fund would become the largest by 1996, supplying the liquidity needed for Merrill Lynch's and other investment banks' activity (Fredman 1997).

In light of this rising competition, concerns over competitive inequity through regulation, repeatedly voiced by banks, came to be increasingly shared by bank regulators seeking to accommodate banks' requests for competitiveness from the late 1970s onward (Reinicke 1995, p. 59f; Singer 2007, p. 46; FCIC 2011, p. 31; Tarullo 2015).

Both banks and their regulators started to clamor for deregulation of prior limits on bank activities as well as limits on interest rates on deposits to be able for banks to compete with these nonbanks. The initiatives for deregulation were successful in the 1980s, with a first act of deregulation in 1980 (Depository Institutions Deregulation and Monetary Control Act) that abolished parts of Regulation Q, allowing banks to compete easier for the customer base. It was followed by the Saint Germain Act in 1982, which broadened the types of loans and investments thrifts could make. Starting in 1982, banks were also allowed to offer money market deposit accounts, giving them a chance to compete with MMMFs. However, even though banks could now pay whatever rates they wished, the yields on money market deposit accounts were generally lower than those on MMMFs because of the higher operating costs of banks (Fredman 1997, p. 22).

At the same time that liquidity would move from banks to MMMFs, these funds would emerge as the most important buyers of commercial papers, largely owing to regulatory restrictions, which increased the possibilities for refinancing through that instrument. Given the institutional support the banks had granted to the commercial paper market in 1970 and the continuous growth of MMMFs,[9] which acted as steady buyers of commercial papers, the commercial paper market would continue its ascendance growth from 1970 onward, growing from $121 billion in 1970 to $959 billion in 1997 (Stojanovic and Vaughan 1998). Banks would respond to this threat of disintermediation, which, at the same time, meant the growth of commercial paper market liquidity through financial innovation, namely the ABCP market. The incidents propelling this innovation were the financial turbulences of the 1980s, which would bring about harsher bank regulation.

The Financial Turbulences of the 1980s and the Birth of the ABCP Market

In 1980, the Fed decided to get serious about domestic inflation caused by its incapacity to control the expansion of credit (Konings

---

[9] MMMF assets were to grow at an average annual rate of 13 percent over the quarter century from the end of 1983 to the eve of the Lehman crisis (McCabe 2010, p. 3).

2011).[10] The sudden hike of short-term interest rates induced by the Fed from 1980 onwards (the Volcker shock) caused massive problems for savings banks and thrifts, the local banks in the US responsible for mortgage lending, as their refinancing costs suddenly shot up. It would also throw the solvency of Latin American countries, which had taken up sovereign debt in dollars, into doubt. These loans had been largely provided by money center banks in New York, which, in order to face the domestic competitive threat, had massively increased their leverage and engaged in lending to foreign countries, in particular in Latin America and Eastern Europe. With the outbreak of the Latin American debt crisis, which started in 1982 as Mexico announced that it was no longer able to repay its debt (Diaz-Alejandro et al. 1984), these banks would be directly affected

To counter this increased risk-taking by banks and the financial turbulences it caused, core capital requirements, which were first formally adopted in the USA by the FDIC in 1981, would increasingly gain in importance. Specifying how much equity a bank needs to hold with respect to each and every asset it holds on its balance sheet, these regulatory requirements heavily intervened in banking business, wherefore the Federal Reserve had hitherto refused to impose statutory equity requirements on its large BHCs. However, it was forced to do so in 1983 so as to appease a congress up in arms about bailing out money center banks due to the fallout of the Latin American debt crisis (Reinicke 1995, p. 146f). Being forced to bail out US banks through loans to Latin American countries, Congress demanded in 1983 that higher core capital requirements be imposed on internationally active commercial banks in order to prevent future bailouts.[11] Being a rather coarse measure, bankers complained about excessive equity charges for activities that they perceived as rather risk-free, such as short-term lending to customers. These new measures would make the off-balance-sheet engagement of banks increasingly attractive, as long

---

[10] Ironically, it is the financial innovations adopted by the banks and permitted by the Fed, such as the use of the eurodollar market, which severely limited the capacity of the Fed to constrain inflation (Konings 2008).

[11] The Fed then engaged in international diplomacy with the Bank of England in order to generate an international Accord that would spread such higher core capital requirements to the global competitors of their banks also, in particular Japanese banks (Kapstein 1991). The result was the first Basel Accord, which was adopted in 1988 to be put into force by 1992. Chapter 5 will focus on these transnational dynamics.

as no capital requirements were attached to it. Starting at 3 percent, these newly imposed capital requirements would rise to 6 percent by 1987, reducing permitted leverage and putting further pressure on the business model of money center banks (Gart 1994).

As a consequence of these rising capital requirements, and seeking both to generate fee income and to satisfy customer requests, money center banks pushed further into off-balance-sheet business. Large money center banks in this respect had support from the Federal Reserve, which supported the fee business of its banks in order to increase the capacity of its BHCs to compete with investment banks. In this vein, it had already ruled in 1980, rather counterintuitively, that the underwriting of commercial paper by commercial banks did not constitute the issuance of securities and, thus, constituted a permitted activity for commercial banks. While this decision was challenged in court by broker-dealers and initially defeated in 1981, a higher court ruling in 1982 upheld the opinion of the Federal Reserve, allowing commercial banks unfettered business in this market (Reinicke 1995, p. 59f). In this context, coupled with the newly imposed core capital requirements, in 1983, the asset-backed commercial paper market was born.

The Emergence of the ABCP Market in 1983

Citicorp, the largest money center bank in New York, which would dominate the ABCP market for the next decade, started to set up ABCP conduits for its clients in the spring of 1983 to grant them capital market access, where refinancing rates for their loans would be lower than if refinanced by bank credit. Investors would prefer such short-term investments in order to deal with the volatility of interest rates in that era (Kavanagh et al. 1992, p. 108). For banks, the attraction of this financial innovation lay in the fact that it allowed them to maintain contact with their customers and, at the same time, earn a fee for facilitating capital market access. Given the new capital requirements, such a way of financing became more profitable.

The legal engineering involved in the setup of ABCP conduits was a straightforward application of the principles of regulatory arbitrage in the realm of corporate law. To avoid core capital requirements, banks had to ensure that the ABCP conduit was not consolidated as a subsidiary of the bank. In 1983, according to the then-valid accounting standards, this meant to avoid any indicators of control in legal form. Instead of exerting direct control, Citibank specified, with the help of contracts, all relevant actions by the special-purpose entity (SPE). In this way, any possibility of consolidation on the balance sheet of the banking conglomerate was avoided, transforming the SPE into an "orphan company" (see PwC 2005, p. 36). This was important, as regulatory accounting by banking regulators was strongly coupled with financial accounting (Interview, former Federal Reserve regulator, March 14, 2016). Hence, gaining this off-balance-sheet status was a precondition for the viability of the business model of ABCP conduits at that time.

At the same time that Citibank exerted no direct control, it undertook all the business activity of the SPE for fees and provided liquidity guarantees in case of the SPE experiencing difficulty selling its short-term debt. At that point, concrete banking regulation for these activities was, in fact, nonexistent, and banks were free to structure liquidity lines such that, in effect, they were credit guarantees, further increasing their fee income (Interview, Wall Street lawyer, March 23, 2016). Asset-backed commercial papers were a financial instrument sold in financial markets. Thus, the primary regulations structuring the market at that time stemmed from the US financial market regulator SEC and its subordinated Financial Accounting Standards Board (FASB). In addition, the private rating agencies imposed constraints for action through their ratings, which were deeply coupled with the regulations that constrained the investment choices of MMMFs. The SEC and the rating agencies, in line with their mandates, focused on investor protection and on investor protection only, ignoring the dangers stemming from risk exposures of the banking system.

However, this is not to say that there were no regulations that affected banks' structuring activities. In particular, the regulation of MMMFs was an important factor. As the volume of MMMFs grew, so did the regulation by the SEC. To be able to fulfill their promise of daily redemptions, these funds were forced by Regulation 2-a 7 in 1983 to invest in safe, short-term assets. To ensure that customers could withdraw their money at any time, the SEC imposed regulations guaranteeing that the value of the assets purchased by MMMFs would at least be equal to the money paid in. In addition, informally, the sponsors of these funds promised that the funds "would not break the buck"; that is, they promised to support their funds and ensure the full value of the money paid in, should there be a run (FCIC 2011, p. 29f).[12] At the time, however, regulatory treatment of these MMMFs was based on the presumption that investors had knowingly purchased equity and were willing to bear the losses, should there be any.[13] Hence, sponsors of these MMMFs, initially mainly broker-dealers, would not have to consolidate these MMMFs on their balance sheets, even if they implicitly protected them.

To comply with this new MMMF regulation and hence to be eligible for MMMF investment, commercial papers had to attain the highest ratings. Such a rating (termed p1 by Moody's, in contrast to the usual AAA for long-term ratings) indicated that the probability of loss to investors is minimal. This regulation directly favored the asset-backed Commercial paper market, which owing to bank sponsor support, was consistently able to achieve such a rating. Sponsor support, explicit or implicit, was an important element of this rating, as acknowledged by Moody's (1993). As matters stood, the fact that Citicorp's contractual structure with the conduit had not transferred the risk to institutional investors but, rather, retained it was not a reason for concern for rating agencies or the SEC. Instead, it was the basis of the highest rating for these investments, as they posed no risk to investors. Evidently, the safety and soundness of the banking system was of no concern to SEC or rating agencies.

First Regulatory Dialogues

The focus on the risk for the banking system stemming from these conduits was hence left to the supervisors of these large banks, mostly the Fed. Yet, while already well established during the 1980s (Interview, former rating agency employee, February 15, 2016), the ABCP market was so small not to be subject to any specific regulatory regime by the Federal Reserve up until 1992. There was no specific regulatory guidance on the ABCP market, and banks at this point in

---

[12] While this promise was legally not binding, hence, implicit, recent studies have shown several hundred occurrences of such sponsor support (McCabe 2010; Moody's 2010).

[13] Again, as in other instances, regulators and legislators had taken contractual obligations at face value, discounting market usances, such as the "don't break the buck" promise of MMMF sponsors (interview with French financial market regulator, April 19, 2011).

time did not have to approach the regulator before setting up a conduit. Instead, following the general regulatory guidelines on securitization was seen as sufficient to ensure appropriate capital treatments (Interview, Wall Street lawyer, March 23, 2016). Approaching the regulator with regard to these structures was something that was avoided, unless one thought it very likely to violate the rules and hence wanted regulatory approval (Interview, Wall Street lawyer, March 23, 2016).

Nevertheless, there were some supervisory interventions in the ABCP market in the 1980s in the context of a growing general concern regarding the increasing off-balance-sheet activities of banks (*American Banker* 1985a). Regulators were particularly critical of the structuring activities by Citicorp, which aggressively sought to move assets off balance sheet, while retaining credit risks through contractual structures, practices that were forbidden by the regulators (*American Banker* 1985b). Following the introduction of core capital requirements, off-balance-sheet commitments of the five largest BHCs, including standby letters of credit as well as interest rate swaps, had grown from $909 billion in 1985 to $1.2 trillion in 1987 (equal to more than twice their total assets; *American Banker* 1987). These off-balance-sheet exposures, regulators worried, could expose banks to large liquidity strains in times of crises, in particular referring to standby letters of credit and other similar exposure to credit risk (BCBS 1986, p. 4).[14] Therefore, they considered the option to impose reserve requirements on these activities (*American Banker* 1986), an option finally discarded.

Instead, the Federal Reserve would seek to clamp down on these practices by developing risk-based capital standards that were seeking to define the credit-equivalent amounts of risk exposure stemming from off-balance-sheet transactions (*American Banker* 1985b). These activities received the support from the highest levels, as Fed president Volcker clearly embraced this approach (*American Banker* 1985b). The focus of the Fed's concerns were orphan finance companies, which were founded by banks but not owned by them and into which banks were depositing their assets in order to lower core capital charges (*American Banker* 1985b).

---

[14] Tellingly, the Bank for International Settlements (BIS) study group, which issued these stark warnings, was headed by an employee of the Federal Reserve of New York.

This work of the Federal Reserve, which honed in on the dangers of hidden credit enhancements, was to become important to the formulation of the Basel I Accord. This accord, completed in 1988, was the first global regulatory agreement on capital requirements that the Fed and the Bank of England had begun to negotiate from 1986 onwards. It aimed at raising capital requirements globally and leveling the playing field (Kapstein 1991).[15] During these negotiations, regulators were very aware of the structuring attempts by banks (see the famous "Cross-Report" by the BIS in 1986); hence they sought to curtail these off-balance-sheet activities. However, regulators, both domestically in the USA as well as in the global accord, left liquidity facilities below one year without capital charges while applying credit conversion factors to all other forms of contractual structures. Regulators were arguing that these generally "only carry low risk" (BCBS 1988, p. 13). This would make the distinction between liquidity facilities and credit lines the crucial regulatory distinction in the years to come, and once the negotiations for Basel I were completed, the Federal Reserve Regulators immediately sought to enforce this distinction. With respect to ABCP conduits, supervisors were particularly worried about credit guarantees of banks to ABCP conduits, which were disguised as liquidity facilities in order to avoid core capital requirements.

The Formulation of the First Regulatory Framework: 1988–1992

As a consequence of their analysis of the structuring practices by Citicorp, the Federal Reserve in 1988 threatened to revoke the exemption of core capital requirement for the ABCP conduits that Citicorp had set up (Interview, Wall Street lawyer, March 23, 2016). Through that intervention, the Fed at that point clarified that liquidity lines that provided credit enhancement would not remain free of core capital charges. Citicorp reacted to these interventions through contractual adaptations of existing contracts and the industry as a whole began to develop new contractual structures in order to alleviate regulatory concerns (Interview, Wall Street lawyer, March 23, 2016).

---

[15] For more on the Basel Accords and the effects they had globally for the growth of the ABCP market, see Chapter 5.

Reengineering was complicated by the fact that while seeking to retain capital relief from banking regulators, the banks were at the same time facing the requests of rating agencies for credit enhancement to achieve the highest ratings. In order to balance these competing requirements, a new structure that would satisfy both requirements was developed. It would provide the conduit with a 10 percent credit enhancement and a 100 percent liquidity facility for the entire conduit. This allowed for the commercial papers to be issued by the SPEs to maintain the highest credit rating without having to hold capital against all – but only 10 percent of assets.

Another outcome of the increased capital requirements and the hardening stance of regulators was the creation of a form of SPE operating in financial markets by Citicorp in 1988, which were established to place assets with high asset quality outside of the banks' balance sheet (Ehrlich et al. 2009; Mason 2009). The first structured investment vehicle (SIV), Alpha, refinanced only about a quarter of its assets with commercial paper. The rest would be refinanced issuing medium-term notes. Much like a bank, structured investment vehicles would have an equity of about 10 percent. By using this amount of equity, a refinancing mix focused on medium-term notes and clear investment policies into the highest-grade papers, the debt issued by these entities received the highest ratings (Tabe 2010). Given the reduced exposure to rollover risks in the commercial paper market, Citicorp only needed to provide a 360-day liquidity line to the vehicle – but only for 10 percent of the volume of assets held by the vehicle and no credit guarantees.

The provision of only partial credit guarantees (called a "partially enhanced conduit") or the creation of SIVs were only the first steps in the ongoing regulatory dialectic between banking regulators and banks with respect to the support structures that banks would provide to their conduits. In this way, while regulators were trying to reduce off-balance-sheet exposures of banks and sought to limit their exploitation of coarse rules, the raising of the capital requirements in the Basel Accord only increased the growth of the ABCP market. But, this is not to say that regulators weren't aware of the dangers; instead, it speaks to the fact that industry responded. These institutional innovations would lay the groundwork for the expansion of the ABCP market in the next decade, an expansion that was very much driven by the new capital rules enshrined in the Basel Accord.

Here, a first paradox emerges. While regulators were trying to limit off-balance-sheet financing (BIS 1986), the Basel I accord in its final version (1988) would provide strong incentives for US (and non-US) banks to place short- and long-term assets into SPEs and to refinance them in the ABCP market. The combination of higher capital requirements of 8 percent, in conjunction with the 0 percent for liquidity facilities, gave a large impetus to further engagements by US banks, as they were seeking to generate more fee income, providing strong incentives to place short- and long-term assets into SPEs and to refinance them in the money markets (American Banker 1988a; Kapstein 1991). A market of the size of $11 billion in 1988 and almost exclusively dominated by US banks (and here in particular Citicorp, which issued $7 billion of the $11 billion [*American Banker 1988a*]), the ABCP market would grow in terms of what was to be securitized, who did it, and under which rules, becoming much more international in the process.

The evolution of this market in the US from 1988 onwards, still seen as a niche market in 1991 (Interview, former rating agencies employee, February 18, 2016) would be exponential in the following decade, moving from less than $5 billion in 1987 to $50 billion in 1992 to $350 billion in 1998 (Moody's 1993, 1998). On the supply side, its evolution was determined by both the core capital requirements that the new Basel Accord had set and the incentives it provided to banks, foreign and domestic, to enter that market as well as the market turbulences of the 1990s. On the demand side, the continued growth of the market would be supported by a further tightening of Regulation 2a-7 by the SEC in 1990, which substantially lowered the amount of commercial papers MMMFs could buy without the highest rating (Cook and Duffield 1993, p. 165). This strongly coupled the growth of MMMFs to ABCPs which, thanks to the support by bank sponsors, were uniquely placed to produce these highest ratings.[16] On the supply side, it meant a diversification of assets to be securitized and a lengthening of their maturity.

This growth in volume and the extended maturity of assets started to arouse further regulatory interests and regulatory interventions by

---

[16] This tightening was caused by a further default of a large commercial paper issuer during the recession in 1990, which had raised another threat of a run on MMMFs in 1990 (Investment Company Institute 2009).

the Office of the Comptroller of the Currency (OCC) and the Federal
Reserve. So, they would take different measures in order to deal with
this expanding market. One aspect that the Fed saw as critical was the
rigid and outdated accounting rules of that period, which determined
whether ABCP conduits were independent entities or subsidiaries of
the bank.[17] The guidance by the Fed on the treatment of securitization
activities (Federal Reserve 1990) expressed a certain regulatory discontent with developments in the financial accounting realm, which
failed to address the problem properly. While the SEC had considered
issuing a more stringent rule for orphaned securitization conduits in
1989, it had abstained from it after months of deliberation (*American
Banker* 1989), most likely due to pressure by industry. This inaction
meant that up until 1996, the FASB didn't provide any clear guidance
regarding the consolidation of SPEs (Hartgraves and Benston 2002,
p. 247).

Any statements issued prior to that by the Emerging Issue Task
Force, a body of mostly public accountants linked to the FASB or the
SEC, while indicating awareness and concerns about off-balance-sheet
financing of banks, were also indicating clear pathways for banks to
avoid consolidation (Hartgraves and Benston 2002).[18] In order to deal
with the structuring practices of banks in securitization to avoid the
on-balance-sheet status of assets, the Federal Reserve specified that
it had the right to demand consolidation of securitization vehicles in
case the debt was guaranteed by the sponsor (Federal Reserve 1990,
p. 11), even if nonconsolidation was accepted under US Generally
Accepted Accounting Principles (GAAP). This legal change would

---

[17] Although the SEC had considered issuing a more stringent rule for orphaned
securitization conduits in 1989, it had abstained from it after months of
deliberation (*American Banker* 1989), most likely due to pressure by the
industry. This inaction meant that up until 1996, the FASB didn't provide any
clear guidance regarding the consolidation of SPEs (Hartgraves and Benston
2002, p. 247). Any statements prior to that, issued by the Emerging Issue Task
Force, a body of mostly public accountants linked to the FASB or the SEC,
while indicating awareness and concerns about off-balance-sheet financing of
banks, were also indicating clear pathways for banks to avoid consolidation
(Hartgraves and Benston 2002).

[18] The most famous of these bright lines was the stipulation in 1990 by the
SEC that outside parties holding more than 3 percent equity of a conduit
are sufficient to avoid consolidation (EITF 1990-15), a guideline that would
structure much of the accounting practices (Hartgraves and Benston 2002,
p. 252f).

open a venue for requesting the regulatory consolidation of ABCP conduits on banks' balance sheets, an issue that was heatedly debated within the Fed (Interview, Federal Reserve regulator involved in rule making, March 15, 2016).

Furthermore, in 1991, both the OCC as well as the Federal Reserve investigated the risks emanating from the ABCP market, with the OCC in particular being concerned about interest rate risks that stemmed from the lengthening of the maturity of assets inside of the ABCP conduits (*American Banker* 1991b). Their interventions clarified to the banks once more that liquidity facility, ostensibly just credit guarantees in disguise, had to be backed up by higher core capital, leading again to further restructuring (*American Banker* 1991a). The Fed's conversations with banks concerning their liquidity exposure to the ABCP market led Citicorp and other large players to invite other banks, most notably Japanese banks, to provide liquidity backup facilities for their ABCP conduits (*American Banker* 1991a, c; Interview, former rating agency employee, March 21, 2016), further promoting the internationalization of the market.

The first specific guidance by the Fed on the ABCP market, published for its bank examiners in 1992, put these ad hoc interventions on a permanent basis (Kavanagh et al. 1992, pp. 107, 109). Resulting from an intense internal debate, it specified that liquidity facilities should not fund against assets in default and employ an asset quality test, thereby ensuring that it was not a credit enhancement in disguise. In effect, this meant that industry practices were approved of by the regulator. Should the examiner identify it as such, it could be declared as a credit guarantee. The guidance also required that banks prove that they have sufficient self-regulatory capabilities to deal with the risks emerging from these programs (Federal Reserve 1992).

This final ruling was the outcome of an internal fight, as a certain faction within the Fed involved in the investigation sought to classify ABCP conduits as subsidiaries of banks, thereby forcing banks to consolidate them on their balance sheets. However, these attempts encountered the resistance of chairman Greenspan, who favored deregulation. A Fed regulator involved in these debates remembered,

Historically, the loss rate was ridiculously low, like basis points. In fact I remember [chuckles], I remember when I was trying to get them consolidated as affiliates back in the early '90s, Greenspan looked at me and he said, "What's the loss rate on this?" And, I had it and was like, "One basis point," and he said, "Why are you bothering these people?" [laughs]. I mean, historically, the loss rates were extremely low. (Interview, Federal Reserve regulator, March 15, 2016)

It was hence the new leader Greenspan and his antiregulatory stance (as compared to the much more interventionist stance of chairman Volcker) and the low loss rates that decided the battle in favor of non-regulation. The report by the Federal Reserve Board from the same year documents the awareness of the regulators regarding the regulatory arbitrage that drove the growth of the market.[19] They observed these activities and approved of them, as they agreed that the core capital requirements for short-term revolving loans of clients were too high in the Basel requirements (Kavanagh et al. 1992; Interview, Federal Reserve regulator, March 15, 2016).

This regulatory stance is a reflection of the regulatory principles embraced by the top managers at the Fed at the time. It espoused an ideology that believed in market discipline, letting market forces sort out and solve the problems these markets posed themselves (Greenspan 2008).[20] Since 1987, when he first became chairman of the Fed, A Greenspan had especially argued for the need to remove outdated regulatory constraints and to stop equating the lack of government regulation with the complete lack of regulation. If markets were to undertake their due diligence and discipline too-risky behavior, this would be seen as potentially more efficient than having regulations distort market signals and generate incentives to shift these tasks to regulators (Mallaby 2016, pp. 663, 665). This view equated the pursuit of self-interest by investors with the achievement of a larger societal goal without questioning whether this alignment might always come about or whether there might be instances in which the public interest and the interest of investors actually deviate. This decision meant that, despite its legal prerogatives, the Fed would largely continue to follow

---

[19] Kavanagh et al. (1992) also emphasized the increasing restrictions for MMMFs with respect to their investment into commercial papers, fuelling the growth of the market from the demand side.

[20] Nobody else would come to represent that attitude better than the group of high-level policymakers in the USA in the 1990s, which came to be known as the "three marketeers" (Treasury Secretary Rubin, his deputy Lawrence Summers, and Alan Greenspan, known as "the maestro"), as they were called by the *Times* in 1999.

financial accounting decisions with respect to ABCP conduits in most instances (Interview, former Federal Reserve regulator, March 14; Interview, Federal Reserve regulator, March 27, 2012) and leave ABCP conduits largely untouched in terms of core capital requirements.[21]

There was hence a particular ambivalence about the regulation of ABCP conduits. The Fed was, on the one hand, condoning the use of these conduits to finance trade receivables in a way that was cheaper than the Basel Accords permitted on-balance sheet, and, on the other hand, was insisting on the distinction between credit enhancements and liquidity facilities that were enshrined in the Basel Accords. Any further action of the Fed would be impeded by internal contradictions within the Fed, contradictions between forces seeking further regulation of the risk exposure of banks to the ABCP market, in particular the liquidity risks and others observing no dangers (Interview, banking regulator, March 15, 2016). This lack of decisive regulatory intervention would mean that regulation would infringe on market developments only at the margins, which is to say in the supervisory practices. In the meantime, as the market actors got more accustomed with the technique, they started to expand the range and maturity of assets they were to refinance.

Changes in the ABCP Market in the 1990s and Regulatory Unease

In 1992, the Fed (Kavanagh et al. 1992) characterized the assets refinanced by ABCP conduits as mostly short-term trade receivables, an observation that at that time was already belied by the increasing length of maturity and diversifying asset classes (Interview, former Moody's employee, February 17, 2016). It is a picture that is more appropriate for 1988, when the vast majority of programs were still multiseller programs, which refinanced short-term self-liquidating loans (Interview, former ABCP conduit manager, March 18, 2016). The latter were investment grade, or if not investment grade, were provided credit enhancement to achieve this status. Companies sourced for assets would usually be highly graded firms able to bear certain risks on their own.

---

[21] In essence, prudential consolidation of conduits by the sponsoring bank would be required only in the most blatant cases, when the debt transferred to a securitization vehicle was, in effect, directly guaranteed by banks.

With the expansion of the ABCP programs, the competition increased and conduit managers lowered credit quality expectations to find more loans to refinance from noninvestment-grade clients. In this vein, Citicorp opened a conduit in 1988 that could refinance noninvestment-grade clients and their loans (*American Banker* 1988b). This trend would accelerate in the 1990s, with different assets that before had not been seen as suitable included in ABCP programs, such as student loans and mortgages rather than trade receivables alone. It started again with Citicorp, which founded McKinley Triangle in 1992 to refinance longer term credit card receivables with ABCP, because of the fear that the term ABS might be too small a market (*American Banker* 1992). This lengthening of maturity mismatches did not present a problem to the rating methodology of rating agencies: as long as the investors were protected from losses, lengthening maturity mismatch didn't matter.[22]

To be able to securitize such riskier assets without having to provide more credit enhancements, banks and their lawyers started to structure liquidity facilities such that they provided credit enhancements without core capital charges (Moody's 1997). These liquidity facilities, which were structured to achieve credit enhancement without classifying as such, would be a topic for regulatory dialogues in the next decade in one form or another (Interview, former Moody's employee, February 17, 2016; Interview, former S&P employee, March 2016, Wall Street lawyer, March 23, 2016). In this respect, rating agencies always qualified their position as interested bystanders (Interview, former rating agency employee, February 17, 2016; Interview, second rating agency employee, February 18, 2016), worried only about the repayment of loans, but not worried about whether and in how far the economic substance of regulation was followed. If liquidity facilities somehow could do the job without requiring higher credit enhancements, that was completely acceptable.

However, despite their signaled neutrality to market solutions, in the mid-1990s Moody's employees started to discuss at industry

---

[22] As Moody's emphasized when exposing its methodology for ratings, a prime rating was based on the capacity of the issuer of ABCP (i.e., the ABCP conduit) to access funds "other than the sale of new ABCP" (Moody's 1993, p. 5) to repay maturing investments, not on the quality of assets itself. That means that a prime rating always relied on the support of some third party, most often the sponsoring bank, be it through credit enhancements or liquidity facilities.

conferences these issues of "trick liquidity" (Interview, former Moody's employee, February 17th, 2016, former S&P employee, March 21, 2016). Toning down the negative wording, they renamed these contractual schemes as "structured liquidity facilities" and published a report on these techniques in 1997 (Moody's 1997). The Federal Reserve was also aware of these practices and sought to operate against them in its examinations, seeking to limit liquidity facilities to market disruptions (Interview, former Federal Reserve regulator, March 14, 2016). This stance is evident in the guidance issued by the Federal Reserve to its examiners in the banks in 1997, where it is stated that

> Furthermore, banking organizations that extend liquidity facilities to securitized transactions, particularly asset-backed commercial paper programs, may be exposed to high degrees of credit risk which may be subtly embedded within the facilities' provisions ... *depending upon the provisions of the facility – such as whether the facility covers dilution of the underlying receivable pool – credit risk can be shifted from the program's explicit credit enhancements to the liquidity facility. Such provisions may enable certain programs to fund riskier assets and yet maintain the credit rating on the program's commercial paper without increasing the program's credit enhancement levels.* (Federal Reserve 1997, emphasis mine)

Such provisions were to be classified as credit facilities, increasing capital requirements for the bank. This stance was influenced not only through the detection of these practices during on-site examinations but also by the observation of industry publications, such as Moody's, by Federal Reserve experts (Interview, former Federal Reserve regulator, March 14, 2016). Furthermore, regulators were attending industry conferences, where these practices were discussed.[23]

Nevertheless, despite this awareness of structuring practices, there was little in terms of binding regulation (Interview, former employee Standard and Poor's, March 21, 2016). This unregulated situation of the market was rather unsatisfactory for the examiners on the ground. However, the discomfort was soothed by a belief in market discipline within the Federal Reserve. As a Fed examiner working on ABCP conduits in the late 1990s recalled,

---

[23] Industry participants were, of course, not happy about the discussion of such issues in front of regulators, but that did not prevent their discussion (Interview, former Moody's employee, February 18, 2016).

But, you know, there was some comfort in knowing that although there might not be explicit contractual recourse to the bank that there were, you know, there were investors, institutional investors, there were rating agencies, there were, you know ... you know, so ... the capital requirement for off-balance sheet was, you know, driven by, you know, intelligent form of market forces. (Interview, former Federal Reserve regulator, March 14, 2016)

This ideological embrace of the self-regulatory power of markets prevented forceful, preventive action by supervisors. The Fed's director of banking supervision summarized this culture in 2010 when he stated that "supervisors understood that forceful and pro-active supervision ... might be viewed as i) overly intrusive, burdensome and heavy handed, ii) an undesirable constraint on credit availability, or inconsistent with the Fed's public posture "(FCIC 2011, p. 54). As this statement indicates, the general culture climate was not conducive to aggressive intervention by supervisors (see also Goodstadt 2011). Given this stance, market developments at this point in time were not for the most part driven by regulatory interventions. Indeed, if anything, the repeal of Glass–Steagall in 1999 would only cement the legitimacy of commercial banks action in capital markets, a move supported by the Fed that forced the hand of Congress when it approved the merger of Citigroup with Travellers Insurance in 1998 (*Wall Street Journal* 1998; Konings 2011).

Rather than regulatory interventions, it was the financial turmoil of the late 1990s, during which the ABCP market held up astoundingly well (Moody's 1998), which proved to be much more important to the development of the ABCP market. The turbulences in capital markets, experienced in the wake of the East Asian crisis, the Russian ruble crisis, as well as the collapse of Long-Term Capital Management in 1998, led to the cancellation of the issuance of many asset-backed securities. In contrast, the ABCP market would prove to be a reliable refinancing source during this turmoil. Lacking demand, the issuers of longer term asset-backed securities turned instead to warehousing these asset-backed securities in ABCP conduits, waiting for buyers. Additionally, as the direct sale of asset-backed securities failed during the financial turmoil, more issuers perceived conduits as a profitable venue to refinance these securities, even while holding on to them.

Hence, 1998 witnessed the emergence of many new conduits pursuing a buy-and-hold strategy, arbitraging long-term interest rates with short-term rates (the securities arbitrage model) and those conduits warehousing ABS before they would be repackaged and sold on to other investors. Moody's calls it "a whole new ball game" as the ABCP market emerges unscathed from the financial markets turmoil (Moody's 1998). Given these developments, the ABCP market grew threefold from $256 billion to $745 billion from 1997 to 2001, making it represent in 2001 for the first time more than 50 percent of the commercial paper market (Moody's 2002). This rapid growth further increased the supervisory discomfort of the faction within the Fed worried about the ingenuity of banks operating off balance sheet in the ABCP market. However, it did not find any expression in domestic interventions immediately. Instead, it expressed itself on the transnational level, using the window of opportunity that opened when the negotiations for a new Basel Accord (named Basel II) were initiated by the Federal Reserve in 1998 (Tarullo 2008; Goldbach 2015).

These negotiations were set off by concerns in the regulatory community over the financial turmoil in developing countries from 1994 onward as well as by desires of the US banks to integrate newly developed internal risk models into capital requirements, the revisions to the Basel Accord (known as Basel II). These negotiations were largely driven by the Federal Reserve and their agenda, which featured both a belief in market discipline (what was to become pillar III in Basel II) and a belief in a qualitatively intense supervisory review process (pillar II). In the context of these negotiations, the critical faction within the Fed, unable to generate domestic action, inserted their discontent over off-balance-sheet financing techniques of its banks in the global regulatory discourse.

The Basel II Negotiations from a US Perspective

Already in the first consultative paper for the revision of the Basel Accord, in 1999, the case is made for limiting the regulatory arbitrage by large banks off balance sheet. The paper points to the exploitation of the 0 percent capital charge for liquidity lines below one year and suggests instead a 20 percent conversion factor for these liquidity lines (BCBS 1999a, p. 32). That this proposal indeed is linked to the critical stance of examiners of the Federal Reserve to the ABCP market can be seen from the first working paper by the Basel Committee (BCBS 1999b), one published two months before the first draft of the new Accord. Basing itself on "information collected by US regulators *through on-site examinations*" (BCBS 1999b, p. 21, emphasis mine), the study shows the degree to which some US financial institutions had become engaged in the ABCP and CLO markets, seeking advantages from regulatory arbitrage. It also indicates accelerating possibilities for such regulatory arbitrage (BCBS 1999b, p. 25). They write,

> On the basis of the available information, the securitisation activities of these companies loom large in relation to their on-balance sheet exposures. As of March 1998, outstanding non-mortgage ABSs and ABCP issued by these institutions exceeded $200 billion, or more than 12% (25%), on average, of the institutions' total risk-weighted assets (loans). For several institutions, the combined issuance of ABSs and ABCP approached 25% (50%) of total risk-weighted assets (loans). (BCBS 1999b, p. 24)

The report strongly attacks the circumvention of core capital requirements of large banks through their off-balance-sheet business. In particular, the ABCP market is singled out as one of those activities "to be motivated heavily *by capital arbitrage considerations*" (BCBS 1999b, p. 26, emphasis mine).

Yet, while the critical section of regulators in the Fed could thereby strongly influence the "global" regulatory debate, domestic regulatory action pointed in the opposite direction. Instead of implementing this proposed measure domestically, the Fed initially chose to implement measures that were accommodating banks' requests to converge risk-based measures within the Basel Accord with industry practices, an endeavor that they had pursued since 1997 (Goldbach 2015, p. 88).

Thus, in November 2001, the Federal Reserve introduced the advanced framework concerning capital requirements for securitiza-tion, one that it had developed in the context of the Basel II negotiations. Bringing substantial core capital relief to all balance sheet positions regarding securitized products, the rule also sought to lower capital charges for banks' credit enhancements for ABCP conduits (Office of the Federal Register 2001, p. 59627).[24] At the same time that they

---

[24] To do that, it allowed banks to evaluate the credit enhancements they had granted to their conduits using the Internal Ratings Based Approach, based also on the external ratings of assets inside of the conduit, a measure announced in 2000 (*American Banker* 2000). If after undertaking such a stock-taking exercise, the bank deemed its risk exposure based on the

installed these beneficial rules based on self-regulation, the regulators noted the ingenuity of the new financial structures and reserved for themselves the authority to determine on a case-by-case basis whether the appropriate capital requirements and credit conversion factors were applied (Office of the Federal Register 2001, p. 59624f).

Interview sources at the Fed spoke of an ongoing conversation about liquidity lines, which could not be resolved yet, but that it was debated was announced to industry participants (Interview, former Federal Reserve regulator, March 14, 2016, Federal Reserve regulator March 15, 2016). Again, an issue of particular concern was the distinction between credit guarantees on the one hand and, on the other hand, contractual guarantees on nondefaults that in economic substance are hardly distinguishable (*American Banker* 2000).The deadlock that gripped these internal regulatory debates in 2001 would come undone with an external event that would shake up the ABCP market and permit pro-regulation forces within the Federal Reserve to gain the upper hand. This event was the implosion of Enron in December 2001 and the accounting scandals following it (such as WorldCom in 2002), which forced both accounting and banking regulators to face the issue of off-balance-sheet financing techniques.

Enron and the Ensuing Uncertainty in the ABCP Market

Enron, a Texas-based energy company, had exploited off-balance-sheet rules to beautify its balance sheet aggressively, which permitted its rise to one of the highest valued companies in the 1990s and caused its sudden demise in the last months of 2001 (Dharan and Bufkins 2008). When Enron filed for Chapter 11 bankruptcy in December 2001, as off-balance-sheet debt returned to its balance sheet, the US accounting standard-setting body, FASB, was propelled into action to develop more appropriate accounting standards for off-balance-sheet business. In this moment, the issue of SPEs came on top of the agenda of the Financial Accounting Standards Board (Moody's 2003a). A consolidation project addressing SPEs had been worked on by the FASB from 1994 on (Hartgraves and Benston 2002, p. 255), without any tangible

underlying collateral to be BBB or better, it only needed to withhold 8 percent of the equity; if it deemed it worse, the charge could double or even go up to 100 percent of equity.

results. As public pressure was mounting, activities of the FASB on this front were accelerating, seeking to close the regulatory loopholes that had permitted such egregious misstatements of earnings and risk.

In that moment, owing to the direct coupling of national accounting rules and regulatory capital requirements, banking regulators vigorously had to confront the issue of consolidation (Adelson 2003b). According to adamant critiques (Adelson and Cho 2002; Saunders, Banks: The Next Enron? Unpublished paper 2002), the prior neglect of the off-balance-sheet question led to leverage ratios that bank regulators used to regulate rather muddled capital requirements, making capital requirements inadequate. The critiques bemoaned that FASB Accounting Standards and Capital rules distinguished between ABCP and on-balance-sheet transactions, as the risks in economic substance were the same. While the final outcome of the accounting rule changes by the FASB did not move the situation closer to the economic substance of the transaction, as we will see, the faction within the Federal Reserve in favor of regulation used this window of opportunity in negotiations with the industry.

By August 22, 2002, the FASB had developed an exposure draft in order to deal with the problem of off-balance-sheet SPEs, positing the new concept of variable interest entity (VIE) to decide whether SPEs should be consolidated. That concept abolished the considerations of equity ownership, hence, visible control alone. It removed major prior guideposts such as the 3 percent equity stake for a third party that was needed to avoid consolidation, as Enron had exploited this bright line within the rule to hide accelerating debts from its balance sheet. Instead, it sought to capture the variable interests: the exposure of the larger entities to the economic fate of an SPE. The rule demanded that the entity that was exposed to the majority of variable risks and rewards from the SPE had to consolidate it on its balance sheet, independent of the legal links that it entertained with the SPE. It required consolidation if a party was providing most of the financial support, even if that support did not exceed 50 percent.[25]

Reactions requesting changes and clarifications to the proposal were numerous, those from industry mostly critical and those from banking regulators encouraging. In 2002, the Accounting Policy Group of the

---

[25] The new approach should especially be applied when the equity such an SPE held was insufficient to deal with the risks to which the entity was exposed.

Fed, a group in frequent contact with the FASB (Interview, former Federal Reserve regulator, March 14, 2016) sent a comment letter to the FASB on this issue, commending it for seeking to provide greater clarity with respect to off-balance-sheet items and encouraging it to follow a risk-and-reward analysis, just like its own approach (Federal Reserve 2002, p. 7).[26] After a very short comment and revision period, the new rule, FIN 46, was issued in January 2003. The rule had an immediate impact on the securitization activities of banks in the USA, halting expansion and leading to massive restructuring of securitization programs in order to avoid on-balance-sheet consolidation (see Bens and Monahan 2008, p. 1027).

When introduced in January 2003, the new rule abolished the 3 percent capital rule and instead focused on the question of which corporation held the majority of risks and rewards emanating from the entity (Moody's 2003a). Focusing on economic substance rather than legal form, FIN 46 stipulated that if an entity cannot self-determine its course of action, or if another entity is exposed to the majority of risks and rewards, it should be consolidated on that entity's balance sheet. ABCP and CDO conduits would be clearly affected by this measure. Auditors were initially asked to undertake a qualitative assessment, which if no results could be produced, should be followed up by a quantitative approach. The quantitative approach asked the auditor to evaluate the majority of risks and rewards in quantitative terms, providing *clear bright lines* (Adelson 2003b). The contractual setup of the entity was to be analyzed and fixed fee income, such as for servicing fees, to be included to determine the rewards, an inclusion that evoked industry opposition (Morgan Stanley 2003).[27]

Following this introduction, industry then set out the search for the Holy Grail: avoid diminishing risk and rewards while avoiding the on-balance-sheet status implied by the new regulations (Adelson 2003a;

---

[26] The letter further clarifies that the Federal Reserve was focusing on equity masquerading as debt and hence on investors rather than sponsors of SPEs, which meant that nearly always there would be off-balance-sheet treatment for sponsors of conduits (Interview, former Federal Reserve regulator, March 14, 2016).

[27] Despite these far-reaching changes, the final FIN 46 measure already had dropped several of the more demanding initial requirements, such as the need to reassess continuously the exposure of banks to SPEs in order to determine consolidation. Instead, auditors were asked to establish who was exposed to the majority of risks and rewards only at the setup of the conduit.

Interview, former rating agency expert, February 18, 2016; Interview, Federal Reserve regulator with special accounting focus, March 27, 2012). Initially, credit arbitrage conduits and SIVs, which at that time issued more than $200 billion worth of ABCP, wanted to move to the alternative regulatory status of qualifying SPEs but were effectively barred from doing so when FASB issued an interpretation to the contrary in March 2003. One response to the threat, then, was to move from full liquidity to partial liquidity and increasingly to use instruments such as medium-term notes and extendible commercial papers, in order to shift risks to the investors (Adelson 2003a), partially explaining the rise of SIVs from 2004 onward.

The main response by industry, however, would reside in using the quantitative measurement of risks as the loophole to escape consolidation (Moody's 2003a, p. 4). By selling expected loss notes, which would cover 50 percent of the expected losses to outside investors, banks were able to shift the measured majority of risks away from them. At the same time, using the ratings-based approach and internal risk models to calculate the losses to be expected, the regulated were capable of justifying expected loss tranches that had the size of 0.1 to 0.2 percent of the assets in the conduits. Despite paying 15 to 25 percent on these notes (Moody's 2003b), these costs were marginal to the business model of ABCP conduits (Interview, former Federal Reserve regulator, March 14, 2016).

In September 2003, the FASB put the rule on hold and issued a new exposure draft. This decision was partially due to industry complaints about inconsistencies and partially due to its own dissatisfaction with a mainly legalistic implementation focusing on the quantitative bright lines within the rule. In its final December 2003 revised version (FIN 46 R), the FASB sought to act against the merely quantitative implementation of the new standard in practice. Against industry complaints (see PwC 2003) that opposed qualitative analysis as impractical, the FASB emphasized the need to combine qualitative and quantitative analysis. Nevertheless, it left the quantitative analysis as such untouched (Adelson 2003b). Owing to this loophole, FIN 46, even in its revised form, was failing to lead to major consolidation of ABCP conduits from 2003 onward (Interview, Wall Street lawyer, March 23, 2016).

As a Federal Reserve regulator pointed out, by 2005 "almost all of them [ABCP conduits] had been structured to achieve off-balance sheet treatment under FIN 46" (Interview, Federal Reserve regulator March 27, 2012).[28] This was confirmed when the SEC assessed the impact of these new off-balance-sheet standards and their effects and noted that much structuring had occurred ex ante to prevent consolidation (SEC 2005, p. 92). Justifying its measures, the FASB responded that the problem of the litigious culture required it to employ bright lines in its approach to consolidation, even if a pure risk-and-reward approach might be more satisfying (FASB 2006).[29] Thus, in the end the litigious culture and the strong sway of industry over FASB prevented any major consolidation of ABCP conduits in the accounting realm. However, in the meantime, the change coalition within the Fed had effectively used the threat of consolidation to bring about change on a different front.

In the period from 2002 to 2004, there were multiple meetings between rating agencies, banks, and the banking regulator concerned about the expected impact of consolidation upon the industry (Interview, Federal Reserve regulator, March 15, 2016), at the same time that the regulator was consulting industry on how to implement Basel II (Interview, Federal Reserve regulator, March 18, 2016). There was much fear that the beneficial regulatory treatment for ABCP conduits would be abolished and the market would come to a halt (Moody's 2003a; Bens and Moynihan 2008). Industry players that were particularly important in that discussion with the Fed were MMMFs, which were concerned about the amount of assets eligible for their investment. As the most important stakeholder in the ABCP market, their position would prove crucial for the negotiations, as a Federal Reserve regulator involved in the negotiations pointed out:

One of the points they made was that they needed these assets, money market assets because they had all this money they had to put at work and there was nowhere else to go, so if half of the commercial paper market disappeared because the ABCP disappeared ... then they would have nowhere to put money that they consider, you know, basically restrained. There just wasn't

---

[28] With follow-up interpretive work undertaken by the FASB, these weak standards would be even further diluted, e.g., when specifying that those servicing fees that were not absorbing any variability of the entity should not be taken into account when calculating the variable interests (FSP FIN 46r 6, 2006).

[29] Available at www.fasb.org/news/nr021606a.shtml.

enough. There was more demand for money market than there was assets to buy. (Interview, former Federal Reserve regulator, March 14, 2016)

The regulator thus faced a situation in which the abolishment of the beneficial capital treatment for ABCP conduits might hamper the prospects of the entire MMMF industry. These deliberations were one reason why, in the wake of the announcement of FIN 46, regulators announced that they were considering excluding conduits consolidated according to the new accounting rules from core capital requirements (Office of the Federal Register 2003). In October 2003, the US banking regulators issued a temporary exemption of newly consolidated securitization SPEs from the calculation of core capital requirements, an exemption that was made permanent in July 2004.

To critics, the US banking regulators thereby made "a material distinction between two kinds of activities with essentially identical risk" (see Adelson 2003b, p. 6),[30] confirming the regulatory loophole that allowed banks to evade core-capital requirements. Instead of aligning their regulatory accounting protocol with FIN 46 or even tightening it, the regulator preferred an unusual differentiation between accounting and regulatory rules (Interview, Federal Reserve regulator, March 27, 2012). This announcement by the OCC proposal did allay much of the FIN 46 concerns of the industry (Moody's 2003a). When responding to FIN 46, regulators clearly took into account international competitiveness concerns of the banks, just as Moody's (February 2003) had assumed, as any unilateral action will have negative competitive consequences. As a former Fed official confirmed, "It was certainly one of the issues the banks made very clear, because this FIN 46 was only applied by FASB in the US and most ... a lot of the activity was done by non-US banks" (Interview, former Federal Reserve regulator, March 14, 2016).

But, international competitiveness concerns were not the only reason. Instead, banking regulators were basing their perception of the market on the historic losses the industry reported, which were in the amount of basis points. The final ruling of the Federal Reserve on July 28, 2004 confirmed the exception clause for consolidated conduits. As Adelson (2003b) put it, in this way, regulators found a way to avoid

---

[30] On the one hand, corporate lending secured by customers receivables and on the other hand, asset-backed commercial papers.

having to apply Basel I to ABCP conduits as they saw the charges as excessive.

However, in the same ruling, the Federal Reserve introduced a 10 percent credit conversion factor for liquidity lines with less than one year maturity, which was a major step forward in the regulation of the market. While the Federal Reserve had initially proposed a 20 percent credit conversion factor, in accordance with the provisions in the final revised version of the Basel Accord (see BCBS 2004a, p. 125 for the standard approach, p. 138 for the advanced approach), in the end, it settled for 10 percent. Justifying the lower capital charges for liquidity facilities, the regulators cited the following reasons:

> Seven commenters stated that the proposed 20 percent credit conversion factor for short-term liquidity facilities was too high given *the low historical losses* and the overall strength of the credit risk profiles of such liquidity facilities ... One commenter noted that the *proposed capital charge would put U.S. banks at a competitive disadvantage relative to foreign banks and non-bank funding sources.* The agencies generally agree with these commenters. (Federal Register 2004, p. 44910, emphasis mine)

Here again, competitive disadvantages as well as low loss rates convinced the regulator to lower the requirements. However, despite being lower than the rules envisioned in the Basel Accord, this introduction of a 10 percent credit conversion factor was still an important victory for the change coalition. It was the outcome of a shrewd bargaining tactic, where the critical voices within the Federal Reserve had used the pending accounting rule changes as a bargaining chip in order to overcome a longstanding internal and external blockade concerning their unease about the lack of core capital charges on these liquidity lines. In these negotiations, they allowed industry to exclude consolidated conduits, but requested the 10 percent liquidity line charge in return. At the end of the process, when the toothless character of FIN 46 had become clear, industry negotiators wanted to renegotiate the terms of the deal struck, but the regulator clarified to them that it was too late (Interview, Federal Reserve Regulator March 18, 2016).

The hardened bargaining stance of the Federal Reserve was the outcome of a longstanding unease at the Fed about the complete exclusion of liquidity lines. One regulator explained,

> At least some people at the Fed staff were concerned that a liquidity facility was really a credit facility. As soon as it's exercised, then it becomes a credit

facility. And so, this kind of minimum capital charge was a way to recognize it. (Interview, Federal Reserve regulator, March 18, 2016)

The 10 percent core capital charge then was a compromise of different fractions in the Fed, some of which opposed any capital requirements for liquidity lines, while others wanted convergence with Basel II at that moment. As an examiner stated,

Well ... there was a ... it's not really a process ... I think it is consensus building. I think the people that were concerned about this, you know, they were appeased because this met ... You had a capital charge on liquidity for the first time and you know, so the ... the risk weight ... maybe was less important than to actually have a capital charge on a short-term liquidity facility. (Interview, Federal Reserve regulator, March 15, 2016)

The fact that there was to be a charge meant that new information would be generated and that liquidity facilities would become subject to more scrutiny. As the same regulator explained,

There weren't a lot of very bright lines or good data points under which to say that, you know, what the capital charge should be. But, once you have some capital charge, then you have a lot of information, because now you have something you can just definitively measure, and we certainly could change that at a later point if needed. (Interview, Federal Reserve regulator, March 15, 2016)

These consecutive regulatory pronouncements and the ongoing deliberations that they reveal point to the delicate environment within which regulators were operating. They were seeking to impose some regulations while not unsettling the market, always in deliberation with the industry.[31]

From this moment onward, no further regulations were imposed on the market in the USA, and the ABCP market would slowly regain

---

[31] In addition to the new rules on liquidity lines, the rule from July 28 introduced the concept of an eligible liquidity facility in which assets that were to be funded had to be subject to an asset quality test that sought to prevent the funding of assets that were already in default, in fact tackling a practice of providing credit guarantees through liquidity lines (Sissoko 2013). The rule clearly shows awareness among regulators about the rule circumventing uses of liquidity facilities, such as when assets near default are bought from specific pools, funded by liquidity facilities. The follow-up guidance from March 2005 again sought to limit this practice (Joint Bank Regulators 2005, p. 30f).

the momentum it had lost. The growth of SIVs in the USA was quite pronounced in that period, in contrast to the growth of securities arbitrage conduits, which was rather limited. This differential can be linked to core capital charges on liquidity lines from 2005 onward, by which SIVs were much less affected than securities arbitrage conduits, hence becoming more attractive.

This chapter has detailed the evolution of the ABCP market in the USA, the largest and oldest market. It has embedded it in the increasing hybridization of financial markets and banking business and pointed to the internal struggles within the Fed seeking to regulate it. Notably, while blocked internally, the critical faction of the Federal Reserve used the global negotiations as a way to insert its critical stance and, then, to use the negotiated transnational accord nationally as a reference point for domestic negotiations. While global competitiveness concerns did play a role in these actions, the transnational level present can be perceived as a tool for domestic policymaking.

What was the impact of these transnational agreements on other countries' regulation of the ABCP market? Which impact did it have on its growth and evolution? As argued in Chapter 3, the engagement of banks from different countries in this market can be understood only through the Basel Accords and the attempts of different national regulators to interpret and to update these requirements – an interpretation that, in turn, would be shaped by the international regulatory context within which it evolved. It is with these questions in mind that we turn to Chapter 5.

5 | *In the Shadow of Basel*

What if global governance mechanisms undermined the capacity of national banking regulators to deal with the deviant activities of their banks? Such was the case, this chapter argues, with respect to the Basel Accords and the regulation of the bank-based shadow banking system in Europe. The ABCP market has been identified as problematic by the international regulatory community since 1999 (BCBS 1999b), motivating reforms in Basel II (BCBS 1999a). This chapter shows that, nevertheless, regulatory loopholes that allowed banks to engage in these activities without core capital charges persisted in almost all Western jurisdictions precrisis. It lays emphasis on the global nature of the ABCP market in conjunction with its national regulation, and shows that these national regulations on the fringes of global banking regulation were driven by competitiveness concerns. The Basel Accords were central in this dynamic, as they guaranteed the global nature of this market and gave national banking regulators the leeway to exempt short-term securitization activities from global regulation. Established to level the playing field, the Basel Accords channeled them to its fringes, where the ABCP market resided. There, it introduced a regulatory race to the bottom.

That cognitive capture alone cannot explain the absence of regulation of shadow banking is strongly suggested by evidence for regulatory awareness about regulatory arbitrage in that sector. Such evidence can be found at the national as well as the international level already in the 1990s. In 1995, the Deutsche Bundesbank linked the sixfold growth of securitization from 1980 to 1995 to the reduced regulatory burdens in this field as compared to bank credit, which created incentives for "innovations for circumvention" ("Umgehungsinnovationen," Deutsche Bundesbank 1995, p. 21). The first working paper of the Basel Committee in 1999, whose members were mostly from Anglo-Saxon countries yet included a member from the Netherlands, goes even further than that when evaluating the impact of Basel on bank behavior.

The authors note large-scale and accelerating acts of regulatory arbitrage in the field of securitization. They find it to be most pronounced in the field of asset-backed commercial paper conduits, where banks transferred assets into special-purpose entities (SPEs), which refinance them with the help of commercial paper. They argued that this form of securitization allowed banks to reduce the core capital they were required to hold, without changing the risk exposure of the bank (BCBS 1999b, p. 24; see also Jones 2000; Balthazar 2006, pp. 33–35).

Their conclusion is rather dramatic:

> The available evidence suggests, therefore, that the volume of regulatory capital arbitrage is large and growing rapidly, especially among the largest banks. Securitisations are motivated by a number of factors ... in many cases the effect is to increase a bank's apparent capital ratio relative to the riskiness of its actual book, which is making the ratios more difficult to interpret and in some cases less meaningful. (BCBS 1999b, p. 26)

In this document, the fact that banks were hiding their true risk exposures with the help of securitization, in particular the ABCP market, is clearly communicated, as is the fact that the numbers used by regulators to manage risk exposure become less meaningful. This means that knowledge about the negative consequences of regulatory arbitrage occurring within the realm of securitization activities of banks was disseminated in a BCBS working paper in 1999, almost a decade before the financial crisis.

Regulatory arbitrage in the realm of securitization was one factor that motivated the process of revision of the Basel Accords that started in 1998 (see Balthazar 2006; Blundell-Wignall and Atkinson 2010, p. 10; Goldbach 2015). These debates, driven by the US regulators, produced concrete proposals to close certain regulatory loopholes in the area of securitization from 1999 onward, some of which were incorporated in the revision of the Basel Accords (Basel II) in 2004. These international debates, although initiated by the USA, cannot be treated as exogenous to national debates in Western countries, whose banks started to engage massively in the ABCP market, starting from the mid- to late 1990s (*American Banker* 1993). Regulators from these nations are members of the Basel Committee and thus part of these debates.[1] It is, therefore, highly unlikely that they have not been aware of the international debates on acts of regulatory arbitrage in the field of securitization and the proposed measures to remedy the situation. At the latest, by 2004, when the new measures are agreed on, such awareness must have been the case. Nevertheless, most regulators did not act up until 2008. One reason for this inaction, as will be shown in the text that follows, stemmed from national competitiveness concerns that the Basel Accord was supposed to overcome.

How the Basel Accords Furthered the ABCP Market and Limited Its National Regulation

It is well known that the introduction of Basel I, and – in particular – the core capital requirements accelerated the development of securitization in general (see, e.g., Balthazar 2006) and the ABCP market in particular. Securitization SPEs such as the structured investment vehicles (SIVs) were invented by banks to deal with the new core capital requirements (see Ehrlich et al. 2009), and those countries that did not have a regulatory infrastructure in place in order to permit the transfer of bank assets from balance sheets came under pressure by their domestic banks to achieve such regulation, like Japan did (Kapstein 1991, p. 28). But, there are two further linkages between the Basel framework and the development of the ABCP market that need to be appreciated in order to understand the widespread regulatory exemption for these activities. These regard both the global nature of the market for securitization where banks are buying up credits from their customers and are transforming them into securities and the fact that conditions under which banks compete in it are determined nationally.

Kane (1987, p. 114) comes closest to the structural critique developed in this chapter when he argues that the inevitable time gap between the evasion of regulation by private firms and the closure of these loopholes by the supervisors (what he calls the "regulatory dialectic") is greatest when the rule maker is an international body. This

---

[1] Indeed, all of the four countries that are investigated in depth in this book have been members of the Basel Committee that debated this framework between 1998 and 2004. In addition, Belgium, Canada, Italy, Spain, and the UK were members.

statement seems to be borne out by the fact that, while regulatory arbitrage in securitization was identified as a problem the latest by 1999, it still took nine years for the revised Basel Accord to become operative. What Kane does not consider is the *national* regulatory reaction to regulatory arbitrage during this time gap in which an international response is prepared. This reaction, I posit, is structured by competitiveness concerns of regulators for their domestic banks, reinforced by the limiting effects the Global Accord has on the regulatory powers of national regulators.

It is in particular the rule of home country regulation, a primary element of international banking regulation since the first Basel Concordat in 1975 (see Herring 2007, p. 202f), which undermines the capacity of national regulators to impose common regulation for domestic and foreign banks in the securitization business on national grounds. The rule of home country regulation implies that by signing up for the Basel Accords, one accepts the banking regulations of other countries as appropriate if they are deemed to be in compliance with Basel and one does not impose additional charges for their operation domestically (see Pistor 2010 for an in-depth treatment).[2] This implies that if foreign banks have comparatively more lax regulation for issues outside of the global accords, they can securitize local credits according to their domestic rules, which carry fewer costs for supervision and, therefore, can outperform domestic banks in the local market for securitization.

The capacity to impose market access restrictions has been identified in the literature on regulatory competition as the lever that permits regulatory convergence toward a higher common denominator, as nations with large domestic markets can impose their views on other countries through the threat of market access restrictions (see Murphy 2004, p. 13 and Simmons 2004, p. 50 for the US position on core capital requirements; see also Drezner 2007). However, what has not been considered in this literature is that once the threat of market access restrictions has been used to achieve global legislation, it cannot be used again. Domestic supervisors, even those of states with large

---

[2] This exemption of host country regulation applies in particular to branches of foreign banks used for securitization, whereas subsidiaries could be subject to additional regulatory charges. Complete acceptance of foreign banking regulation was instituted in the EU in light of the implementation of Basel I with the banking passport in 1990 (see Pistor 2010).

markets, no longer have the leverage to force foreign overseers to raise regulatory costs on financial innovations that emerge to evade the global accord. Furthermore, introducing measures that go above and beyond the global accord to deal with the risks generated by this financial innovation generates will impose a competitive disadvantage on domestic banks in these global markets without impacting the operation of foreign banks at home. This helplessness is aggravated by the fact that the Basel Accord operates on "dependent rules" (Pistor 2002, p. 107f), where fundamental terms used in global standards are defined by national laws. For the case of the ABCP market, the crucial national laws defined the perimeter of banking supervision and the construction of consolidated balance sheets.

In 1979, the Basel Committee had introduced the concept of consolidated supervision, based on consolidated financial statements. This move toward consolidated supervision was motivated by the fact that with the increasing internationalization of banking business, banks had used foreign subsidiaries to evade costly banking regulation (see Herring 2007, p. 203). Thus, banking regulation increasingly relied on consolidated balance sheets. Hence, the quality of banking regulation became increasingly coupled to – and limited by – the quality of accounting standards and their actual implementation with respect to capturing all the subsidiaries of the bank, over which the parent bank has control and to whose risk the parent bank is exposed, thereby determining the actual size of the banking conglomerate and its exposure to risk.

The Basel Accord in 1988 followed this convention and made it mandatory to supervise banking conglomerates on a consolidated basis (including all financial subsidiaries) built on the consolidated financial statement of banking conglomerates (see BCBS 1988, p. 3, point 10). However, it did not specify under which conditions a company qualifies as a subsidiary of a conglomerate, nor did it determine when such a subsidiary is deemed a *financial* subsidiary. Instead, consolidated balance sheets were constructed based on *national accounting rules*, and this accounting information was then translated into capital requirements according to *national banking laws, which decided if a subsidiary was deemed to be a financial institution or not*. If it was not, then the subsidiary falls outside of banking supervision, which means that no core capital requirements will be applied to the assets of that subsidiary. The decision to change these frameworks, however, lies entirely in the realm of the national legislative.

Basel corrects neither for the differences between national accounting frameworks nor for the national differences regarding the scope of banking supervision. Instead, the international accord was placed on these national rules, thereby imposing heterogeneous production process regulation on off-balance-sheet financing activities of banks.[3] Heterogeneous production process regulations have been identified as the key feature for inducing a competition in regulatory laxity (Murphy 2004, p. 6), as banks in jurisdictions with very loose national regulations gain a competitive advantage in the securitization business. We, thus, find in the center of the international banking accord, which sought to reduce competitive inequities globally and was hailed for doing so (Kapstein 1991, p. 24), a source of such inequities that could not be influenced by the international accord itself, threatening the leveling of the playing field at the margins (see also Scott and Iwahara 1994; BCBS 1999b, p. 41). The accord did not resolve the problem of competitive inequities, but instead shifted the problem to the perimeter of supervision and the perimeter of consolidated financial statements, the outer margins of the Basel Accords where national supervisors had to decide how to regulate. At this point, heterogeneous production process regulation, coupled with the impossibility to impose market access restriction, shifted the balance of power between industry and national regulators in favor of the former.

National Inaction at the Margins of Basel

Owing to the specific constellation of international and national rules elaborated on earlier, national perimeters of supervision came under pressure to converge toward an international minimum, as a large perimeter automatically meant a competitive disadvantage for banks from those countries. The question of regulatory exemptions became virulent regarding the use of SPEs by banks for securitization purposes, which are used for the ABCP market. As an organizational form, these entities were used to circumvent the Basel rules, but their capacity to do so depended on their exemption from the national perimeter

---

[3] The international diversity on consolidation regarding securities activities and other financial entities and the role of national law in determining what will be consolidated for regulatory capital purposes is acknowledged in the revised Basel Accord (see BCBS 2004, p. 7). However, the problem is not rectified.

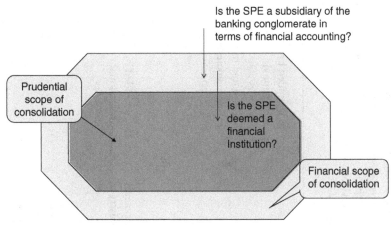

Figure 5.1 The two-level process to recognize SPEs in banking supervision.

of supervision. For the reader to understand the mechanics involved better, the sequence of steps that include national accounting rules and national banking laws in the regulatory treatment of SPEs used for securitization are shown in Figure 5.1.

The first step asks whether or not the accounting framework requires the consolidation of these SPEs in the financial statement (financial scope of consolidation). A second step asks if these entities are considered a credit or financial institution according to national law. If they are, they have to be supervised by national banking regulators or national financial market regulators respectively, but if they aren't, they have to be ignored, even if they appear in the financial statements of banks. If the answer to either one of these questions is no, banking conglomerates from these countries do not have to withhold core capital against these SPEs. As will be seen in Tables 5.1 and 5.2, the national perimeter of supervision shifted almost uniformly in favor of the exclusion of SPEs.

In the following, I will document variation in national regulatory regimes,[4] yet we can observe a general trend toward regulatory exemption for the activities of banks in the ABCP market. This trend can be explained only if the structural mismatch between the scope of regulation – national – and the scope of market activity – global – are taken into account, a mismatch paradoxically aggravated by the global Basel

---

[4] Notably, I will do so for France, Spain, and Portugal.

Table 5.1 *Classification of Securitization SPEs in Western European EU Members, Canada, and the USA*

Country	SPEs Considered a Credit Institution	SPE Considered a Financial Institution	SPE under the Supervision of the Banking Supervisor/ Financial Markets Supervisor	State Supervision
USA	No	No	No	No, if funded by professional investors
Canada	No	No	No	No (delegated to credit rating agencies, which approve them)
Austria	No (explicit in banking law since July 1, 2005), before yes	No	No	No
Belgium	In principle yes, but thanks to by Royal Decree of July 7, 1999, no (EFMLG 2007a, p. 27)	No	If funded by the general public, the ministry of finance	No, if funded by professional investors
France	Yes, but implicit exemption for French SPEs	No, but the fund who is managing the SPE is	Custodians of SPEs are supervised, by banking and financial supervisor	Yes

Germany	No	No	No	No
Ireland	No	No	No	No
Italy	No	Yes	Banca d'Italia (information on notes and assets)	Yes
Luxemburg	No	No	Yes, the financial supervisor, if issued to the public (i.e., not to professional investors)	No, if issued irregularly or to professional investors
Netherlands	Yes, but exemption in banking law that allows it to be considered not as a credit institution, if it is selling only to professional investors	No, unless it is a credit institution	No; unless deemed a credit institution	No
Portugal	No, but the fund who is managing the SPE is considered to be a financial institution		Yes, if the sponsor is a bank, then both by financial and banking supervisor	Yes

(continued)

Table 5.1 (*cont.*)

Country	SPEs Considered a Credit Institution	SPE Considered a Financial Institution	SPE under the Supervision of the Banking Supervisor/ Financial Markets Supervisor	State Supervision
Spain	No	No, but the fund who is managing the SPE is considered to be a financial institution	Financial market supervisor	Yes
England/Wales	No	No	No	No

Sources: Chant (2009); EFMLG (2007b); Synthetic Assets (2009).

Table 5.2 *The Consolidation of Securitization SPEs in Financial Accounting Terms and Their Inclusion in the Scope of Banking Supervision, EU Nations, USA, and Canada*

Country	Accounting Rules Regarding the On-Balance Sheet Status of SPEs	The Question of the Inclusion of SPEs in the Scope of Banking Regulation
Netherlands	**Medium** Accounting policies: since 2001 explicit accounting rule to capture SPEs; however, because of governance problems fully applied only by 2005 (Interview, regulatory advisor, Amsterdam, October 6, 2011).	**SPEs are not included.** since 1997 (DNB Memorandum in zake securitizatie) not translated into prudential regulation (Interview, Dutch banking manager, December 6, 2011).
Germany	**Easy** Until 2009, securitization SPEs were usually not captured in German GAAP; in 2005, introduction of International Finance Reporting Standards (IFRS).	**SPEs are not included.** Link between German GAAP and banking regulation was severed at the moment consolidation became possible in German GAAP in 2010.
USA	**Medium** Until 2003 securitization SPEs were usually not captured, only when FIN 46 is introduced.	**SPEs are not included for the calculation of core capital charges, but** assets of consolidated SPEs are translated into simple leverage ratio.
Italy	**Easy** Until 2004, securitization SPEs were usually not captured in Italian Generally Accepted Accounting Principles (GAAP); IFRS is introduced in 2005.	**SPEs are not included.** Link between accounting and prudential consolidation is severed in March 2006 (Schiavello and Mimun 2007).

(continued)

Table 5.2 (*cont.*)

Country	Accounting Rules Regarding the On-Balance Sheet Status of SPEs	The Question of the Inclusion of SPEs in the Scope of Banking Regulation
Canada	**Medium** Very relaxed until 2004, until Accounting Standards Board Guideline 15 (AcG-15) is issued, transposing FIN 46 into Canadian law.	**SPEs are not included for the calculation of core capital charges, but** assets of consolidated SPEs are translated into simple leverage ratio.
Belgium	**Easy** Until 2004, Securitization SPEs are not captured in Belgian GAAP; IFRS is introduced in 2005.	**SPEs are not included.** When consolidation occurs in financial accounting, only the equity of SPEs is consolidated in prudential terms, as they are not banking institutions (see Dexia 2009, p. 11).
UK	**Easy** Relaxed before 2004; IFRS is introduced in 2005.	**SPEs are not included.** Excluded from the calculation of core capital requirements according to FSA rules (see RBS 2009, p. 5).
Spain	**Difficult** Before 2005, securitization SPEs were usually not captured in Spanish GAAP. Since 2005 strictest rules in Europe, due to intervention by Spanish banking regulator, goldplating IFRS rules.	**SPEs are included from 2005 onward.** Strict link, nonpermissive: if SPE is consolidated, core capital charges are applied.

Table 5.2 (*cont.*)

Country	Accounting Rules Regarding the On-Balance Sheet Status of SPEs	The Question of the Inclusion of SPEs in the Scope of Banking Regulation
France	**Difficult** In 1999, an accounting rule is introduced by the banking regulator to capture SPEs on the balance sheet, until 2004 (under French GAAP for banks); in 2005, introduction of IFRS	**Yes (from 1999 until 2004)** French banking regulator delinks the prudential treatment of securitizations SPEs from their accounting treatment in 2005 (see Amis and Rospars 2005), after losing the battle for strict accounting standards.
Portugal	**Difficult** Before 2005, securitization SPEs were usually not captured in Portuguese GAAP; banking regulator was goldplating IFRS (see Millennium BCP 2011, p. 9).	**Yes (from 2005)** Since 2005, strict use of consolidated SPEs for prudential regulation, nonpermissive.

Sources: Acharya and Schnabl (2010); Banco de Espana (2008, Circular 3/2008); Bank of England (2007, p. 60); BDO (2011); ECB (2001); Thiemann (2012). PWC (2006). The categories easy/medium/difficult are meant to measure the difficulty to achieve off-balance-sheet status for SPEs in these jurisdictions.

Accords. The case of the bank-based shadow banking system reveals the inevitable shortcomings of that accord. What we observe is an iterative process in which the Basel Accord provokes financial innovation for the purpose of regulatory arbitrage at its outer margins, where global regulations do not apply and that, thus, needs to be regulated nationally. At the same time, the markets that are created by such regulatory arbitrage are global markets because Basel grants banks complying with it the right to operate in all countries where the regulation is implemented.

Competitive inequity concerns, which the global Basel Accords seek to overcome, thus reemerge with a vengeance at the margins, as the global accords prevent countries from closing their markets to competitors that carry a lighter regulation. The lack of common regulation for activities at the margin of global regulation at the same time that conglomerates from these different regulatory backgrounds are free to compete with each other imposes the structural conditions for a regulatory "competition in laxity" (Murphy 2004). That is to say, independent of the attitudes of national regulators to these financial innovations, these structural conditions favor lax supervision. These conditions were most acute for the countries within the EU, where the Basel Accords had been implemented as European Directives in 1989, becoming the foundation for the European financial market. Hence, it is no wonder that we find a strong degree of exemption and of the growth of the ABCP market there.

The first arena in which we find a widespread trend toward regulatory exemption is national banking laws, where the classification of securitization SPEs as credit institutions, financial institutions, or neither of the two became the crucial issue. This classification had important consequences for the supervision of these entities, as it determined which regulators were responsible and which regulatory requirements applied. Including SPEs in these registers would have both meant an automatic increase in regulatory costs and made much of the capital relief aspired to by the banking industry impossible. As Table 5.1 shows, national regulation posed only few, if any, difficulties in this regard.

Table 5.1 documents a trend toward regulatory exemption, where SPEs are treated in no jurisdiction as credit institutions and only in very few as financial institutions. The exemption of SPEs from the status of credit institutions and financial institutions required special derogations and exemptions. These practices clarify the legal accommodation of nation-states to the practices of securitization as the decision to treat securitization SPEs explicitly not as credit institutions *is the regulatory foundation, the sine qua non of the securitization business for the purpose of regulatory capital relief.* If SPEs were treated as credit institutions, any reduction of core capital through the process of off-balance-sheet financing would have been impossible.[5]

---

[5] A simple Dutch SPE, issuing $50 million (a rather small sum) was operating with a leverage of 1:2770.

Arguably, one can make the case that securitization SPEs engaging in the selling of ABCP and buying up loans or ABS should be qualified as credit institutions. For example, the European banking directive specifies that if an institution takes in deposits or other repayable funds from the public and grants credits for its own accounts (see 77/780/EEC Article 1, becoming part of 89/646/EEC, 2000/12/EC, 2006/48/EC[6]), it is a credit institution and needs to comply with all banking regulations, including the ownership of sufficient core capital.[7] Securitization SPEs, however, operate on minuscule equity that is incompatible with its status as a credit institution. In order to facilitate these operations, states were changing their laws (Austria in 2005, the Netherlands in 1997),[8] or opened up loopholes, as in France, where the rules classifying the acquiring of receivables on a regular basis as a credit operation are not applied to domestic securitization vehicles, based on the implicit derogation that they do not constitute credit institutions (see EFMLG 2007a, p. 26).

As securitization SPEs were not considered credit institutions, they were excluded, in principle, from the "taking of repayable funds from the public" by the European Banking Directives (see EFMLG 2007a, p. 26f). Nevertheless, in order to allow SPEs to sell ABCP into financial markets, most European legislators chose to limit the investor base of securitization SPEs to institutional or professional investors (see EFMLG 2007a, p. 28), rather than the general public. Doing so allowed the circumvention of the prohibition in the European Directive as well as the relaxing of the regulatory supervision to minimal to none

---

[6] These acronyms stand for the first and second directive on the coordination of laws, regulation and administrative provisions relating to the take-up and pursuit of the business of credit institutions from 1977 and 1989, the Second Banking Directive from 2000 and the Capital Requirements Directive from 2006. All of these documents are available at http://eur-lex.europa.eu/fr/index.htm.

[7] When the SPE buys loans or an asset-backed security from a seller, it is at least indirectly linked to a credit activity. The question is, does such indirect linkage constitute credit activity or not? In the case of France, for example, "acquiring receivables on a regular basis constitutes a credit operation" (see European Financial Markets Lawyers Group 2007a, p. 26, in the following EFMLG 2007a).

[8] This was the direct motivation of the regulatory changes in the Netherlands, as a Dutch banking manager confirmed (personal correspondence, Dutch bank manager, December 7, 2011).

(EFMLG 2007a, p. 28; see Table 5.1).[9] But, in most jurisdictions, the exemption of securitization SPEs from regulation went even further than that, also excluding them from the status of a financial institution. Since the Second Directive of the European Community in 1989, an entity should be classified as a financial institution if it is trading for its own account or for others in transferable securities (89/646/EEC, Annex). Securitization SPEs are trading in transferable securities for themselves or for others, thus requiring remarkable legal ingenuity to avoid that status for SPEs. Nevertheless, only four of the fifteen countries analyzed classified them as financial institutions (see Table 5.1). This lack of supervision reduces the regulatory burden on securitization SPE and, thus, the costs for the securitization business, but it also reduces the information available to regulators.

The next issue, after the regulatory treatment of SPEs themselves, regards the treatment of the link between SPEs and their sponsoring banks. Banks would structure their relationship with SPEs to make sure that these would fall outside of the financial scope of consolidation, so that they did not have to record them on their balance sheet, while benefitting from their business. If the accounting rules were not explicitly changed with respect to SPEs, they were incapable of capturing the assets placed into SPEs as part of the banking group. In those systems, where banking regulation was directly coupled with accounting rules, this meant that these assets would not be taken into account for the calculation of regulatory capital charges. This coupling between national accounting rules and international banking regulation created specific concern over competitiveness attached to accounting rule changes for consolidation (Bens and Moynihan 2008; Interview, French banker, March 25, 2011; Interview, banking regulator in Germany, July 1, 2011; Interview, banking regulator in the USA, March 27, 2012; PwC 2006, p. 3).

Any reform of national accounting standards that could force securitization SPEs of their sponsoring banks forced national banking regulators to answer the question if capital charges should be applied to the newly consolidated assets or not. This question became charged with concerns over international competitiveness of the domestic financial sector, as it directly threatened the profitability of securitization business. It is, thus, not surprising to see the USA as well as

---

[9] The measure copies US regulation, which, since the Investment Company Act of 1940, exempts institutional investors from supervision (see Horsfield-Bradbury 2008, p. 24f).

most European banking regulators to give a negative answer to this question (see Table 5.2).

As can be gauged from Table 5.2, stringent regulation was imposed only in France, Spain, and Portugal, where accounting standards made the achievement of off-balance-sheet status difficult. If conduits were deemed on balance sheet, core capital requirements were applied to them. In the other seven cases, accounting standards were either not modernized, or if so, conduits were consciously exempted by the regulators.

The persistent exclusion portrayed in Table 5.2 is no coincidence; instead, eight out of ten regulators consciously decided to exempt SPEs from core capital requirements, when accounting rule changes threatened their inclusion in the perimeter of banking supervision. In Chapter 4, the case of the USA was reviewed. European banking supervisors were also confronted with this question in 2005 when all large European Banks had to apply the International Financial Reporting Standards (IFRS) (see Gilliam 2005, p. 315). As it is more difficult to achieve deconsolidation in IFRS than under US rules (see Adhikari and Betancourt 2008), European banks were about to suffer an automatic competitive disadvantage with respect to their American competitors in the securitization business, favoring exemption. Domestic preferences of banking regulators, in the final instance, shaped the transition to IFRS differently (see Enria and Texeira 2011, p. 9), but preferences favoring prudence had to overcome domestic opposition from banks and finance ministries generated by competitive inequity concerns, as will be shown in the next chapters.

This trend toward regulatory exemption can also be seen with respect to the early adoption of regulatory measures, which were developed during the revision of the Basel Accord (1999–2004) designed to limit regulatory arbitrage in the securitization sector. The most important measure in this respect in the revised Accord was the proposal to impose core capital requirements on the liquidity lines banks had granted to securitization SPEs, which, owing to a maturity of less than one year to that date, had been exempted. It envisioned a 20 percent conversion factor for the assets that are guaranteed by the liquidity lines of a bank operating in the simple ratings-based approach and a slightly lower measure for those banks operating in the internal ratings-based approach. In addition, a framework in which only a significant risk transfer from the banking conglomerate to the SPE permitted regulatory capital relief was established (see BCBS 2004a, pp. 116–139).

Table 5.3 *Entry Point 3: Application of Core Capital Charges to Liquidity Lines*

Country	Application of Capital Charges to the Liquidity Line with Less than One Year (Credit Conversion Factor)
Netherlands	**Latest possible entry date 2007/8 (20%)**, before 2008 0%
Germany	**Latest possible entry date 2007/8 (20%)**, before 2008 0%
USA	2004 (10%)->, below the 20% envisioned in Basel II
Italy	**Latest possible entry date 2007/8 (20%)**, before 2008 0%
Canada	2004 (10%)->, below the 20% envisioned in Basel II
Belgium	**Latest possible entry date 2007/8 (20%)**, before 2008 0%,
UK	**Latest possible entry date 2007/8 (20%)**, before 2008 0%; see FSA (2001, p. 119),
Spain	2002: 100% (see Acharya and Schnabl 2010); 2007/8 (with a 50% conversion factor, no 20%, see circular 3/2008 of Banco de Espana 2008)
France	2002 (20%)
Portugal	2002: 100% (following Spain) 2007/8 (50%)

Sources: ECB (2001); Commission Bancaire (2002); Bank of England (2007, p. 60); Banco de Espana (2008, Circular 3/2008); Acharya and Schnabl (2010); BDO (2011); Thiemann (2012).

This measure was initially proposed in the first consultative paper by the BCBS, published in 1999. In the interim period from the first draft in 1999 to January 1, 2008, regulators had the choice to implement elements of the framework ahead of time according to domestic preferences. The widespread lack of core capital charges on liquidity lines with the duration of less than one year before 2008, as depicted in Table 5.3, is revealing in this respect.

In most countries, these measures were implemented at the latest possible date, with a 0 percent conversion factor before that. Imposing a level of regulation stricter than the international requirements of the time implied a cost disadvantage for domestic banks, which is why most regulators did not adopt the measures before 2008. As can be seen from the preceding, this process was very pronounced in the EU, where but for France, Spain, and Portugal, no regulatory adjustment occurred.

Overall, in the EU, only Spain, Portugal, and France increased costs to their banks by applying core capital charges to consolidated conduits and by introducing core capital charges for the liquidity lines below one year in 2002 (Commission Bancaire 2002; Banco de Espana 2008, Circular 3/2008 for Spain; Acharya and Schnabl 2010 for Portugal). Following a recommendation by Bank for International Settlements (BIS) and Committee of European Banking Supervisors, the other five EU countries decided to exempt consolidated conduits from core capital charges (CEBS 2004). And, they also decided to wait until the introduction of a core capital charge until 2008, when Basel II entered into force. Plus, with respect to core capital charges for those conduits consolidated on the balance sheet of banks, only France (2000) and both Spain and Portugal (2005) decided to apply core capital charges. All other countries exempted them. With French and Spanish regulators being more interventionist than, for instance, the German or Dutch regulators, how can we explain these differences? One reason can be linked to the different belief systems and traditions in these countries, with a more market-shaping approach in these Latin countries (Quaglia 2010), an issue that expressed itself in supervisory practices, which I will return to in Chapter 6. However, another reason for this different degree of action, I argue, is structural, stemming from the increasing banking system competition in the EU and the alignment of banks and regulators it produced. It seems, then, that it is the better positioning of Spanish or French banks in this competition that allowed regulatory space for action.

The Bank–Regulator Alignment in the Process of European Financial Integration

Financial integration in the eurozone has two distinct dimensions, both of which accelerated from the mid-1980s onward (Jabko 2006, p. 16). In the first, the introduction of the euro, enshrined in the Maastricht Treaty of 1992, meant that from 1999 onward, an important barrier to a pan-European market would be removed (Galati and Tsatsaronis 2003). In the second dimension, the creation of a European financial market for credit institutions, regulatory harmonization was needed to allow banks from foreign jurisdictions to operate beyond national borders. Here, the countries failed to delegate the regulatory function in terms of rule making and supervision to the European level.

Instead, the eurozone countries found a particular compromise in the Second Banking Directive in 1989, agreeing on the mutual recognition of national regulation, the predominance of home country regulation, and harmonization according to certain minimum standards (Story and Walter 1997, p. 17). Harmonization in terms of minimum requirements was based on the capital requirements of the Basel framework, which participating European nations had to translate into national law by 1992. While this largely facilitated the negotiations between European countries (Muegge 2006, p. 1006), it meant that additional regulations had to be undertaken nationally, installing regulatory competition right at the heart of the European integration of the banking systems (Jabko 2006).[10]

Since the late 1980s, this ensuing European integration led to a common perception both in the banking industry and among national banking regulators that the chance of surviving the impending consolidation in the European banking space could be ensured only by growing to a large enough size that would prevent hostile takeovers, a task often achieved through mergers and acquisitions (Walter 2004). By breaking down the barriers for competition in Europe, the competitive situation for large national banks thus changed completely (Walter 1999).[11] The established "conceptions of control" (Fligstein 1996, p. 658) of national incumbent banks that established a certain status hierarchy, stabilized competition, and ensured incumbent rents had to change in order to survive on the European stage. Size and the retail presence in several European markets were seen as necessary to reach European incumbent status, which implied the growth in foreign retail markets.

In the process of reaching this status, low stock market valuation of a bank and large, but limited size were a dangerous characteristic, as such banks were becoming the target of takeover attempts in a European competitive space imagined to be soon dominated by a few

[10] As Jabko points out, commission officials were hoping for a process of regulatory convergence to regulatory minimum standards because of regulatory competition (Jabko 2006, p. 79).
[11] Initially, national countries in the EU opposed this process of breaking down the barriers to competition. The European Commission overcame national opposition by forging alliances with big multinational banks looking for liberalization as well as reform-minded state officials. They were invoking global financial liberalization as a constraint, which made the European integration look like a necessary adjustment to an inevitable dynamic (Jabko 2006, p. 61). The unfolding dynamic of liberalization on the European level soon evoked national resistance, as it was transforming national banking systems to a degree unintended by national actors (Seikel 2014).

large pan-European conglomerates (Walter 2004, p. 76f; Smit 2009, p. 208f). The strategy was to gain dominance in the home market, and to expand from there (Grossman and Leblond 2011, p. 422).

This dynamic of outward expansion implied winners and losers on the industry level. But, it also implied the threat of takeover of a large share of the domestic banking system by foreign banks, as these were seeking to expand their retail networks abroad. In particular, inefficient bigger banks were likely takeover targets, as foreign competitors were looking for large retail networks in the new market (Koehler 2009, p. 13). A foreign-owned banking system is highly undesirable for a national sovereign in general and for the banking regulator in particular. One reason is the prevalence of home country regulation in the EU that starkly limits the power of the host country regulator in times of crisis (e.g., Spendzharova 2014), as eastern European countries painfully experienced during the recent financial crisis (Pistor 2010).

For these reasons, since the mid-1980s, regulators encouraged their domestic banks to merge domestically (see inter alia Barendregt and Visser 1997; Maes and Buyst 2009, p. 109f; Slager 2004, p. 245f, for the cases of the Netherlands, Belgium, and Austria, respectively), sometimes even coordinating these attempts, as in the case of France (Coleman 2001) or Spain (Perez 1997). In the process of domestic consolidation, furthermore, incumbent banks were encouraged to acquire banks in other countries in the EU in order to generate a size that would allow them to compete on the unified European market and to fend off foreign competitors (for the Netherlands, Barendregt and Visser 1997; for the case of France, Coleman 2001). This process of foreign acquisitions, however, was itself repeatedly obstructed by foreign regulators in nontransparent review processes of foreign takeovers (European Commission 2005; Berger 2007; Koehler 2009). Direct state intervention (such as in Italy or France) or protective efforts by national communities of central bankers, bankers, and government ministries, such as in the Netherlands were identified as the driving political factors in this process (Boot 1999, p. 610).

The effect of this attitude of domestic regulators to favor domestic mergers and to limit cross-border mergers was that national banking systems became more concentrated (Allen et al. 2005, p. 6) and populated by large national champions, which, however, had limited foreign presence (Grossman and Leblond 2011). The strategy of protecting domestic banks from foreign takeover through nontransparent merger review decisions, however, came under increasing strain in the 2000s because of the continuous expansion of European competition law that threatened the capacity of domestic governments to protect their national financial systems (Carletti et al. 2006; Seikel 2014).[12] This diminishing capacity of national regulators to protect their incumbents from foreign takeovers made regulatory leniency even more attractive as a particular form of industrial policy.

Structural Reasons for the Differential Regulation of the ABCP Market in the EU

A cross-case comparison of the competitive situation of the seven continental banking systems with banks involved in the ABCP market, as plotted in Table 5.4[13] reveals that the decisions on these two regulatory measures are highly correlated with the competitive position of incumbent banks in the European space and the alignment of the interests of regulated and regulators that it caused. The table lists different aspects of national banking systems (such as the size of the home market and concentration, overall profitability) in 2004 as well as the stock market value of incumbents, their price-to-book ratio, and their capacity to open up a second retail market. Lastly, the capacity of the national banking regulator to intervene in foreign takeover attempts in that year is portrayed.

Using variables to assess the vulnerability of incumbents of a given national banking system, we can see that at this critical juncture in 2004, French and Spanish incumbents were not vulnerable to foreign takeover because of the size of incumbents, price-to-book ratios, and the capacity of the banking regulator to intervene. The Italian and Dutch banks, conversely, were vulnerable, and their vulnerability is thus assessed as medium, but for different reasons. In Italy's banks, profitability is high, but the stock market value of banks is medium, as is their price-to-book ratio. What lowers the vulnerability is the

---

[12] This came to the fore when the Bank of Italy blocked takeovers of domestic banks by Dutch banks in 2005, which led to a large scandal that ended in the reduction of the powers of the regulator to interfere in the process by the end of 2005 (Carletti et al. 2006).

[13] Finland, Portugal, and Luxembourg, the other continental "Western" European banking systems, are excluded from the comparison as none of their banks ever engaged in the ABCP market, making a regulatory update unnecessary. Portugal's update stemmed from an institutional linkage to decisions of the Bank of Spain (Acharya and Schnabel 2010).

Table 5.4 Structure of Domestic Banking Systems and Protective Capacity of Banking Regulator

	France	Spain	Italy	Netherlands	Austria	Germany	Belgium
Return on average assets (1999–2007), EU 11 average: 0.6%[a]	0.489%, below EU-11 average	0.776%, above EU-11 average	0.649%, above EU-11 average	0.476%, below EU-11 average	0.49%, below EU-11 average	0.176%, below EU-11 average	0.447%, below EU-11 average
Size of home market 2004 (bn of Euro)	3,642.8	1,551.3	2,330.9	2,198.4	308.13	5,604.4 (but limited due to three pillar system)	930.6
Concentration of five largest banks in 2004 (%) (ECB data)	49.2	41.9	26.8	84.5	44.4	21.6	84
Average market value of three largest banks 2004	High (37.39 billion euro)	High (50.5 billion euro)	Medium (20.85 billion euro)	High (41 billion euro)	Low (9.486 billion euro)	Low (18.66 billion euro, outlier Deutsche Bank)	Medium (20.98 billion euro)
Price to book ratio	Medium (1.85)	High (2.7025)	Medium (1.63)	Medium (1.99)	High (2.83)	Low (1.18)	Medium (1.78)
Second largest retail market[b]	No	Yes, Latin America	No	Yes, Belgium	Yes, Central and Eastern Europe	No	No

(continued)

Table 5.1 (*cont.*)

	France	Spain	Italy	Netherlands	Austria	Germany	Belgium
Capacity of regulator to protect banks in merger review process 2004[c]	Medium (0.60)	High (0.9)	High (0.92)	Low (0.12)	Low (0.12)	Low (0.12)	Not computable[d]
Vulnerability of incumbents of national banking system	Low	Low	Medium	Medium	High	High	High
Regulation above Basel I for ABCP market	Yes	Yes	No	No	No	No	No
Exposure to ABCP market	Low	Low	Low	High	Low	High	High

[a] Return on average assets, rather than return on equity (RoE), is employed for two reasons. First, return on average assets shows the underlying profitability, excluding leverage. Second, the hypothesis of the paper is that banks and regulators were colluding to produce high RoE; therefore RoE cannot be used to measure the alignment of regulators and regulated.

[b] The banks from Table 4.4 were used to calculate the exposure. For the case of Spain, the third largest bank was excluded, as it was a local savings bank. In Austria, only two private banks were used, as the third bank was too small to be considered an incumbent. Data from The Banker and Annual Reports, author's calculations.

^c Author's own calculation, using data from Koehler (2007) and Carletti et al. (2006). Aggregate Approval Requirements Index (Koehler 2007, p. 31) is multiplied by the status of the competition enforcer (=1 if antitrust-authority, 0 if no competition control, see Carletti et al. 2006, p. 8). Final result is computed by 1– (computation).

^d Koehler does not provide data on the Aggregate Approval Requirements Index. However, in Belgium only the antitrust authority is involved in the competition review, indicating a weak position of the banking regulator to influence the process.

Sources: OECD Database on banking profitability; Slager (2004); EC (2005, p. 13); Carletti et al. (2006, p. 8), ECB Statistical Data Warehouse; Schoenmaker and van Laecke (2006, p. 27f); V-Lab Beta, author's calculation.

capacity of the banking regulator to protect domestic banks through a nontransparent merger review process. In the Netherlands, profitability is below average and the capacity of the banking regulator to protect banks from mergers is limited. However, Dutch incumbents are large and ING especially has a high price-to-book value. Nevertheless, the largest Dutch bank by asset size, ABN Amro, has a rather limited price-to-book ratio and is, thus, vulnerable to takeover attempts. German, Belgian, and Austrian banks have high vulnerability. In these countries, the banking regulator has limited capacity to protect domestic banks from takeover; banks are small-to-medium-sized and profitability is below average. The vulnerability of the national banking system correlates highly with the leniency of regulation of the ABCP market. The more endangered the banking system, the more lenient the regulation.[14]

In the following, I will seek to substantiate and to elaborate on these structural findings from the cross-case comparison through within-case analysis for Germany, France, and the Netherlands, engaging in what Mahoney (2003, pp. 361ff) has called "pattern matching."[15] The analysis will show that these competitive pressures did, indeed, play a role for the evolution of the regulatory regimes in these countries.

France

Following a comprehensive and anticipatory strategy (Coleman 1996, p. 14), the overall merger activity coordinated by the French government during and after the 1991 reprivatization of public banks resulted in an oligopolistic structure and welcome profitability in a home market large enough to sustain pan-European banks (Interview, French economist, December 15, 2010). The unification and privatization of mutual banks into two large players in 1988 (Credit Agricole and Credit Mutuel) is paradigmatic for this change. The government also had a clear protectionist stance, as was demonstrated during the 1998

---

[14] No country with stringent regulation has a high exposure to the ABCP market, and three out of five countries with lenient regulation have high exposure. Only in Italy and Austria is there limited engagement, despite lenient regulation.

[15] Pattern matching is the search for within-case evidence that investigates if those variables that seem to have a causal effect in the cross-case analysis can be found to exert such an influence in the within-case analysis.

sale of CIC to Credit Mutuel rather than to the Dutch ABN Amro, the breakup of Credit Lyonnais in 1999, and the crisis of Société Générale in 2008 (Koehler 2009, p. 40; Jabko and Massoc 2012; Woll 2014). These institutional facts put the independence of large French banks beyond doubt and eased regulators' concerns about the competitive disadvantages that French banks might face in the shadow banking sector. The French banking regulator, independent from the ministry of finance since 1993 (Coleman 2001), entertained an even more prudent approach to the links of domestic banks to the shadow banking system than their US peer, but these preferences again had to overcome domestic opposition from banks and finance ministries generated by competitive inequity concerns. It tightened regulation of the ABCP market in 1999, 2000, 2002, and 2003, despite industry complaints of competitive disadvantages in the ABCP market (Interview, French bank manager, March 25, 2011; Interview, French banking regulator, February 3, 2011) and despite the ministry of finance at some point siding with industry (Interview, French state official involved in the process, April 30, 2011). Regulatory action included the imposition of a 20 percent core capital charge on liquidity lines in 2002 (see CB 2002) and the modernization of accounting rules. In 1999, the banking regulator modernized accounting rules in order to control the risk taking of their banks in their securitization business (Interview, representative French Banking Association, May 11, 2011). In collaboration with the French securities exchange regulator, it made the interpretation of these standards even more restrictive (see CB 2002). These rule changes limited profitability, especially of the securities arbitrage business, so that banks had to restructure their ABCP business completely (Interview, French bank manager, March 25, 2011), closing all securities arbitrage conduits in 2002. A final accounting rule change in 2003, as a reaction to the Enron scandal, made off-balance-sheet securitization by the banks even more difficult. This and the impending introduction of IFRS led to a bundling of forces of those concerned over competitive inequities for banks in the securitization business.

An alliance of banks and the ministry of finance orchestrated an attack on off-balance-sheet accounting rules for securitization (Interview, member French accounting standard setter, January 27, 2011). French banks and the ministry of finance feared that the banks would lose market share to foreign competitors (Interview, French banking regulator, February 3, 2011). In particular, this alliance sought to emulate American rules for securitization SPEs (qualifying special-purpose entities, Q-SPEs), which in the USA were excluded from consolidation. Opinion No. 2004-D of the Emergency Committee of the National Accounting Board established this possibility for exemption, defeating the opposition of the banking regulator. This exemption was motivated by "the will of the CNC not to include in the perimeter of consolidation securitization transactions systematically, in order not to threaten the economic advantages stemming there from, and this for *reasons of international distortion of competition*" (Conseil National de la Comptabilité 2004, p. 2,[16] translation and emphasis by the author).

Overwhelmed by this coalition, the French banking regulator in 2005 criticized these new accounting standards as too weak and decided to delink the prudential treatment of securitization SPEs from their accounting treatment (Amis and Rospars 2005, p. 57f). Instead, it introduced the significant risk transfer mentioned in the Basel framework for securitization in 2005 and instituted comparatively high core capital charges in this framework (1,250 percent; see Amis and Rospars 2005, p. 58). While these changes led to less stringent regulation in this area than desired (Interview, French bank manager, member of accounting standard setter, March 25, 2011; Interview, French banking regulator, February 3, 2011; Interview, former French banking regulator, January 30, 2011), these concerns over international competitiveness did not carry sufficient weight for regulators to inhibit action, as incumbent banks were well protected and profitable.

Germany

In the case of Germany, whenever the question arises, banks are persistently exempted from core capital charges for their securitization activities. However, despite evident cognitive capture, and possibly even regulatory capture (Thiemann 2012), these are not the only reason for regulatory laxity. In Germany, the banking regulator is subordinated to the Ministry of Finance and the concern over the internationally low profitability of German banks at the finance ministry made the closure of regulatory loopholes less appealing to the regulator (Interview,

---

[16] see note de presentation, available at www.cnc.bercy.gouv.fr/fonds_documentaire/reglementation/avis/avisCNCompta/2004/note_avis0408-09-10.htm

German financial regulator, July 1, 2011). The general guideline for the regulation of German banks was to apply international standards – but no national regulation that went beyond – in order not to worsen German bank profitability as compared with their international peers (Interview, regulatory advisor, June 14, 2011).

During the 2000s, the German banking system generated consistently lower profitability than the European average. Large German banks were smaller than their European peers because of the fragmentation of the German banking system into three pillars of private, public, and local credit associations (Hackethal 2004). Despite support at the highest political levels (Hakenes and Schnabel 2006), attempts in the 2000s to form a national champion by combining at least two of the three large private banks failed (Slager 2004). The low profitability of German banks was a main preoccupation at the Ministry of Finance (Interview, German banking regulator, July 1, 2011), which saw fee income from securitization business as one means to improve the situation (Asmussen 2006).

Given the comparatively low profitability of German banks, raising the regulatory burden for securitization beyond general European requirements was seen as counterproductive by the Ministry of Finance (Asmussen 2006; Interview, German banking regulator, July 1, 2011; Interview regulatory advisor, June 14, 2011).[17] The comparative weakness of German banks dissuaded the Ministry of Finance from raising the regulatory burden for securitization beyond general European requirements. A regulatory advisor explained this stance thus: "It was always important; it was a unitary market in Europe ... Equal rules should apply, and the German ones should definitely not be stricter than the others" (Interview, regulatory advisor, June 14, 2011). As a consequence of this stance and the fact that the ministry of finance controls the decisions of the financial regulator (the Bundesanstalt für Finanzdienstleistungsaufsicht; see Quintyn 2007), regulatory measures that increased the costs for ABCP business were delayed to the latest possible moment (that is, 2008).

---

[17] The ministry of finance evaluated securitization positively, as a means for German banks to deepen their skills in dealing with capital markets and to increase their fee income (for the position of, see Asmussen 2006). Therefore the finance ministry engaged since 2003 in a pro-securitization campaign, removing regulatory obstacles to securitization.

The Netherlands

Like their Belgian counterparts, Dutch conglomerates in the 2000s were facing low-interest margins in their domestic markets and were having difficulties expanding into western Europe. Characterized as having truly European ambitions (Boot 1999), the conglomerates were looking for a second home retail market large enough to sustain them as large pan-European banks; it was clear to both chief executive officers (CEOs) and banking regulators that without expansion, they would be taken over. Despite pressure from the Dutch National Bank (DNB) on the Bank of Italy and others to allow takeover bids from Dutch banks (Smit 2009, pp. 251, 340), interference by foreign domestic regulators blocked Dutch banks' European expansion. This led these banks to direct their attention to the wholesale market. The CEO of ABN Amro explained to a professional journal in the summer of 2000,

> Germany and France are locked up ... the merger process is making little progress in those countries ... where it is that foreign banks are not really welcome. That's why we've stopped saying that we want to create a second domestic market ... the expansion will come from global wholesale banking. (Smit 2009, p. 168f)

From the 1990s onward, the DNB was supportive of Dutch banks' plans to establish themselves in wholesale finance and the ABCP market (Aalbers et al 2011; Interview, Dutch banker December 6, 2011). By 2007, with no extra regulatory charges, and lenient regulation, Dutch banks had become major players in the ABCP market. Indeed, ABN Amro, the largest Dutch bank by asset size, was the biggest sponsor of ABCP conduits in the world ($75 billion, ING $38 billion, Rabobank $35 billion, Moody's Index Program). The increased fee income from this market gave an important competitiveness boost to ABN Amro, which in the mid-2000s, had a mid-sized market capitalization and underperformed its peers in most of its activities. It suffered from comparatively high cost-to-income ratios (Slager 2004, p. 205), putting its independence into question (Smit 2009, pp. 208–209, 288). In this historical constellation, in 2004, the DNB considered imposing additional capital charges on liquidity lines for ABCP conduits (DNB 2005). It could have tightened measures even without legislative approval (Interview, Dutch banking regulator,

April 11, 2015), but abstained due to its focus on the level playing field for its banks with respect to European competitors (email, DNB manager, April 14, 2015). Instead, reacting to the threat to the independence of one of its large national champions, in 2006 the DNB sought to facilitate a merger between the largest banks, ING and ABN Amro, but failed (Smit 2009, pp. 322ff). Finally, ABN Amro was taken over in 2007 by a consortium led by the Royal Bank of Scotland. In this competitive context, imposing additional regulatory charges on its banking incumbents in a field where they had become world leaders contradicted the interests of the regulator.

Conclusion

This chapter has focused on the structural characteristics of the global financial architecture and the European one in particular, which favored the expansion of the ABCP market. The particular setup of the relationship between national and transnational regulation favored regulatory laxity until transnational regulation was in place to address the identified weak spots of current regulation, around which regulatory arbitrage practices had developed. This structural configuration was particularly detrimental in Europe, where it was coupled with increasing banking competition and sovereigns seeking to protect their incumbent banks. In those countries, where such incumbents were endangered because of their incapacity to reach sufficient size and/ or the lacking capability of the state to protect them, incentives for regulatory forbearance were particularly high. This analysis applies in particular for the period from 2004 onward, when the Basel II Accord was passed and regulatory decisions operated under the knowledge of rules and regulation to come.[18]

---

[18] It is noticeable that Spain, France, and – to a lesser extent – Italy, countries often categorized as forms of "state-enhanced capitalism" (Schmidt 2003) opposed this regulatory drift. This reflects their capacity to "adapt traditional aims, notably the promotion of … international champions, to new conditions" in the EU (Thatcher 2007, p. 1028), where state intervention was facilitating the formation of banks competitive at the European level before full liberalization exposed them to their competitors (Deeg 2012). The capacity of these governments to protect their incumbents from foreign takeovers and to restructure their banking systems in such a way as to establish them at the European level allowed them to ignore questions of competitiveness in the field of shadow banking.

But, what about pre-2004? How did regulators come to form their opinions about this regulatory innovation? How can we understand why the French regulator intervened early on and in such decisive manner in 1999, in 2000, and again in 2002? In other words, what institutional settings in the regulatory process in these different countries allowed the French regulator to detect and to act against these acts of regulatory arbitrage? Note well that the French did not simply forbid the engagement of the banks in this market but, instead, sought to adjust the regulatory costs so that these activities would be included in the framework of banking regulation. While the strength of domestic banks in conjunction with the capacity of the French state to protect their incumbents did take away pressures for regulatory leniency, such a factor is evidently only a necessary but not a sufficient condition.

The following analysis will show that in addition to these structural factors, the embeddedness of regulators within the processes of rule compliance in these three countries made an important difference to the way in which regulators related to this financial innovation. When regulators were absent from these processes within which compliance decisions were produced, they were easily manipulated by the data sent to them and interfered only little in the process. Distance from the processes meant that they had little knowledge of the risks posed and little capacity to intervene. Conversely, when regulators interacted with the banks only in the process of compliance, they were prone to get cognitively captured, developing a view of the risks emanating from ABCP conduits that made regulatory inaction acceptable (the Netherlands). However, as I will show, when regulators were embedded within these processes of compliance, both within the realm of accounting decisions as well as in the realm of banking regulation, early and decisive regulatory action became much more likely (the case of France). Being in close contact with both auditors and the regulated themselves, asking them to explain their decisions allowed these regulators to know the neuralgic points of where and how to intervene.

Understanding this difference in the regulatory stance and the development of the regulatory regime resides in understanding the differential role of these regulators within the realm of accounting, both in terms of rule making and rule supervision. When looking at this, on the one hand, a path-dependent process becomes visible, where inclusive or exclusive structures of standard setting before the 1990s shaped the role of banking regulators while, on the other hand, the interaction between the national and transnational level regarding the regulation of accounting in the EU also comes into view. It was in the transnational space where one of the most potent regulatory innovations to deal with the deviant behavior of banking conglomerates within the accounting realm was developed. This innovation was SIC 12, an interpretation of accounting rules issued by the International Accounting Standards Council in 1998.

While this transnational standard setter generated a measure to deal with the off-balance-sheet behavior of banks, it challenged the role of banking regulators in the realm of accounting regulation, whereby intense maneuvering by the banking regulators became necessary to secure a role within this realm. This chapter addresses this process, in which the French regulator maintained his role in the accounting realm and transferred the most modern accounting rule into French law while the Dutch banking regulator got delegitimized and excluded from the accounting realm and the German regulator never really entered into it. Chapter 6, then, will focus on the realm of the supervision of compliance supervision and the different effect that this insertion of the regulator within this realm had on the evolution of the market and the impact during the crisis.

6 | Converging Procedures or Standards?: The Challenge of the IASC and Domestic Pathways to SIC 12

In this chapter, I embed the regulation of the off-balance-sheet status of ABCP conduits in France, the Netherlands, and Germany in terms of accounting and banking regulation in the evolution of the respective national systems of accounting standard setting from the 1980s onward. Challenged by an emerging (European) transnational system of accounting standard setting, these systems would be reformed in order to increase their legitimacy at the transnational level. This chapter focuses on the adaptation of accounting standard setting in terms of procedures and legitimate members at the national level resulting from these transnational pressures in the Netherlands, France, and Germany. It inquires how these changes affected convergence with the contentious transnational off-balance-sheet rule SIC 12. It thus investigates how changes in how and by whom national accounting standards were set ended up limiting or fostered the convergence process.

It argues that the reconfiguration of domestic governance architectures had a decisive impact on these processes. Counterintuitively, copying goals, membership, and procedures of the transnational, private International Accounting Standards Committee (IASC) limited the chances of rule convergence, as it threatened to deinstitutionalize the standard-setting role of an important national champion of rule convergence, the banking regulator. A strong coalition, however, is needed to overcome vested business interests favoring convergence with transnational templates for legitimacy gains at the same time that they oppose convergence to contentious rules that limit their business activities. Banking regulators were hence to play an important role in this dynamic, as it was their intervention that would tip the balance of power in favor of more or less permissive off-balance-sheet rules. Before we turn to their role in the evolution of off-balance-sheet accounting standards, a look at the history of accounting harmonization in the EU and the ascendance of the International Accounting

Standards Council in the 1990s as the most likely transnational source of such standards is necessary in order to understand the larger context of the transformation of national accounting standard-setting systems.

This chapter is structured as follows: I first review the literature on the political economy of regulatory change at the national level and the challenges posed by transnational developments. Next, I situate the three cases with respect to the developments on the EU and international level in the time between 1983 and 2005. Here, the challenge the IASC posed to the architecture of standard setting and its content is clarified. I subsequently analyze the reconfiguration of domestic governance architectures and the impact it had on the struggle over the convergence to SIC 12 in my three chosen cases. In the discussion of findings, I employ a cross-case comparison so as to understand how the convergence of the French, German, and Dutch accounting standard setters with the IASC template in terms of procedures and membership impacted rule convergence. Bringing out the salient features of the association between the two processes in the three countries, I point to the impact the processes of de- and reinstitutionalization of the role of banking regulators in accounting standard setting in these three countries had on the process of rule convergence.

National Regulatory Change and Transnational Challenges

Regulation is a highly political process, one with direct economic consequences for both those regulated and society as a whole. But, while political, it often does not get the general public's attention because of the complexity of the issue and the negligible immediate impact regulations have on the public. Instead, the regulated, directly and immediately concerned, often organize as a collective to influence the regulatory process in their favor (Pelzman 1976). As a consequence, the resulting regulation often benefits groups of firms charged with defending the existing rules. To bring about change in such a situation, it takes either private or public entrepreneurs of change, who forge a coalition based on a new insight or idea, a calamity, or some other event that puts the regulatory status quo into question (Mattli and Woods 2009, p. 17). Putting the deficiencies of existing regulation on the rule-making agenda of the domestic rule-making process is a first step in the direction of change. However, placing these issues on the agenda and negotiating a new rule does not yet constitute successful change, as a change of the rules in the books without any impact on practice is nothing else but a masked continuation of the status quo.[1] Effective change comes about only if the political will and the institutional capacity exist to implement, to monitor, and to enforce the new rules.

Ideas that challenge the national status quo may stem from the transnational space, where international institutions or transnational standard setters develop rules. For transnational standard setters, which often have extremely limited leverage over national jurisdiction, persuasion and normative influence are the main transmission mechanisms.[2] At the same time that transnational rules challenge national ones, the national institutional context of rule making itself is put into question by transnational rule-making organizations. This challenge adds another dimension to the complex bargaining game where firms, public agencies, and professional groups seek to control "regulatory governance and hence the substance and form of regulatory outcomes" (Abbott and Snidal 2009, p. 70). The recent literature on transnational governance and its impact on national institutions has pointed out that the latter are open systems interacting with and subjected to change from the transnational level (Djelic and Quack 2008, p. 317f; for the case of accounting, see Noelke and Perry 2007). Rather than emphasizing path dependency based on institutional complementarities (Hall and Soskice 2001), this literature has pointed to the coevolutionary interaction between transnational path generation and national path transformation (Djelic and Quack 2007, p. 162; see also Morgan 2005, p. 441). As Djelic and Quack (2007, p. 162) put it, "transnational rule-making is shaking and shaping national institutional trajectories," undermining the stability of national arrangements based on policy feedback and power.

Analyses of transnational governance formation point to the destabilizing effects that transnational standard setters have on national institutional configurations, in particular when the former

---

[1] As research on the national implementation of such rules has pointed out, domestic actors shape the meaning of such standards in local practices (Malets 2013, p. 320), and domestic institutions often inhibit effective rule change of contentious rules due to the power of organized interest groups at the national level (Mosley 2010, p. 754).

[2] An example is when nation-states model their rules according to what are perceived as global norms (Halliday and Carruthers 2007, p. 1173).

become focal actors in the rule-making process (Buethe 2010a, b; Buethe and Mattli 2011). National institutions, conceptualized as "standardized interaction sequences" (Jepperson 1991, p. 145), are challenged by newly emerging sequences on the transnational level, in particular when transnational standard setters and their rule making become focal.[3] Old sequences of rule making are deinstitutionalized, and new processes and new players included in the organizational arrangements that link private actors, their competencies, and their interests with state agencies (what Mayntz calls the national governance architecture; Mayntz 2009, p. 80f) in order to gain legitimacy in the transnational realm. These isomorphic pressures can be coercive (such as EU regulation making certain procedures binding), normative, e.g., via rooted cosmopolitans, members of "transnational communities," and national communities at the same time (Ramirez 2010; Djelic and Quack 2011, p. 89f), or when in situations of high uncertainty, transnational models are copied, mimetic (DiMaggio and Powell 1983).

National governance architectures should, thus, not be seen as static, as who is legitimate in standard setting and who is seen as interfering varies over time and between jurisdictions (Cooper and Robson 2006, p. 425). Change at the national level can also be initiated strategically: to increase institutional complementarity with the transnational standard setter (Büthe and Mattli 2011, p. 12f), as national actors seek to upload their preferences at the transnational level. Such change seeks to increase legitimacy in the eye of the transnational agency as well as to align work practices in order to be able to provide quicker and more effective input into the transnational rule-making efforts. In this way, a specific transnational form of private standard setting, one concerning actors involved and procedures employed, imposes itself on the national level, a trend called meta-standardization. Accounting standards have been identified as one of the prime examples of this increasing influence of transnational standards and transnational standard-setting procedures (Martinez-Diaz 2005; Noelke 2005; Botzem and Quack 2006; Buethe and Mattli 2011). As the International Accounting Standards Committee (IASC), a private body existing since

---

[3] Focal refers to the holding of uncontested authority on the transnational level. Büthe (2010b) analyzes the stages and mechanisms of how a transnational standard setter reaches such a focal position.

1973 and renamed the International Accounting Standards Board in 2001 (IASB), has become the predominant source of international accounting standards since 2005, its influence over national standard-setting procedures increased.[4]

As several accounting scholars have noticed, most national configurations in Europe have moved in the direction of the IASC/B over the last decade in terms of both their due process and the legitimate members of standard setting (Baker and Barbu 2007, p. 607; Chantiri-Chaudemanche 2009, p. 1118; Colasse and Pochet 2009, p. 50; Botzem 2012, p. 122). This standardization of standard-setting bodies shows the clear impact of the ascendance of IASC/B on national standard-setting bodies. However, this research has not linked these isomorphic tendencies regarding procedures and actors involved to the question of convergence in terms of content of accounting standards. These changing settlements over legitimate members and procedures at the national level might impact the output and the implementation of the rules issued. In particular, the creation of actor mismatch between those actors considered crucial to the implementation of a law and those formulating them can lead to disengagement of the former or outright rejection of the law,[5] thereby weakening implementation along with the monitoring and enforcement of compliance with these rules.[6]

Regarding the convergence of rules, the findings of change are more mixed. Convergence of national with international accounting standards was desired but not prescribed by EU directives, making its occurrence contingent on the national political alliances that sustained such projects. Such rule convergence with transnational rules is a politically contested issue, as it challenges the way in which economic activities are regulated and undertaken nationally. The demanded convergence of standards thus has to overcome the opposition of the political and economic forces that generated the domestic rules and

---

[4] Up until 2001, the body issued International Accounting Standards (IAS). Since 2001, its standards are called the International Financial Reporting Standards (IFRS). Posner (2010) provides a good description of the ascendance of the IASB.

[5] For the case of global law, see Halliday and Carruthers (2007, p. 1152); Halliday (2009, p. 277).

[6] On this point, see Abbott and Snidal (2009, p. 46). Regarding the implementation of global norms in local contexts, see Mosley (2010, p. 725f).

benefit from the status quo in the first place (Hall and Thelen 2009). This was also the case for SIC 12, the new off-balance-sheet rule issued by the IASC in 1998 that made it more difficult for conglomerates to transfer debts off balance sheet into special-purpose entities (SPEs). It was threatening the status quo for domestic interest groups invested in off-balance-sheet financing, a potentially very large and powerful group. Because of its limiting effect on debt-financing practices, convergence to the standard was certain to encounter resistance.

As will be shown in the following, moving in the direction of the organizational architecture and procedures of the IASC did not automatically lead to convergence, as it weakened the national alliances in favor of convergence. National opposition to the adoption of the template of standard setting of the IASC, conversely, did not exclude rule convergence either, as the case of France demonstrates. The next two sections are devoted to outlining the sequence of events that turned the IASC into a focal transnational standard setter and the specific configuration of actors that shaped the specific setup of that body. Before discussing their direct impact on the three countries studied, I will then present how these challenged national ways of setting standards.

The Ascendance of the IASC and Its Challenge to National Standard Setters

Owing to the underdevelopment of capital markets before the 1970s, accounting standards for consolidated financial statements had remained largely underdeveloped in many European countries as compared to their Anglo-Saxon peers. The growing role of capital markets rather than banks for financing investments created the need for more sophisticated standards. In particular, the European Community played an important role in modernizing these rules, seeking to generate common practices that would support the evolution of a common capital market. To this effect, it published the 4th Directive on accounting in 1978 and the 7th Directive for consolidated financial statements in 1983. However, these European Community Directives were constructed in international negotiations between member states, which could be concluded only by including several options, thus allowing member states to block convergence and to maintain national leeway if seen as beneficial to the national interests. By the early 1990s, this fact had caused disillusionment within the

European Commission seeking to achieve the desired harmonization (Camfermann and Zeff 2007, p. 418). Since then, conversations
about the formulation of common European standards were ongoing,
the policy community being in search of an appropriate institutional
mechanism (van Hulle 1993).

In 1995, the European Commission admitted that the harmonization of national accounting standards in Europe via European
Directives had failed and that a new policy was needed (Van Hulle
1993; European Commission 1995). Such a shift in policy became
urgent, as European conglomerates started to list on US capital
markets and, therefore, had to switch to US accounting standards.[7]
The SEC considered European accounting standards for consolidated statement to be underdeveloped, thus refusing to accept them
as equivalent to US Generally Accepted Accounting Principles (GAAP)
(Camffermann and Zeff 2007, p. 314). It became clear that consolidated accounting statements in Europe needed to reach an equivalent
status to US GAAP quickly or else more conglomerates would switch.
Without influence over the developments of US GAAP, this idea was
politically unpalatable and another, equivalent accounting framework
was sought (Camffermann and Zeff 2007, p. 329). The European
Commission weighed several options but, then, suggested clearing the
way for the application of International Accounting Standards (IAS),
issued by the IASC (EC 1995, p. 6f). From this point, the question
arose how European nations would exert influence on the IASC, a
standard setter that was, itself, in the midst of reform to streamline
its rules and to widen their applicability. The Commission restated
its commitment to IAS in 1999 and 2000, and in 2002, it declared
that IAS would be applied by all European conglomerates listed on
stock exchanges from 2005 onward (see European Commission 1999,
2000a; European Parliament 2002).

These developments were attentively observed by European nations,
as they wanted to maintain influence over the accounting standards
for their large conglomerates. The debate over the future governance
of the IASC, where the congregation of national standard setters was
seen as likely (Camfermann and Zeff 2007, p. 314), led to an empowerment of national standard setters (Benston et al. 2006). The search

---

[7] Daimler's switch to US GAAP in 1993 is seen as a major event in this respect
(see Camffermann and Zeff 2007, p. 314).

for voice in international negotiations over European Accounting Standards drove the bulk of these national reforms, which owing to the different understandings between them and the IASC regarding who should be involved in standard setting and what the goals of these standards should be was a major challenge for many continental countries (Biener 2000; Hoarau 2010).

The institutional configuration of standards, standard-setting procedures, and actors of the IASC evolved over the course of thirty years from a lack of political legitimacy, the subsequent need for public endorsement, and close linkage to the Anglo-Saxon tradition of accounting (Botzem 2012, p. 29f). As several authors have noted, the IASC has technical legitimacy due to the presumed expertise of its members (Botzem and Quack 2009; critical Burlaud and Colasse 2010). At the same time, it has a lack of political legitimacy (Colasse and Pochet 2009, p. 34f), as it is questionable if the standards take into account the concerns of the stakeholders. The IASC has dealt with this problem by developing an elaborate due process in the formulation of new accounting standards, one that involves consultation periods before and during the standard setting so as to give voice to stakeholders. Analysis of the due process shows, however, that it has limited impact on rule making (Botzem 2012, p. 117ff), allowing the IASB to maintain the principle of expertise while showing some openness regarding the concerns of stakeholders (Botzem and Quack 2009, p. 994; Richardson and Eberlein 2011, p. 224f).

The IASC also developed a conceptual framework, another feature typical of an Anglo-Saxon body lacking political support (Walton 2008). It narrowed the supposed addressees of the standards to investors, claiming that the needs of all other stakeholders can be satisfied by focusing on the needs of this group (Chantiri-Chaudemanche and Pochet 2012, p. 152). Adopted in 1989 (IASC 1989), this framework allowed the IASC to align the rules with the interests of such powerful third parties as the International Organization of Securities Commissions (IOSCO) and the Securities and Exchange Commission (SEC), whose endorsement it won in 1995 (Tamm-Hallstroem 2004). As Martinez-Diaz (2005, p. 20) points out, the endorsement of IASC by global stock market regulators encouraged a particular choice of standard setting "based on technical expertise, functional representation and private authority, while rejecting a model with public sector participation and based on the representation of a wider set of stakeholders."

The IASC, its institutional configuration, and the rules it produced posed greater or smaller challenges to national standard setters based on their distance from the Anglo-Saxon tradition. There are many national differences among our three cases, but a general distinction can be made according to the role of the state in the accounting standard-setting process: either as facilitator of negotiations France), as final arbiter (Germany), as rather absent, or delegating standard making to professional bodies or private standard setters as in the Netherlands (Colasse and Pochet 2009). Regarding the content of the rule systems, France and Germany have been treated in prior literature as largely similar with respect to the origins and the driving motivation of the accounting system (Germany and France; see inter alia Mattli and Buethe 2005, p. 255). The Netherlands, though, is seen as much closer to Anglo-Saxon accounting (Zeff et al. 2002). These differences are viewed as stemming mostly from the code law tradition that is anchored in France and Germany and the deriving legalistic character of the accounting rules that have problems accommodating Anglo-Saxon principles, mainly its placement of economic substance over legal form (Ballwieser 2010; Bocqueraz 2010).

The off-balance-sheet rule that SIC 12 issued in 1998 by the IASC's Standard Interpretation Committee (SIC) to amend the international standard on consolidation, IAS 27 is paradigmatic for this economic substance-over-law approach. Given the growth of SPEs and their growing abuse for off-balance-sheet financing in the 1990s, the technical committees of large accounting firms from Europe informed the IASC's SIC about the exploitation of rigid off-balance-sheet rules for SPEs (Interview, member IASB, January 21, 2011). Considering this information, the SIC of the international accounting standard setter, itself consisting mostly of auditors, was impelled to rewrite the rules. In order to cut through the abuse of rules, the IASC installed a principles-based economic substance analysis as to whether or not the assets or debts should be put on the balance sheet by asking who was exposed to the majority of risk and rewards of these assets, independent of the legal status of the subsidiary. Such reasoning is akin to the "purposive, teleological and consequentialist mode of reasoning" of banking regulators (Black 2008, p. 26).

During its deliberations, the SIC concluded that it was impossible to provide clear, detailed regulation on what needed to be consolidated (Interview, SIC member, February 2011). The members of the SIC believed that clear rules would just trigger the development of new contractual structures falling outside the criteria, which would again qualify SPEs as off balance sheet. Therefore, in contrast to the US standards regarding off-balance-sheet decisions, SIC 12 stipulated that consolidation would no longer be based on detailed rules or calculative guidelines but, rather, on principles and indicators; specifically, if the majority of risks and/or rewards of an SPE was seen to lie with one entity, that entity needed to consolidate the SPE (PwC 2004).[8] SIC 12 thus made the consolidation of an SPE an issue of ownership in economic substance – who benefits most from the SPE and who is most exposed to the risks – rather than ownership in legal form. Evaluating compliance now required the judgment of accountants and auditors on the basis of a principle and avoided the mechanistic rule-based check-boxes that had previously bound auditors' decisions.[9]

This standard interpretation was developed without much lobbying pressure by the banks because, at that moment, the accounting standards of the IASC still had no binding force (Interview, member IASB, February 3, 2011). And, even in this situation, the comment letters of banks received by the IASC concerning SIC 12 were extraordinarily negative, and it was only the insistence of the IOSCO, the international body of securities supervisors, to pass strong standards that kept the IASC on course (Larsson 2008). Once the rule threatened to become binding in 2002, bank lobbyists fought for the repeal of it on the EU level, criticizing it as the strictest off-balance-sheet rule in the world (European Securitization Forum 2002; Jeffrey 2002). Owing to the tight coupling between accounting and banking regulation, the

---

[8] The new rule reads, "An SPE shall be consolidated when the *substance* of the relationship between an entity and SPEs indicates that the SPE is controlled by that entity" (EC 2009, p. 1, emphasis mine).

[9] As a result, auditors and banks needed to form common interpretations of the distribution of risks and rewards of an SPE to decide whether to include it in the balance sheet (Interview, French auditor, January 21, 2011). This also meant that, once introduced, the interaction of accounting advisors, lawyers, bank accountants, and auditors intensified accordingly, including heated debates over the off-balance-sheet status of conduits (Interview, German legal advisor, November 6, 2011; Interview, German auditor May 3, 2011; Interview, French auditor, March 23, 2011; Interview, Dutch auditor, July 2011).

reappearance of assets on the balance sheet of banking conglomerates threatened the economic rationale for much off-balance-sheet financing, which resided in the reduction of core capital requirements (Acharya and Schnabl 2009; Hellwig 2010). Accordingly, banking conglomerates together with other agents engaged in off-balance-sheet financing opposed national convergence with the rule. As we will see, they were favored in their attempts by the reconfiguration of the institutional context due to transnational pressures.

The Netherlands

The Netherlands has a very peculiar system of accounting standard setting. Although its content has always been very close to Anglo-Saxon accounting standards (Choi and Meek 2005, p. 85), the rules of the Dutch standard setter (the Raad voor de Jaaresver-slaggeving, RJ hereafter) are nonbinding for the corporations in their accounting decisions. Auditors do not report on compliance to these rules, and in 1990 only 2 out of 119 companies stated that they were in compliance with Dutch GAAP (Camffermann and Zeff 2007, p. 414). Besides the few accounting rules specified in the Dutch Civil Law, which are binding, the question of whether or not the consolidated statements depicted a conglomerate truthfully could be decided by judicial review only after contestation by shareholders in a special court. Commenting on that period, a Dutch regulatory advisor remarked, "Dutch GAAP was a very loose block of regulation. My American colleagues said you can drive a truck through all the possibilities of Dutch GAAP. It has so much room to maneuver; it has so much element of choice" (Interview, regulatory advisor, October 6, 2011).

This lack of enforcement capacity in the domestic framework, however, did not apply to banking conglomerates in the period from 1979 and 1993. In the revised Act on the Supervision of the Credit System 1978, which went into force on January 1, 1979, it was specified in Section 11.2. that "The Bank (DNB) shall, after consultation with the representative organizations concerned, lay down the model for the annual accounts, which may vary for different groups of credit institutions" (DNB 1979). While not unlimited,[10] the DNB had a large

---

[10] Consultation also included the general accounting standard setter (Interview, former president accounting standard-setting body, August 16, 2011).

degree of power over how banks would report their balance sheets to the regulator and which rules they should apply.

This great degree of power over the accounting framework for banks was reduced gradually until it vanished in 1993. As a relatively small economy, the Netherlands was in favor of internationalization of accounting standards already in the early 1990s (Interview, former president of the Dutch auditors' association, March 8, 2012). In the process of the increasing orientation of the Dutch accounting standard setter toward the goals of the IASC – namely, investor-oriented accounting – the DNB lost much influence until the early 1990s because of the goal conflict between prudent and neutral accounting. A former president of the Dutch auditors' association described the process as follows:

We have had some discussions with the central bank because the bank wanted to influence Dutch accounting standards for banks from their supervisory role; ... it was finally decided that there was a different perspective from the banking supervisor and the accounting standard setter, ... *they were being more interested in prudence and conservatism, while the Dutch accounting standards board said we like, we want neutral accounting and not prudent accounting.* (Interview, former president of the Dutch auditors' association, March 8, 2012)

These discussions led to the exclusion of the DNB and its underlying value orientation of conservatism and prudence from Dutch accounting standards. While this conflict first erupted over the measurement standards of banks, which was decided in favor of uniformity across all different groups, it left a certain policy instrument untouched. A former president of the standard setter noted,

They (De Nederlandsche Bank, M.T.) were part of the special committees preparing standards ... and then there was a discussion between people in that special group preparing standards ... this sort of discussions came into the general meeting of the RJ, ... there was a sort of difference of opinion of how to deal with the measurement standards of banking *and in that discussion it was decided that the view of the Dutch central bank would not be applied in accounting.* (Interview, former president accounting standard setting body, August 16, 2011)

Made in the Dutch standard setter, this decision to exclude the view of the Dutch Central Bank from Accounting was the beginning of the exclusion of the DNB from standard setting. Its role, which was already largely diminished by 1990, came to an end in a dispute over the undisclosed loss provisioning for banking conglomerates, which was a central component of the special accounting regime for banks the DNB had instituted. The Dutch Central Bank sought to maintain this hidden loss reserve in Dutch accounting but was defeated by the Dutch accounting standard setter, which, because of its influence, convinced the Ministry of Justice to change the laws in their favor. Reflecting back on this process, a former Dutch president of the accounting standard-setting body recalls:

And, there has been a lot of discussion with the central bank ... but *finally we decided that transparency would be more important and that we would not accept it anymore and also the ministry of justice changed the law saying that a provision against general risks was not appropriate,* only a reserve would be acceptable. (Interview, former president, accounting standard-setting body, August 16, 2011)

The exclusion was achieved through the auditors' association and the accounting standard-setting body turning against the role of the DNB and upholding transparency as the central value to be pursued by accounting standards. It was completed with the implementation of the Directive EC 86/635 into Dutch law in 1993. In this new legislation that sought to harmonize the rules for consolidated statements of banking conglomerates with all other conglomerates, there was no formal role left for the DNB. This decision in 1993 ended the role of the DNB in the subcommittee of the Dutch Accounting Standards for all accounting standards concerning banking conglomerates.

   Large preparers (including banks) and auditors remained the predominant forces in the standard setter (Interview, Dutch auditors' association, July 5, 2011). When the Dutch standard setter converged its goals with the IASC in 1996, adopting the 1989 IASC conceptual framework, this sealed the exclusion of the Dutch banking regulator from the policy network. The sole focus of the framework on the concerns of investors meant that after this decision, any link between the DNB and the standard setter were severed, with the DNB losing any active position or link with the RJ (Interview, former president accounting standard-setting body, August 16, 2011). This development had important implications for the way an SIC 12–like rule would be monitored and enforced, once it was introduced in the Netherlands.

The Transition to an SIC 12–Like Rule

In 2000, it was clear that the International Accounting Standards were becoming the accounting framework of reference for large Dutch conglomerates. As a reaction, the Dutch standard setter became a rather reactive member of the standard-setting community, as its work mostly consisted of considering translation of the latest IASC/IASB standards into Dutch GAAP, based on the potential impact on the Dutch economy (Interview, member of the Dutch auditors' association, July 5, 2011). In 2001, after reviewing the SIC 12, the RJ decided to translate it and to include it in its Guidelines for Annual Reporting.[11] When the SIC 12–like rule was introduced in the Netherlands in 2001, some auditors claimed that it was not a direct translation of SIC 12 and thus permitted their clients to continue not to consolidate their off-balance-sheet vehicles.

This misapplication of the SIC 12–like rule was detected by the RJ, and a footnote issued in 2003 clarified that the rule was indeed a direct translation (Interview, Dutch regulatory advisor, October 6, 2011). However, given the nonbinding nature of the standards of the RJ and the fact that neither the auditors' association nor the financial market supervisor nor the central bank had an institutionalized role in intervening and correcting auditors' interpretation of standards, the effect of this clarification was not an immediate increase in consolidation. Instead, there was a silent agreement between auditors and conglomerates to apply the new auditing standards in full force once the International Accounting Standards became binding in 2005 not and to consolidate until then, as this quote from a regulatory advisor illustrates:

And, then, in practice, everyone looked forward to the IFRS implementation and, in general, not a lot happened in between. Everyone – how do you say that? –it is typically Dutch to do that. You do something wrong, but everybody allows it, and everybody understands it. (Interview, regulatory advisor, October 6, 2011)

---

[11] See Guidelines for Annual Reporting 2001, Chapter 2.14 Article 203 and 203c.

The Dutch auditors' association refused to intervene in this process of the interpretation of a standard, as it saw the responsibility for this task solely residing with the standard setter (Interview, Dutch auditors' association, July 5, 2011). Since its exclusion from accounting matters, the Dutch central bank was also missing as an agent monitoring and enforcing these contentious rules. Being disengaged from accounting standard setting, the banking regulator followed the suggestions of American and British colleagues and the Dutch banks themselves not to apply core capital charges to the newly consolidated entities, which meant that in terms of banking regulation, they remained off balance sheet (Interview, bank manager, the Netherlands, December 6, 2011). This was not a stance shared by all banking regulators, and it decisively relates to their role in accounting standard setting. In the French case, where the banking regulator maintained a central position in the standard-setting procedures, the early convergence with SIC 12 was championed and used for core capital requirements the moment that it was introduced.

France

The French standard-setting process for industrial corporations since the Second World War has been dominated by two special characteristics. First, many different stakeholders are included in the process of standard setting and, second, these standard-setting procedures are undertaken in a collegial style, meaning that all relevant stakeholders are included in the National Council for Accounting (Conseil National de la Comptabilite [CNC]) where they are supposed to debate the standards until a new standard can be formulated unanimously.[12] This need to include all stakeholders and the need for lengthy debate, however, severely hampered the efficiency of the body because of the lack of expertise and number of members (Interview, CNC member, November 27, 2011, interview member of Order of French Accountants, March 21, 2011). Formulated as a response to the pressure that emanated from French conglomerates using US GAAP, institutional changes at the CNC in 1996 and 1998 aimed at streamlining the process by reducing the numbers of members and increasing the speed of operations.

---

[12] Hoarau (2010, p. 312) emphasizes the great variety of interests and collegial deliberation.

In these reforms, the membership of the CNC was reduced by half and different standard-setting regimes were united in the CNC, including the accounting standard setting for banking and insurance standards (Hoarau 2010, p. 316). Until then, accounting rules for banks and other financial institutions were written under the auspices of the banking regulator in a special committee on banking and financial regulation.[13] While the special accounting standards for banks and insurance companies remained in force, new standards were now to be debated and set in the CNC. These reforms implied a large upgrading in terms of the power for the national accounting standard-setting body, an upgrade motivated by the need for quicker and more efficient standard setting (Hoarau 2010, p. 316).

This reform process was driven by rooted cosmopolitans, members of the French accounting community, which at the same time, had been involved in leading positions in the IASC. In 1996, a new president was named. For the first time ever, the president was no longer a former state employee but a former partner at Arthur Andersen, George Barthès. He was also a former president of the IASC (from 1987 to 1990) and favored speedy convergence with the international standards (Interview, member of the Order of French Accountants, March 21, 2011). His prior position as a high-ranking official in one of the two auditors association of France (the "Ordre des experts comptables") allowed him to bring the French auditing communities' financial support and expertise to the project of convergence (Interview, member of the Order of French Accountants, March 21, 2011). While convinced of the goals of the IASC regarding the predominance of shareholder interests, Barthes did not fundamentally challenge the role of the banking regulator in standard setting for banks.

While the banking regulator's predominant role in accounting standard setting for banks was deinstitutionalized, its role in accounting standard setting became reinstitutionalized in the general standard-setting body. With the changes to the accounting regime in 1996, the regulator changed its observer status in the National Body to member and became a leading presence in the subcommittees dealing with the accounting standards of greatest concern to banking

[13] This committee was called "Comité de la Règlementation Bancaire et Financière."

conglomerates (Interview auditor, member of the CNC working group for banks, March 22, 2011). In this subcommittee, auditors, financial regulatory agencies, and banks negotiated new rules in a setting that featured monthly discussions into the late evening, discussions aiming to reach a consensus guided by the commission (Interview, banking manager and member subcommittee, March 25, 2011; Interview with two officials of the CNC, April 2, 2011; Interview, high functionary of CNC, June 2, 2011). The fact that the French banking regulator was so centrally involved in the standard-setting process guaranteed that these standards were often in accordance with prudential preferences. The goal of the accounting department of the banking regulator in these negotiations was "to pass accounting rules which are amenable to the goals of prudential accounting" (Interview, French banking regulator, February 6, 2011).

The Transition to an SIC 12–Like Rule

One of their most significant achievements in this respect was the convergence of the French standards for the determination of the boundaries of banking conglomerates with SIC 12. The French standard-setting body passed two rules in 1999 and one in 2000 concerning consolidation, all modeled according to SIC 12 but with certain deviations, thereby continuing the tradition of different regimes of accounting for different segments of industry that had existed before 1998. The first rule, CRC 99-02[14] applies to all companies, except for banks and insurance companies; it is almost identical to SIC 12, but it requires a capital link between parent and subsidiary (in accordance with the general provisions of the 7th EU Directive). This convergence was one of the first results of the presidency of George Barthès and his personal efforts regarding this matter (Interview, CNC member, January 21, 2011).

The second rule, CRC 99-07, which applied only to banking conglomerates, was similar to 99-02 but dropped the capital link. It was crafted in the special committee for the banks where the input of the banking regulator was central in fighting to make the standard for

---

[14] CRC refers to the comité de la règlementation comptable that transposed proposals by the CNC into law. The full text of the CRC 99-02 is available at: www.articles.exafi.com/compta/ComptaTextes/CRC99-02.htm

off-balance-sheet accounting as strict as possible. A member of that committee at the time remembered,

It was the CNC who formulated it, but I would say the input of the Commission Bancaire for the 99-07 for the banks was crucial; one can say that it is evident ... [t]he 10052 for the banks, this is where the Commission Bancaire has pushed. (Interview, auditor Big Four Paris, former member of the CNC Working Group for Banks, March 22, 2011)

The 10052 was where the risk-and-reward approach to SPEs was introduced. This passage, which can be seen as the core of SIC 12, could be introduced for banks but not for other conglomerates because of the way the 7th European Directive on accounting was implemented in France. In 1983, only the banking regulator decided to use an option in that directive[15] to drop the requirement of a capital link for the consolidation of subsidiaries. A former banking regulator explained, "For the banks, it was considered that, given the financial engineering which already existed at that time, one possibly had to foresee cases where the capital link was not the case" (Interview, former banking regulator and CNC member, January 30, 2011).

When leading the charge for convergence of French GAAP with SIC 12, the French banking regulator could point back to that decision and, in 1999, achieve already almost complete convergence for banks. Convergence for other conglomerates was achieved only in the wake of the Enron scandal, as the French parliament passed a law in 2003.[16] This involvement in the regulatory process stands in sharp contrast to the German case, where there was no tradition of any involvement of the banking regulator in accounting standard setting. As a result, those favoring convergence with SIC 12 in Germany were lacking an important ally and would have success only after the financial crisis.

Germany

Before 1998, there was no specific standard-setting body for accounting standards in Germany; instead, changes to the accounting standards in

---

[15] 7th EU Directive, Article 1.c, available at: http://europa.eu/legislation_summaries/internal_market/businesses/company_law/l26010_en.htm
[16] Loi n° 2003–706 de sécurité financière, available at: www.assetrecovery.org/kc/node/2cb8acd0-a34a-11dc-bf1b-335d0754ba85.0;jsessionid=4B6D2DB9CC618947BD24825FD-304DEC0

German commercial law were undertaken by the Ministry of Justice in close coordination with the large business associations and the concerned ministries. This sparsely populated policy network with few resources allotted to accounting standard setting resulted in very few very large projects, among them the modernization of the accounting rules in 1985 and again in 2009 (Interview, German accounting professor, June 30, 2011). There was no official independent standard-setting body, either private or public. Rather, a system of continuous adjustment and interpretation of the existing rules by practitioners and academics was in place (McLeay et al. 2000), with the German auditors association, IDW, playing a lead role.[17] This weakly institutionalized framework would be reformed to answer the pressures that emanated from the lacking quality of German GAAP and the subsequent need for influence at the IASC.

In 1998, the governance of the IASC was seen as moving toward a body of national standard setters (Camffermann and Zeff 2007, p. 314), and the ministry of justice was granted two options to fill that void. It could set up either a private standard setter or a collegial-style state organ including the financial and banking regulator, the ministry of justice, and the finance ministry.[18] The ministry of justice chose to sign a contract with the private German Accounting Standards Board (the GASB), as the goal of gaining influence at the IASC was seen at risk through the inclusion of state organs (Interview, German financial regulator, July 1, 2011; Interview, board member German auditors' association, May 3, 2011). After all, the SEC had requested the IASC to be modeled as an independent body of experts (Camffermann and Zeff 2007, p. 14). The GASB was thus set up to answer the question "where the German private standards setter was" (Benston et al. 2006, p. 130). This meant that at a critical juncture in the transformation of the German institutional context of accounting standard setting, transnational pressures prevented the inclusion of the banking regulator, although the latter directly depends on German accounting standards for its supervisory work.

The tasks of the GASB were to offer advice to the Ministry of Justice on reforms to improve the rules for domestic consolidated

---

[17] In the realm of consolidated financial statements, the German auditors association (IDW) informally filled this void by providing statements on questions of accounting (called HFA RS).
[18] The different options were enshrined in § 342a and § 342b of the German Commercial Code.

accounts[19] and to represent Germany in the IASC. While the German standard-setting body did not face any state interference when submitting comment letters to the IASC/IASB, it remained dependent on the approval of the Ministry of Justice to change domestic standards. While this leads to a constant exchange between the two bodies with the representative of the Ministry of Justice attending some board meetings (Interview, official of the Ministry of Justice, May 4, 2011), at the same time, the Ministry of Justice continues directly to involve business associations in the process of rule formulation, as prescribed by the common procedures of the German ministries. The new standard-setting body was thus in an incredibly weak position to push for contentious convergence projects. This weakness was further aggravated through its rivalry with the national body of auditors (IDW), which felt that the new body was encroaching on its turf and blocked convergence projects (Interview, auditor and member of DRSC, February 21, 2011; Interview with IDW officials, April 14, 2011; Interview with IDW board member, May 3, 2011).

The (Blocked) Transition to a SIC 12–Like Rule

In December 2001, for the first time, the German accounting standard setter requested from the Ministry of Justice convergence of the German standards for consolidation with SIC 12.[20] This attempt was motivated by the failure of Enron in the fall of 2001 and consequent reactions within the auditing community (Interview, board member of the German standard-setting body, December 11, 2010). In a remarkable deviation from its French counterpart, the German banking supervisor was opposing the proposed rule changes, lobbying the Ministry of Justice directly on this issue. Its opposition was motivated by the fact that changing the rules for consolidation might have an impact on the core capital requirements of banks in prudential regulation, the exact size of which could not yet be estimated.[21]

---

[19] At the time of its founding, there were expectations of a large-scale reform to converge the rules for consolidated final statements upon IAS, if possible, until 2002 (see Biener 2000, p. 63).

[20] See E-DRS 16. Available at: www.drsc.de/docs/drafts/16.html

[21] The German text can be found at www.standardsetter.de/drsc/docs/comments/016/bakred.html

While it cannot be established in how far this intervention was driven by regulatory capture, the degree of surprise caused by this proposal at the German banking regulator can be seen in its reaction. Instead of being asked for input beforehand, the regulator is confronted with the proposal once it is already published. It, therefore, does not have the time to calculate how much new core capital the consolidation of special-purpose entities would require. In an interview at the financial regulator, two officials emphasized the length of time that an inquiry into the impact of new consolidation rules on core capital takes and the difficulties of assessing these issues without data prepared by the banks themselves (Interview, German financial regulator, July 1, 2011).

This surprise can be linked to the fact that the GASB was set up in line with the goal of gaining legitimacy and influence at the IASC. Modeled along the IASC template, the members of the council of the GASB are all either auditors or preparers of financial statements. There have never been any state officials inside the body. The due process for setting standards starts, just as the due process of the IASC does, with a draft of the rule by the standard setter. In this constellation, there is no stable link with the banking or financial regulator. Indeed, the stance of the standard-setting body toward the banking regulator might be described as ignoring its concerns, given the conviction that it is the concerns of financial investors that matter. The orientation was toward London and the IASC with its due process that kept the influence of state agencies at bay. This orientation was supported by overlap in staff, most prominently by the current president of the DRSC, who was the technical director at the IASC from 1995 to 1999.

For this reason, the domestic financial regulator was not perceived as an important stakeholder in accounting standardization who needed to be included. This view is expressed by a long-term member of the GASB. Asked about the interaction with the banking regulator during the time when the GASB fought for the introduction of SIC 12–like regulation, this member replied, "The contemporaneous BaFin, as this is today a part of BaFin, so the regulators we have never cared about, never interacted, we did not care about them" (Interview, member DRSC, December 6, 2010). This lacking interest and connection meant that the GASB was missing an important ally in the convergence process, an ally that could have helped it in its push for reform. Instead, it remained largely isolated in the German governance network, pushing for change when large conglomerates were opposing it.

The private standard setter continued to push for a change in the consolidation rule according to SIC 12. It criticized the accounting reforms by the Ministry of Justice in 2003 and 2004 as insufficient and submitted a proposal for the modernization of the code of commerce in May 2005, requesting the convergence with SIC 12. The process of accounting standards modernization, announced in 2002, however, was completed only in 2009. Neither the first nor second draft of the proposed reform bill included any proposal for convergence with SIC 12, the result of a forceful opposition to such changes which began even before the first draft of the modernization law was written. Reflecting on why a rule similar to SIC 12 was not in the first draft of 2007, an auditor involved in drafting the reform bill reflected,

There was a lot of thinking, back and forth, but ... already there were interest groups saying, "Nonsense, we do not need that"; then, we have to suddenly consolidate our SPEs. That was especially the association of savings banks and credit unions, "let that be, we do not do IFRS, so we do not need that." And, these are very powerful groups, as you can imagine. (Interview, auditor, May 30, 2011)[22]

As German savings banks and credit unions do not fall under IAS, they fervently defended the old rules that made the continuation of off-balance-sheet activities much easier. These banks, the leasing industry, and its manifold users (SMEs and large conglomerates) formed the powerful political alliance that blocked convergence. Only in 2009, in the aftermath of the crisis, caused by off-balance-sheet activities of banks, did convergence occur. The auditor involved in writing the law described the events thus:

There was suddenly this implosion in the capital markets... The Sachsen LB and the IKB imploded, every politician realized this risk is real and can threaten the existence, and so suddenly a slot is open, a time window, I can make a regulation which otherwise would not be possible. (Interview, auditor, May 30, 2011)

It was only the financial crisis which disturbed the power equilibrium within the German political economy that made convergence largely

---

[22] A banking manager from a private bank also pointed to public banks as the main lobbying force (Interview, July 12, 2011).

impossible. In this moment in time, members of the German auditors' association, IDW, played a prominent role in pushing for more stringent regulation in influential trade journals (Börsen-Zeitung), highlighting its clout as a body of expertise and the importance of a unified front of auditors to achieve accounting change. The delay in Germany was the success of an economically and politically entrenched opposition and a splintered framework for accounting rule setting, where there were many points at which proposed changes could be vetoed. It, therefore, took significantly longer for German accounting norms to converge to international standards, as compared to France or the Netherlands.

Discussion and Conclusion

This chapter traces the deinstitutionalization and reinstitutionalization of the role of the banking regulator in accounting standard setting in national frameworks and the process of convergence toward SIC 12 in the French, German, and Dutch cases. Transnational isomorphic pressures were common to the three cases investigated, as accounting standards and the way of setting accounting standards were deemed as unfit and outdated and the EU exerted pressures toward harmonization. The way that these pressures played out, however, was markedly different as this chapter shows. If banking regulators obtained or preserved a role in standard setting, their inclusion in the policy network meant the installation of a force pushing for prudent accounting standards.[23]

The rule investigated here, SIC 12, which is principles based and puts economic substance over legal form, is challenging to all continental-European Accounting standards systems with the exception of the Dutch one. As the difference between France on the one hand and Germany on the other shows, it is not accounting tradition per se which can explain convergence or the lack thereof but, rather, how this tradition is shaped and transformed by the actors in the policy network. Transnational developments disrupt national regulatory frameworks, but they also offer opportunities to install regulatory regimes that are more favorable for prudence. How regulatory agencies adapt to these changing circumstances is decisive.

---

[23] This finding also holds for the Spanish and Portuguese cases in the positive and the Belgian in the negative.

They can maneuver to gain a central place in the new configuration and appropriate the rules that emerge from a transnational context they deem appropriate, as in the French case. Institutional toolkits and traditions can play a supportive role in this quest, as evidenced by the fact that the French banking regulator could arrange its inclusion in French accounting standard setting based on the collegial style of standard setting that prevailed there. Such a culture was not present in the Netherlands or Germany. Conversely, the complete convergence of the Dutch accounting standard setter in his goals toward the IASC, installing a completely different due process that is more exclusive of stakeholders of accounting standards led to the permanent deinstitutionalization of the Dutch central bank in standard setting. This fact points to the due process in particular as an important element for the de- and reinstitutionalization of the banking regulator.

A comparison among France, the Netherlands, and Germany regarding the changing institutional contexts in which the convergence projects took place reveals the impact the reconfigurations caused by transnational pressures had on the convergence project. Alignment with transnational standard setters in terms of general goals and due process directly influenced the inclusion or exclusion of the banking regulator and, thus, the coalition for rule change. Table 6.1 illustrates the impact the convergence of national with transnational due processes and goals had on the coalition for change.

In Germany, due to strategic considerations of the government and industry, a private standard setter is created following an IASC-style due process. This leads to the fact that the banking regulator is informed only once the intent for rule change is already announced, causing surprise and opposition. In the Netherlands, the convergence of the Dutch standard setter with the goals of the IASC excludes the banking regulator from accounting standard setting. As a consequence, the Dutch banking regulator loses all institutionalized linkage points with accountants and in matters of accounting. While it observes the introduction of an SIC 12– like rule, it does not take it into account as a tool for effective prudential regulation. In both cases, changes in the institutional context remove accounting as a responsibility and weaken relationships with the standard setter. Actor mismatch between those agencies dependent upon the rules in their daily work and those formulating them weakened the likelihood for convergence.

Table 6.1 *Institutional Contexts and Coalitions for Change*

	France	Netherlands	Germany
Convergence with the IASC standard-setting architecture	No, due process remains collegial, banking regulator is not excluded from standard setter, goal of prudent accounting remains important	Yes, state agencies are excluded, due process and goals are Adopted	Yes, creation of private standard setter, mixture of IASC due process with national due process
Role of banking regulator in convergence	Crucial, reinstitutionalized his role in subcommittee of new standard setter, pushes there for convergence	No role: gradually loses its role in accounting, which ends when Dutch standard setter copies concept framework of IASC (1996)	Blocks convergence, never included in accounting standard setter, as the model of IASC is copied in 1998. He is surprised by call for convergence and opposes it.
Coalition against reform	Split, due to different accounting rules for banks and nonbanks	Split, as Dutch central bank allows banks to ignore rule for core capital	United, accounting rules apply to all conglomerates; opposition especially strong by those conglomerates that continue to apply national rules
Collaboration between auditors' association and standard setter	Supportive	Indifferent	Adversarial

In contrast, by reinstitutionalizing its role in the newly empowered accounting standard setter, the French banking regulator maintains its accounting expertise and its interest in the subject matter. In addition, the maintenance of the collegial-style due process and the separation of accounting rules for banks and other entities forced the banking conglomerates opposed to change into direct negotiations with the banking regulator, thereby facilitating convergence. Conglomerates other than banks were not concerned by the rule change and, thus, did not seek to block it until 2003 when the French legislator decided to bring about rule convergence for the remaining sectors of the economy. In this sense, the splitting of accounting rules, which stands in contrast to the universalism of IAS, allowed stepwise convergence, thereby splintering the opposition to rule change and reducing its force.

There is, thus, a certain degree of path dependency in the role of the banking regulator in accounting standard setting and the evolution of the regulatory treatment of SPEs, as the implementation of the 7th Directive for banking conglomerates shows. An independent accounting regime for banks and the thoughtful implementation of the 7th Directive for banks in the 1980s in France proved beneficial for a decade after it was enacted, permitting the regulator to adapt the accounting rules to new constructs of regulatory arbitrage. In contrast, changing German accounting rules for banks was harder to achieve as rule changes automatically applied to all conglomerates, and the implementation of the 7th Directive made consolidation without a capital link impossible until 2003. Furthermore, there was no tradition of involvement for the banking regulator in the accounting standard-setting process.

These different paths taken in the interaction with external directives, whether shaped by the intervention of banking regulators or not, impacted the timing of the convergence to SIC 12–like rules and the use of the accounting information for core capital requirements. It appears as a self-reinforcing process in which banking regulators at the heart of the accounting standard-setting regime make decisions today, which will be beneficial for future regulatory action. Such good decision making is possible because of their position in the network issuing accounting standards, but it does not automatically follow from that position.

Instead, what informs this decision making is the supervision of developments in the banking realm, including the monitoring of the interpretation of accounting standards and the enforcement of accounting decisions. Only by being involved within the field of compliance can banking regulators derive the information necessary to update regulation. As we will see in Chapter 7, this embeddedness was a crucial factor in the differential buildup in the off-balance-sheet position in the ABCP segment in the different countries. The latter cannot be explained by these accounting rule changes alone (n.b., the early introduction in the Netherlands). Pushing the interpretation of SIC 12 toward prudence and intervening in the interpretation of banking regulations regarding liquidity lines was another task that differentiated the French banking regulators from their Dutch and German counterparts. In Chapter 7, I will investigate the differential embeddedness of banking regulators in these processes of compliance decisions that both it and the effects these different constellations had on the interpretation of existing rules regarding the ABCP market.

7 | Steering Finance toward Prudence: The Role of Banking Regulators in the Governance of Compliance Decisions

From my point of view, what is important is not to have any more special purpose entities to be orphaned. Wherever they end up, they should not be nowhere ... So I would say, if you have to err, you should err on the side of prudence. (Interview, employee of French banking federation, May 11, 2011, translation by author)

In Chapter 6, we focused on how transnational impulses reconfigured the role of banking regulators in accounting standard setting and shaped the space of maneuver for them to bring about the introduction of an SIC 12–like rule. In this chapter, we will shift the focus to the domestic governance network controlling the application of these rules and the rules for the calculation of capital requirements regarding liquidity lines. The comparison of the different capabilities and capacities of banking regulators allows me to answer the question of why the French banking regulators both became involved with the introduction of SIC 12–like rules at all and updated the interpretation of the liquidity line early on while the German and the Dutch ones didn't. Furthermore, the comparison will show that the efficiency of the SIC 12–like rules to force ABCP conduits on the balance sheets of their banking sponsors as well as the rule for liquidity lines depended on the steering of the interpretation of these rules into an encompassing direction, including all the risks and rewards emanating from these entities, to force compliance officers and auditors in particular "to err on the side of prudence." Steering the application of SIC 12 and the classification of liquidity lines into a prudent direction meant expanding the events, risks, and rewards that needed to be taken into account, thereby sharpening the criteria that a special-purpose entity (SPE) has to fulfill in order to be assigned the status of a stand-alone, independent corporation in terms of core capital requirements.

Regulatory Dialogues: The Fight over the Implementation of Principles-Based Rules

Governance theory emphasizes varying governability of different sectors in the economy in different countries, depending on the capacity of state agencies to involve private actors in the implementation of rules (Mayntz 2009, p. 21). Nonstate actors are seen as more powerful in shaping the implementation of new rules the larger their tacit knowledge (see Mayntz 2009). To reduce this power advantage of private actors, regulators need to gather information about the way in which rules are currently interpreted and how future rules might be interpreted. In such a situation, regulators need to strengthen their ties with the external auditors and the compliance personnel of the banks, engaging in frequent (informal) dialogues with them in order to stay abreast of the most recent contractual innovations in finance and accounting.

This need for dialogue especially holds for principles-based standards emphasizing economic substance over legal form. Accounting and banking regulators often favor an economic substance approach,[1] as a principles-based analysis of economic substance hinders the structuring work of lawyers and regulatory advisors – a process called "stitching on the edge" in interviews, as conduits were constructed to fall right outside of the perimeter of consolidation (Interview, German accounting manager, May 5, 2011). The uncertainty for those engaging in "creative compliance" that is generated by principles-based standards, however, carries a disadvantage for the regulators regarding their capacity to control the compliance process itself. Because much of the decision making in this system is delegated to local compliance officers and auditors, the system's effectiveness in achieving the desired lofty end-goals depends on the interpretation of these principles in the community of compliance officers, internal and external to the firm. The fact that so much discretion is granted in interpreting the rules makes the implementation of principles at least as relevant as their exact wording (Black 1997, p. 31). The delegation of much of the

---

[1] A simple example regards the question of any legally enforceable debts that a company has given to another company. If the other company is nearing bankruptcy, the economic value of that asset is lower than is predicated by the legal form. Economic substance thus aims at taking into account the economic circumstances that surround the contracts.

actual interpretation of the rules to the regulated and local compliance officers which they pay carries the possibility of a most lax, permissive interpretation of these rules. Therefore, regulators dealing with principles-based standards need to follow a strategy of compliance that involves "negotiation, advice, education and compromise with the regulated" by the rule maker in order to achieve effective regulation (Black 1997, p. 29). This necessitates a constant conversation between regulated and regulator in order to achieve the appropriate application of the rules.

As an answer to the problem of how to achieve the desired shared interpretations of general principles, legal scholars have proposed the development of interpretive communities that together define the content of these provisions,[2] characterized by iterative regulatory dialogues between regulator and regulated (Black 2002). There has to be a "dense network of 'regulatory conversations': dialogic, iterative and reflexive communications between regulator, regulatee and others as to the purpose and application of the principle" (see Black 2008, p. 17). These regulatory dialogues should achieve certainty by establishing interpretive communities, a certainty that otherwise is provided by clear rules. As Julia Black, leading legal scholar on these issues explains:

Interpretive communities are a way that mutuality of interpretation could be assumed without further specification by rule. What is necessary then is that the rule maker, the regulated and enforcer share those norms, values, goals that give rise to a shared understanding as to the rule's meaning and application. (Black 1997, p. 33)[3]

In their analysis of various regulatory regimes coupled with principles-based regulation, researchers have differentiated between the formal variant, in which principles are found only in the rule book but are nonetheless accompanied by very strict guidance; the substantive

---

[2] "Certainty in a principles based regulation has less to do with how a particular provision is drafted and more to do with the development of an interpretive community that defines the content of that provision" (Ford 2010, p. 31).

[3] In a similar vein, Ford concludes, "Fundamental to principles based regulation is the development of a functional and effective 'interpretive community' that includes industry participants, regulators and other stakeholders in ongoing communication around the content of regulatory principle" (Ford 2010, p. 5).

one, where rules are applied in a flexible and principles-driven way; and the principles-based regulation based on polycentric networks, where a range of actors develops the interpretation of principles, including nonstate actors who offer guidance. Consultants and voluntarily appointed advisors play a key role in shaping the application of principles-based regulation in this field (Black 2008, p. 24). In particular, in polycentric interpretive communities, there can be different understandings among the regulator and at the regulated and advisors (Black 2008, p. 25), which increases the necessity of an ongoing regulatory dialogue between the regulator and the regulated.

The requirements for principles-based standards to work, especially in polycentric networks, make them extraordinarily prone to failure and require a delicate intervention of the state in the form of the regulator in the system. They require the regulator to have "necessary capacity in terms of numbers, access to information and expertise" (Ford 2010, p. 8), which provides the regulator with a strong voice steering the interpretation of principles (Ford 2010, p. 40). Regulators must be able to scrutinize information independently in order to see if the front-line decision makers have interpreted the rules as desired. Their capacity to do so is enhanced if regulators themselves engage in probing the compliance decisions made by the audited (see Ford 2010). These different requirements clarify that the implementation of principles-based regulation imposes high institutional demands on regulators and cannot be left to the integrity of external auditors alone.

While auditors are legally liable for the correctness of the compliance decisions that they certify, this liability resides in a broad space of legally defensible decisions. The client–customer relationship pushes the interpretation in this space in favor of the corporation with the help of pressures exerted by regulatory advisors, lawyers, and corporations, as detailed in Chapter 3. Auditing networks seek to counter this tendency by installing technical departments that review the legality of the accounting decisions of the business partners of the auditing network. But, even these technical departments have limited capacities to suppress the exploitation of legal rigidities through financial innovations, as the burden of proof regarding the lack in conformity of compliance decisions with the regulatory standards resides with the auditing firm. If auditors cannot find evidence that the decisions of the internal compliance decisions contradict these principles, they have to accept them, leaving the auditors with only the possibility of issuing a dissenting point of view.

In order to provide compliance officers and external auditors with the capacity to constrain the misuse of these innovations, an interpretation needs to be issued by an authority over compliance standards (either auditors' association, standard-setting body, financial regulator, or banking regulator) that directly reacts to these innovations and signals to external auditors and internal compliance officers alike that this innovation is no longer receiving the benefit of the doubt. Early intervention in the development of these practices is important, as nonintervention can lead to strong growth of these contracts, which is based only on the compliance decision. The earlier regulators intervene to stop this kind of behavior, the lower the resistance of the regulated will be. Conversely, if contracts worth billions of euro are signed and entire business models are based on the provision of such contracts, it will be more and more difficult to change these interpretations.[4] This intervention requires the capacity to monitor developments and the capacity to steer compliance officers and their auditors in their decision making through the power of sanctions. In the following, I will detail the different insertion of the banking regulators into these regulatory networks and how their positioning influenced the interpretation of the most crucial standards.

Germany: Ignorance Caused by Distance

The Regulatory Network

In Germany, banking supervision is implemented by a highly fragmented and decentralized regulatory network. BaFin (the Federal Financial Supervisory Authority), an administrative agency operating under the mandate of the Federal Ministry of Finance (BMF), holds the final legal responsibility for banking supervision (DIW 2006; Hartmann-Wendels et al. 2009, p. 104). Despite its key regulatory role, however, BaFin's banking supervision unit has very limited staff and – especially – a lack of qualified accounting personnel,[5] which allows only for off-site supervision: the unit verifies banks' compliance with existing rules based on documents verified

---

[4] Funk and Hirschman make a similar point regarding the development of the FX swaps market in the 1980s (Funk and Hirschman 2014).
[5] At the BaFin, fewer accountants are employed by far than in one large auditors' network in Germany alone (Interview, German banking regulator, July 1, 2011).

by the Bundesbank (the German Central Bank), on those sent by the banks themselves, and on reports from bank auditors. BaFin then crafts administrative sanctions if necessary. On-site supervision and the verification of the accounting numbers reported to BaFin are outsourced to the auditors of the banks and, since the mid-2000s, to the Bundesbank as well.

This delegation of tasks leads to problems in the information flow between on-site and off-site supervision in that before the crisis, the regional Bundesbank official auditors sent reports on which the BaFin acted, but there was no institutionalized meeting between these agents where matters could be discussed further. There is a formal exchange between BaFin and the German auditors' association IDW that is happening at least once a year with specific committees dealing with insurance and banking conglomerates and where views on different topics are exchanged, but these exchanges mostly regard the audit reports for the BaFin, not the financial statements of banking conglomerates (Interview, German banking regulator, July 1, 2011). Besides this meeting, there are no formal or informal conversations of the banking regulator with the auditing networks. The lack of informal conversations with auditors has been identified as a problem by auditors, who desired such an exchange in order to voice their concerns without putting them into writing (Interview, German professor of banking involved in the official investigation of the German banking supervision after the crisis, May 24, 2011). The BaFin is, thus, largely isolated from practices of on-site supervision as well as the current accounting practices, which are left to the auditors.

This structure of supervision is an outcome of the federal structure of Germany as well as the desire to enforce the subsidiary principle and to keep the federal agency at its inception in 1962 as small as possible (Hellwig et al. 2010). The decentralized nature of the German banking regulatory network is further reinforced by the strongly restricted mandates of agencies and their limited discretion in interpreting the law, leading to few inquiries or supervision across divisions and little coordination between the various actors. The regulatory focus on the letter of the law originated in postwar Germany when strict limits on the regulatory discretion of administrative agencies were included in the constitution as checks on excessive governmental power (Hellwig et al. 2010). This constitutional framework emphasizes the liberty of legal entities to take economic risks on their own, making any federal administrative intervention into these decisions subject to extensive justification based on clear legal mandates (Hellwig et al. 2010).

Any transgression of mandates can be legally challenged by the banks in the administrative courts, which since 1949 have remained independent and outside of the executive administration. The strong focus on facilitating private enterprise and limiting supervision to the scope of the law is shared by the BMF, under whose mandate BaFin operates with strict limits on its independence (Hartmann-Wendels et al. 2009). Since the BMF can revoke any administrative ordinances and circulars by BaFin, regulatory action that extends beyond a formalistic interpretation of legal rules has always been strongly discouraged (Interview, German banking regulator, July 1, 2011). As a regulatory advisor explained,

BaFin always has one theme: we are a constitutional state; we have the law for banking supervision; we have a basic framework that is to be applied ... Every bank in Germany could have sued if BaFin had asked for something that went beyond the laws and the decrees. (June 14, 2011, similar points made by banking expert May 24, 2011)

This stance of the regulator to embrace legal form was further reinforced by the insistence of the ministry of finance not to put a higher burden on German banks as compared to their EU competitors. As she added, "It was a unitary market in Europe... [E]qual rules should apply, and the German ones should definitely not be stricter than the others" (Interview, regulatory advisor, June 14, 2011).

Until 2009, BaFin's banking supervision was thus predominantly quantitative in style (DIW 2006; Hartmann-Wendels et al. 2009): using the externally produced bank balance sheets, BaFin would conduct a largely mechanical check of whether the bank's total assets-to-equity ratio matched the minimum levels fixed by law. This reliance on external documents from banks meant that accounting standards and auditor verification played a critical role in banking supervision in Germany. The minimally staffed BaFin, however, lacked the structural capability and expertise to verify banking conglomerates' reporting decisions or to question compliance decisions by auditors (Interview, German banking regulator, July 1, 2011). This shifted almost all responsibility for monitoring banking compliance to the auditors: their reports, either in the form of special audits or annual audit reports for BaFin, became "the main information element of supervision" in Germany (DIW 2006, p. 29). One consequence of this distribution of expertise was that BaFin never overruled the accounting decisions of auditors (Interview, banking managers, July 12, 2011).[6]

The strong focus on legally mandated supervision does not mean that there was no exchange between BaFin and professionals concerned with compliance (Interview, regulatory advisor, June 14, 2011). However, these dialogues were initiated by regulatory advisors and auditors of banks seeking clarification from BaFin; regulators usually did not reach out to the auditors for news of banks' creative means of complying with accounting rules. There was almost no informal exchange on these issues, and auditors were reluctant to report their concerns and doubts about banking practices to BaFin in writing because it could endanger their relationships with clients (Interview, banking expert, May 24, 2011).

The (Absent) Regulatory Dialectic

The first broad regulatory clarification with respect to securitization and ABCPs was published by the BaKred in 1997 (BaKred 1997b). In line with the BMF's strong advocacy of securitization to "strengthen the financial center Germany" (BaKred 1997a), this publication specified how banks could reduce core capital in securitization transactions, providing a checklist of practical requirements that banks had to fulfill. The requirements for setting up ABCP conduits enjoined banks to inform BaKred (BaFin's predecessor) and to demonstrate the conduit's compliance with banking regulations. In practice, however, BaKred (and later BaFin) always approved ABCP conduits, provided that auditors had approved the contractual structure and relationship of

---

[6] This limited capacity of the regulator to challenge accounting decisions also stems from a specificity of the German accounting law: a businessman, for instance, can defend any accounting act as legally appropriate as long as he can find support for his position in the accounting literature, thereby demonstrating that he is applying the principles of proper accounting (Interview, law professor/corporate lawyer, November 6, 2011; McLeay et al. 2000). In this respect, the BaFin has no authority over this interpretation. The only actor with the power to limit these interpretations in German GAAP, at least up until 2006, was the Institut der Deutschen Wirtschaftspruefer (IDW, German auditors' association), as its pronouncements were seen to be binding for the auditors.

the conduits with the bank on the basis of these checklists (Interview, regulatory advisor, June 14, 2011; second interview April 9, 2015). When banks sought to keep their conduits off balance sheet, they and their regulatory advisors mostly negotiated with their auditors and lawyers, thereby following BaFin's compliance assessment to the letter of the law; any liquidity lines below one year were approved by BaFin without opposition (Florstedt 2013). Asked about BaFin's capacity to challenge the off-balance-sheet decisions made between banks and auditors, a regulatory advisor of a large auditor network responded,

It [BaFin] can doubt anything ... But, I'm thinking that if an auditor has looked at the balance sheet part [of the off-balance-sheet decision], then it will be difficult for BaFin to formulate concerns, because the knowledge at the large auditing networks is at least equivalent to that at BaFin [laughs]. (Interview, regulatory advisor interview, June 14, 2011)

BaFin's previous focus on compliance with the legal format of regulation and its arm's-length relationships with auditors placed it outside of the network where discussions about compliance with banking regulation and accounting regulation occurred.

Because off-balance-sheet engagement had become quite prevalent in Germany by 2005, banks started to restructure their SPEs in such a way that their on-balance-sheet status under the International Finance Reporting Standards (IFRS) could continue to be avoided. Banks and their regulatory advisors would work out an initial construction of the contractual relationship of the SPE with the banking conglomerate in such a way that off-balance-sheet status could be achieved even if risk exposure remained. These structures were then presented to the auditors, with whom an intense negotiation on the interpretation of compliance would ensue (Interview, German auditor May 3, 2011; Interview, German legal advisor, November 6, 2011). A legal advisor confirmed the early involvement of auditors in the process, admitting,

A draft is drawn up and sent to the auditors. Then, you ask the accountants, "if we were to do it like this, what would you say to the question of consolidation?" It's a dialogue; the accounting professionals are involved very early on, and often also individuals other than the auditors ... So, you can't say that the legal advisor is developing the structure, and the accountants see it later: it's coordinated beforehand. (Interview, legal advisor, November 6, 2011)

If auditors had compliance concerns, a new round of negotiations and fine-tuning of contracts would start so that the auditors' specific requirements could be satisfied. In the process, banks would often draw on legal opinions crafted in-house or by legal consultancy firms, as a means of strengthening their position with respect to the auditor.

The case of the German bank IKB (Ring 2009) is a paradigmatic example of such negotiation. After receiving negative auditor opinions regarding the off-balance-sheet status of its conduits in 2004, IKB engaged in negotiations with its auditors and regulatory advisors to restructure contractual relations and to maintain the off-balance-sheet status. In the process, it outsourced credit risks related to its large liquidity lines in legal form but kept most of these risks in economic substance (Ring 2009). These contractual changes convinced the auditor to maintain deconsolidation. Asked why IKB did not consolidate its hybrid conduit Rhineland before the crisis, a manager of a large auditing company explained,

No, because this SPE was knitted such that it didn't have to be consolidated. If it is stitched on the edge in that way, you can always debate whether it belongs inside or not, and then, you get the question, "Now tell me how much more risk I need to transfer to somebody else in order for you to accept it, so that I don't have to consolidate it?" And, then, you continue to reflect, and so you develop a model that is exactly on the edge. (Interview, auditing manager, May 3, 2011)

As the quote above shows, IFRS allowed auditors to contradict regulatory engineers and to force them into a negotiation regarding the question of who was exposed to the majority of risk and rewards. Yet, it could not end the creative interaction of the regulated with the categorization efforts inherent in accounting. Instead, banks now engaged in a contractual outsourcing of risk that would satisfy their auditors while maintaining sufficient rewards for themselves.

These decisions by auditors would prove to be important for the interpretation of rules by the regulator beginning in 2006 when the Bundesbank and BaFin started preparations for the 2008 implementation of Basel II, which required banking supervisors to engage in a more qualitative style of supervision (DIW 2006). When the Bundesbank performed a qualitative review of IKB in February 2007, it questioned the legal constructions that IKB had installed as a means of maintaining the 0 percent core capital charge for its large ABCP conduits (Ring

2009). At the end of the evaluation, however, BaFin opted against the economic substance analysis that required the imposition of core capital charges. Instead, it employed a legal form analysis, granting the core capital exemption on the liquidity lines. A constraining element in these decisions was that the auditors had repeatedly confirmed IKB's conduits as independent from IKB itself. Interview sources indicated that the limited legal mandate of BaFin and the fear of resistance from banks and the Ministry of Finance prevented BaFin from challenging the structuring activities of banks (Interview, banking expert, May 24, 2011). An interview with a Federal Reserve regulator sheds interesting light on this dependence of the German regulatory network on auditors:

When the crisis came up, we found out that the liquidity facilities and some of the conduits in Europe, Germany in particular, it was straight out letters of credit, and I would look at one, and I said to my colleague, "This is not a facility, there is no first loss, there is no nothing. It's a straight up guarantee." He said, "No, no, we were told that these are liquidity facilities." I said, "Who told you that?", "The banks." I said, "You believe the banks??" And, then, well, they said, "No, no, the auditors." I said, "Who pays the auditors?", "The banks." I'm like, "And you believe the auditors?" You know, this is what we came across, this came up in Belgium as well." (Interview, Federal Reserve regulator, March 15, 2016)

As the German experience suggests, relying on auditors alone to enforce compliance can be a hazardous decision, as there are evident conflicts of interest. In other words, auditors alone cannot be trusted to protect the interests of the public at large. However, completely excluding them does not necessarily improve the outcome, as the case of the Netherlands shows.

The Netherlands: Cognitive Capture through One-Sided Dialogue

The Regulatory Network

In the Dutch case, the regulatory network concerned with ABCPs is less fragmented and is centered on the Dutch central bank (DNB). The DNB is solely responsible for banking supervision, both on-site and off-site, and enjoys great discretion in the legal interpretation of

existing rules (Seerden and Stroink 2007, p. 194; Jennen and van de Vijver 2010, p. 94). While the central bank does have teams stationed in the large banks, these do not concern themselves with accounting questions, as the central bank lacks the manpower and resources in the field of accounting (Interview, DNB, October 5, 2011). Instead, as in Germany, the DNB has outsourced many tasks related to prudential reporting entirely to the auditors,[7] instructing them what they should do additionally to their auditing work.[8] Auditors had to produce yearly statements regarding banks' compliance with DNB rules in conjunction with annual reports. The DNB has no role in accounting supervision or accounting standard setting, which is fully outsourced to auditors and the Dutch Accounting Standards Board (DASB). As such, the DNB could not detect any irregularities in the field of accounting. In addition, it also lacked any links to actors who did, as the institutional links between the Dutch accounting standard setter and the central bank had been severed in the early 1990s, as detailed in Chapter 6. Following this battle over regulatory turf, the DNB then decided to detach itself entirely from overseeing the actual accounting decisions of Dutch banks (Interview, bank accounting manager, December 6, 2011; Interview, Dutch auditing association, July 6, 2011). While the DNB did have an accounting team, its task was not the auditing itself, but the translation of financial accounting numbers into core capital requirements and the definition of core capital (Interview, DNB, September 9, 2011). This led to a situation where, while largely relying on such information, the DNB had no control over accounting decisions. As a regulatory advisor recalls,

The Dutch central bank did not have any accounting supervision role. They are only responsible for the ratio coverage *which are by the way built on accounting*. The Dutch AFM,[9] they started their accounting supervision three years ago, so at that time, there was nobody else than your auditor who was judging if you applied the rules correctly or not." (Interview, regulatory advisor, October 6, 2011)

---

[7] In recent years, this trend is reversing, with the DNB asking auditors to come in to explain recent market developments (Interview, regulatory advisor, October 6, 2011).
[8] Any expansion of these duties meets fierce resistance by the auditors, as it is unpaid work (Interview, NIVRA, July 6, 2011).
[9] Autoriteit for Financiel Markets, the SEC of the Netherlands.

The Regulatory Dialectic

In the mid-1990s, the DNB developed regulations for securitization transactions in close dialogue with Dutch banks, first on a case-specific basis (DNB, 1997; Interview, bank manager, April 8, 2015) and, then, from 1997 onward, based on a memorandum stating the supervisory aspirations of the DNB with respect to securitization (DNB 1997). In its assessment of the ABCP market, the DNB used two primary information sources: regulatory developments in the Anglo-Saxon context that increasingly relied on the internal risk assessment of banks (Jones 2000) and the banks themselves. While the DNB aimed to ensure the international competitiveness of its banks and perceived securitization as an important area in this respect, it sought to keep abreast of developments in this field as well. As a result, the DNB was generally supportive of bank engagement in the ABCP market (Interview, bank manager, December 6, 2011) and used the interactions with its banks as a "practical class" in securitization, seeking to understand better the developments based on industry experience (email, bank manager, March 16, 2015, March 25, 2015; Interview, bank manager April 8, 2015). The securitization framework in 1997, which essentially formalized the practices developed in these dialogues (email, bank manager, March 23, 2015), shows that the DNB was aware of many of the advantages and risks of securitization and aimed to provide clarity to the banking industry on how it would assess securitization transactions.

One important element of the 1997 securitization framework was that banks had to approach the DNB directly for every conduit that they set up and had to inform the DNB of every securitization transaction on a quarterly basis. The dialogue between banks and the DNB essentially followed a two-step process: first, banks would come with a general overview of the ABCP conduit to be set up; next, after an informal agreement from the DNB, banks would work out the details and come back with a new, more detailed proposal. The DNB would use this proposal to determine the core capital charge of the conduits and could pose additional questions. The process of these discussions was described by bank managers as very constructive and "content-driven," based on new mathematical models that the banks had developed in the late 1990s to argue successfully for core capital reductions of securitized assets that the models showed to be less risky (Interview, bank manager, May 13, 2015). Although these discussions included requests by the DNB that banks adjust conduit structures, banks and their regulatory advisors always had a "knowledge edge" that guided the discussion and exchange (email, bank manager, March 16, 2015). Unlike the German situation, the DNB's decisions about core capital treatment of ABCP conduits relied almost exclusively on information coming from the banks and ignored the accounting treatment of the conduits, with no information or individual assessment by third parties such as auditors.

A good example of these regulatory dialogues was the prudential treatment of liquidity lines of less than one year. In the late 1990s, it was forming its opinion and decision making through conversations with bankers, corporate lawyers, and other regulators, most notably the Financial Service Authority in the UK and the Federal Reserve Bank in the US (Interview, banking manager, Amsterdam, December 6, 2011). In these conversations with corporate lawyers and "financial whizz kids" (Interview, banking manager, Amsterdam, December 6, 2011), the DNB accepted the industry proposition that the liquidity lines for ABCP conduits posed no risk to the banks and agreed to maintain a 0 percent core capital charge on such liquidity lines, a fact which even surprised domestic banking managers (Interview, banking manager, Amsterdam, December 6, 2011). The DNB's decision to accept the industry views that these conduits were only "pipes through which money was flowing" without any risks to the bank was further influenced by discussions with the British FSA and their views on securitization (Interview, bank manager, December 6, 2011).

Because the decisions regarding core capital requirements were disconnected from conduits' accounting treatment, the achievement of off-balance-sheet status in the financial accounts was not the predominant goal of large Dutch banks, so auditors were largely uninvolved in the design of ABCP conduits (Interview, bank manager, December 6, 2011; PwC 2006). The lacking importance of auditors for the DNB in producing data about ABCP conduits was also reflected in the minimal effect the convergence of Dutch accounting rules with SIC 12 had on Dutch banks. When the Dutch accounting standard setter decided to translate the SIC 12 norms and to include them into the Guidelines for Annual Reporting of the Dutch Accounting Standards, reactions were mixed. Some banks simply consolidated these conduits in their annual reports, while others contested the new rule or engaged in restructuring negotiations with their auditors (Interview, regulatory advisor, October 6, 2011). This mixed reaction can be explained by the fact that accounting decisions did not make a difference to core capital charges, as the DNB chose to ignore the accounting information and continued to rely on its own securitization framework, which granted a de facto off-balance-sheet status to securitization transactions if a substantial risk transfer regarding the transferred assets occurred (Interview, DNB, October 5, 2011). This disconnect of core capital treatment from accounting numbers continued when IFRS and SIC 12 were officially implemented in 2005 (DNB 2005) because the DNB accepted the banks' view that all elements of risk had already been included in the direct negotiations (email, bank manager, November 30, 2015).

As the DNB was not involved in accounting standard setting, it was also unaware that the intent of SIC 12 was to push ABCP conduits back on balance sheet when banks were exposed to the majority of the rewards – not just the risks. Discussions between the banks and the DNB focused exclusively on the risks as identified by the DNB and had looked at them through a banking lens of risk management techniques and assessment. The DNB was lacking independent information and, thus, the capacity to challenge their presentations. Regulatory dialogues with auditing experts or the standard setter over problems related to the accounting for ABCP conduits might have further clarified for them the use of these vehicles as a technique of regulatory circumvention. Owing to a lack of critical voices and alternative narratives in their dialogues, the DNB suffered from "cognitive closure," shaped by hegemonic views of finance in the USA and the UK (Aalbers et al. 2011, p. 1790): it considered this banking activity only from the banks' viewpoint and abstained from questioning banks' business models (IMF 2011, p. 59f). The lenient regulation furthered the development of Dutch banking groups as large sponsors of ABCP-conduits[10] and implied that the DNB was not interested in a careful application of an SIC 12–like rule once introduced. This specific position by the Dutch Banking regulator on ABCP conduits was in line with the very supportive stance toward securitization in general, as its

---

[10] ABN Amro, the largest banking conglomerate in the Netherlands, was the largest sponsor of ABCP conduits and provider of liquidity facilities globally in 2007 (see Fitch 2007).

capacity to enhance the credit supply enormously on the one hand and to provide securities of high quality to pension funds and investors on the other hand was seen in a positive light (Interview, banking manager, December 6, 2011).

In contrast to the cognitive capture that occurred on the basis of these regulatory dialogues that included only banking regulators and the banks and further facilitated by concerns over the fate of domestic champions (see Chapter 5), we can see in the French case that such capture can be avoided once the regulator is entertaining relationships to both the internal compliance officers as well as external auditors. Furthermore, we find in the French case the most significant example of regulatory collaboration to intervene in compliance practices on the ground. Within this regulatory network, the French banking regulator was a driving force behind efforts to sharpen the delimitation of the borders of their banking conglomerates. Close collaboration between the two regulatory agencies (the banking regulator Commission Bancaire [CB] and the financial market regulator, until 2003 Commission des Operations de Bourse, afterwards Autorite des Marches Financiers) and the auditing networks (the technical departments in particular) lay the institutional foundation for a further tightening of these criteria.

France: Embedded Regulators

The Regulatory Network

The central player in the French regulatory network during this period was the Commission Bancaire (CB).[11] A part of the Banque de France (French Central Bank), it became independent from the French Ministry for the Economy and Finance in 1993 after a scandal at Credit Lyonnais bank revealed the dangers of political interference in banking regulation (Jean-Pierre 1997; Coleman 2001). The CB was endowed with large regulatory discretion and was involved in both off-site and on-site banking supervision, the latter shared with auditors. In contrast to the Netherlands, however, it also enjoyed a large role in accounting supervision and the process of accounting

---

[11] Today, it is merged with the insurance supervisor and called the Autorite de control prudentiel et de resolution.

standard setting, as it had significant representation in the French Accounting Standard Authority (CNC) along with members of the auditors' association. The CB employed a department of accounting experts that supervised the accounting decisions of French banks and their auditors. It had extensive legal rights with respect to auditors and the accounting decisions of banks so as to provide a complementary guarantee of the independence of the auditors of banks (Commission Bancaire 2002, p. 12). The CB also had its own mandate to take disciplinary action against infringements or violations by the auditors.

The regulatory discretion of the CB, which went hand-in-hand with a strong presence inside the banks (on-site supervision) and a continuous dialogue with the external bank auditors and bank accountants (off-site supervision), fostered a deep understanding of the economic substance of business transactions and the way they were accounted for, as well as a dialogue between different regulators and banks as to how to deal with them. While the CB's off-site supervision consisted of collecting and examining the accounting and prudential documents sent by banks as well as auditors, it also conducted generic or specific on-site qualitative inspections in order to ascertain that the information disclosed by each of these institutions reflected the actual situation of the banks.

In the case of financial innovations, on-site supervision would typically identify potential issues and report them internally to both the bank and the CB. Every six weeks, on-site and off-site supervisors would meet, share information, and debate ongoing developments (Interview, French banking regulator, January 21, 2011). The typical career of a CB employee included both off-site and on-site functions, creating a "revolving door" of practical expertise inside the CB (Interview, French banking regulator, February 3, 2011).[12]

A number of incentives also ensured that the auditors would proactively inform the CB about novel rule interpretations. First, auditors were not obliged to maintain professional secrecy with

---

[12] Some inspectors of the on-site division are transferred after some time into the off-site division, bringing with them their knowledge about the structuring activities of the banks. For example, the career of a director of the accounting division started by two years on-site supervision in Paris, followed by one year on-site supervision in New York, before joining the accounting division (Interview, accounting division of the banking regulator, Paris, February 3, 2011).

respect to the CB and, in fact, were bound to inform the CB of any doubts about the business activities of banks. Second, the French banking regulator had extensive powers to contest and to revoke accounting decisions if it deemed them to violate the spirit of the law. In 1996, the CB was given the authority to hold auditors accountable for signing off on dubious accounting decisions; in June 1999, the CB was empowered to request a change of auditor if that auditor's independence was deemed questionable, and to reject the financial statement of a bank as inaccurate. As a result of these legal powers, which have been put to frequent use by the CB (World Bank Database 2008), banks and auditors frequently discuss and negotiate with each other and the CB concerning accounting decisions.

The Regulatory Dialectic

As early as 1988, the French state set up a comprehensive regulatory framework for securitization (Matherat and Troussard 2000, p. 26),[13] part of the comprehensive reforms by the French administration to foster financial innovation (O'Sullivan 2007; Hardie and Howarth 2013b). Although the framework established clear rules for securitization, it did not restrict the CB's capacity to apply its own discretion and judgment to each case. As the CB put it,

> The general secretary of the Commission Bancaire reserves itself the possibility, as in all matters of core capital requirements, to adapt prudential treatment if a securitization operation presents characteristics which would make such a treatment inappropriate or of a nature which would lead to a mistake in terms of the objectives of prudential supervision. (Commission Bancaire 2002, p. 12)

Given this regulatory discretion and vigilance, it became important for banks to approach the French regulator with new conduit structures early on in order to avoid being hit by core capital charges (Interview, banking regulator, April 19, 2011). As the supervisor said,

> The banks show us, I mean, not all montages. If it is a simple one and it has been approved before, they don't. But, if it is something new, they better do,

---

[13] The framework was revised in 1993, 1996, and 1998.

to their own "peril" if they don't. If they do a complex montage and they haven't shown it and the inspection considers it to be complex, they can ask for a readjustment for the exigencies of capital requirements for the montage *a posteriori*; they requalify the charges, which can be quite problematique for the banks. (Interview, banking regulators, April 19, 2011)

During these institutionalized conversations in the early 1990s between banks, the CB, and bank auditors, the CB became increasingly concerned with the core capital treatment of ABCP conduits because auditors had approached the CB about the dubious off-balance-sheet treatment of securitization SPEs (Interview, CB February 3, 2011). This, combined with its own observation of the structuring activities of banks to achieve off-balance-sheet status and the growing complexity of the contractual structures involved in ABCP conduits, drove the CB to take early action to reduce instances of rule evasion. After the introduction of the new accounting rule in 1999, which was initiated and pushed by the CB, the latter maintained an ongoing dialogue with the banks and auditors about its effects.

Once its interpretation had been made more stringent by a joint recommendation of the banking and securities regulator in France in November 2002, the impact of the French rule 99-07 for consolidation regarding banking conglomerates increased greatly. Both supervisors worried about off-balance-sheet risks after Enron (Interview, high official French financial market regulator, June 10, 2012). But, what exactly motivated this statement by the COB and the CB in 2002 that sharpened the interpretation of 99-07? Besides the startling failure of Enron in 2001 and the supervisory work done on ABCP conduits, it was the consequence of a two-year investigation into the use of SPEs of French banks to hide their potential losses from the Latin American debt crisis in the 1980s during the 1990s. French banks outsourced these debts at depreciated values from their balance sheets into SPEs for which they guaranteed the financing, and they used the provisions that they had built up in order to cover the losses emanating from these credits to invest them into long-running papers, in this way evacuating all evident risk from their balance sheets (Interview, representative of the French Banking Federation, May 11, 2011).

The recommendation also reflected problems with the application of 99-07, particularly with respect to the application of the criteria of the risks and rewards as confirmed by an auditing partner in Paris in a technical department (Interview, auditor, March 22, 2011).In response to these problems, which were partially caused by the novelty of the risk-and-reward framework and to impose stricter rules on the conglomerates, the regulators sought further alignment with SIC 12, as it requested consolidation if either the majority of risks or the majority of rewards were detected with any single conglomerate. In the rule 99-07 itself, both criteria needed to be fulfilled at the same time. The way to achieve that was to impose a specific interpretation between the majority of risks and rewards based on a consequential reasoning. The two regulatory agencies argued that whoever bore the majority of risks also had to have the majority of rewards; otherwise, no professional financial actor would expose itself to these risks and vice versa, reemphasizing the need to apply a risk-and-reward approach.[14] As a partner at a large auditing firm in Paris explained:

"The banking regulator said, 'I am with professionals... I know that these professionals know how to manage their risks ... if they support the majority of risks, it is because they have the majority of advantages.'" (Interview, auditing partner and member of CNCC technical division Paris, March 22, 2011)

But, the new interpretation not only aimed at bringing about complete convergence between SIC 12 and the French rules. More than this, it sought to install a specifically prudent interpretation of SIC 12 itself. IFRS, as any principles-based Generally Accepted Accounting Principles (GAAP), is a rather malleable framework, shaped as much by those applying it as by those setting the standards. Officially, the interpretation is supposed to be shaped only by IFRIC, the standards interpretation committee of the International Accounting Standards Board (IASB), in order to maintain equivalent applications internationally, explicitly not by national regulators.[15] However, in these practices of applying SIC 12, a quite lenient interpretation developed. It had become commonplace for the large auditing networks to focus first and foremost on the residual risks, those which vary with the

---

[14] The French text can be found at www.amf-france.org/documents/general/4388_1.pdf

[15] In Germany, the refusal to seek to influence accounting decisions of auditing networks under IFRS was justified with the need for international equivalence (Interview, BaFin, July 1, 2011; Interview, IDW board member, May 3, 2011).

business success of the ABCP conduit, and to ignore the nonresidual risks and rewards and, here in particular, the fee income (Interview, auditor technical department, Düsseldorf, February 21, 2011).[16]

The recommendation of the two French regulators sought to counter these practices by laying the emphasis on the majority of advantages. This recommendation, then, did not only aim at French GAAP, but also at influencing the way that the international auditing networks in France would apply SIC 12, as the recommendation did not only bring about convergence, but it also sought convergence with a specific interpretation, as the member of the CNCC explained,

It was regarding French GAAP, but this recommendation made a reference to SIC 12, saying this is what is important, saying, *this is how we read SIC 12* ... So, especially an international network, which would read SIC 12 rather from the control perspective, this contradicted their views. (Interview, auditing partner, March 22, 2011, emphasis mine)

By imposing such a strict reading of 99-07, French banking regulation facilitated beneficial innovations regarding securitization while making its use for off-balance-sheet proprietary trading more difficult. Their capacity to detect these conduits as a means of regulatory circumvention stemmed from a good information exchange between on-site and off-site banking supervisors and their strong collaboration with the French authority for financial markets and the auditors' association.

These links are also one reason why the recommendation of 2002 did actually make a difference to the accounting behavior of banking conglomerates, although neither of these agencies has the legal right to specify certain interpretations, a power which resides with the

---

[16] This interpretation was supported by a *tentative* agreement of the IASB to exclude fee income from the considerations of the majority of advantages, as these are fixed in advance (see IASB 2002). While these tentative agreements are neither rules nor interpretations, but instead simple suggestions because the board did not reach a final agreement yet, such decisions are regularly quoted in the accounting guides of the Big Four auditing networks, thereby having impact on auditing practice (Interview, German auditors' association, April 14, 2011). This specific suggestion led to a large degree of deconsolidation, even if the sponsor gained the majority of advantages from the SPE through fees. This disregard for fee income was confirmed for the German case in an interview with bank managers (Frankfurt am Main, July 12, 2011).

National Accounting Standards Setter. The reason for this expansion of regulatory clout resides in the legitimacy the recommendation obtained through the extensive consultation between the regulators and auditing networks. Every year, the financial market regulator AMF, the technical departments of the large auditing networks as well as a specific committee on technical questions at the Compagnie Nationale des Commissaires aux Comptes (CNCC) communicate intensively before the annual recommendation is issued in November, specifying areas where the AMF seeks improvement (Interview, manager French financial market regulator, April 12, 2011). It is a consultative style, which according to a member of the CNCC subcommittee is common to the French regulatory network (Interview, auditing partner, March 22, 2011).

In addition to the legitimacy gained by consultation, the two regulatory bodies have other means for exerting pressure on corporations to adhere to their interpretations of accounting standards as they have the capacity to punish those who do not adhere. Each time that a company wants to issue bonds in the French capital market, it needs approval by the AMF for the prospectus informing potential creditors. This approval might be refused or delayed if the accounting of the corporation is found not to be in accordance with the recommendations of the AMF. As corporations seek to avoid such delays, they conform to these recommendations.

Furthermore, the CB has been granted the right by law to challenge the accounting decisions of the accountants and the auditors of French banking conglomerates (Interview, banking regulator, February 3, 2011), thereby defining what is and what is not acceptable within the framework of the law (Interview, banking regulators, April 19, 2011.)[17] For the question of consolidation especially, the CB acted as a vigilante, as confirmed by the statements of an auditing partner of a large auditing network, who stated,

They were always very present. Absolutely, the auditors, we went to defend our position. Well, defend. We went with the opinion position on why we accepted, for example, the non-consolidation for the large conduits. Always,

---

[17] The banking regulator explained that the fantasy of bankers and advocates is unlimited with respect to structuring activities as this constitutes their source of income. In contrast, it is the task of the banking regulator to define what is acceptable within the framework of the law.

they were always very present ... We had to justify our position, and then, to make the calculus, they were always very present; they never let it go; they didn't do a control every day, but every time one asked the question about these vehicles, they were present. (Interview, auditing partner, March 22, 2011)

Given this presence, when the CB was issuing its point of view publicly, it signaled problems ahead for accountants and auditors if they failed to live up to the recommendation. While such legal action might fail, it strains the relationship between auditing networks, the banking conglomerate, and the banking regulator, and it is perceived as a stigma in the French auditing community. The status of such a recommendation is well explained by a former bank manager and representative of the French banking federation:

One has to know that the document took the form of a recommendation, which doesn't have the force of immediate application, only that the auditors, for them it is totally unthinkable to accept and sign a statement that does not respect a recommendation from the CNC, the AMF and the Commission Bancaire, ... one has to know that the banking regulator has the powers to refuse the statement of a bank. So, imagine a banking regulator publishing a communiqué which states that the statements of Bank X are false for this and that reason ... It is called recommendation, but it could as well be called regulation. (Interview, employee, French Banking Federation, May 11, 2011)

This binding force holds especially as auditors, banking conglomerates, and the regulators take part in repeated interactions in which the banking regulator will have the opportunity for retaliation, especially given that the French regulatory style is characterized by a large degree of discretion in the decision making, as evidenced by the approach to ABCP conduits, which does not force all ABCP conduits to consolidate but requires individual investigation.[18] These institutionalized conversations pushed back against blatant attempts of rule evasion by bankers, supported by the power of the CB as banking regulator, to reject the financial reporting statement

[18] In a public event at Sciences Po on January 25, 2011, a high official of the banking regulator likened the French style of banking regulation to a police officer who assigns different speed limits according to the driver's capability of driving, rather than having a single speed limit for all.

of a bank, an act feared for its reputational effects on banks and auditing teams alike. Furthermore, even if banks managed to achieve deconsolidation with their auditors, the banking regulator reserved the right to take a more precautionary stance on the prudential treatment of these conduits (Commission Bancaire 2003, p. 20). In practice, this meant that the CB verified the auditing decisions regarding conduits and could, at its discretion, either reverse the auditors' decision or treat the conduits prudentially as on balance sheet (Interview, banking regulator, February 3, 2011).

The interaction between these on-site and off-site inspections regarding the topic of ABCP conduits led to an early sensitization of the accounting division toward constructs of sponsoring banks which sought, with the help of ABCP conduits and other SPEs to gain capital relief. In 2001, dialogues between bankers and regulators about ABCP conduits took place on-site, where the bankers were asked to explain the purpose of their conduits and, to some of these inquiries, the bankers could not provide a satisfying answer (Interview, banking regulator, Paris, January 25, 2011). The concerns emanating from the on-site interrogations become the responsibility of the CB having to debate the phenomenon off-site in order to decide how to deal with it. These analyses were then introduced into the meeting between on- and off-site supervisors, which takes place all six weeks in Paris during which the two teams exchange their views on the new phenomena they encounter, and update each other on the newest developments.

In these debates, a decision was made to apply the credit conversion factor to liquidity lines of less than one year which were renewed on the day of expiry for the next year from 2002 onwards, as these were identified as instruments for regulatory circumvention (Interview, banking regulator, January 25, 2011; see also Commission Bancaire (CB) No. 27, 2002, where this rule was first announced). The regulator did not need to change the law in order to make this rule but merely needed to publish it in an annual communication that specified the modalities of core capital charge rules and specified that a renewed liquidity line was to carry a 20 percent credit conversion (CB 2003, p. 20). The accounting rule recommendations from the COB and the CB, in tandem with the changed rules for liquidity lines, forced banks to restructure their contractual relations with ABCP conduits grossly, initially leading to a substantial reduction in their margins (Interview, bank group accounting manager, March 25, 2011) and consequently to a discontinuation of issuance of ABCP by all single-seller, hybrid, and securities arbitrage programs in 2006 (Figure 2.12 in Chapter 2). Most importantly, however, regulatory action was never directed against the ABCP market itself, which was perceived as legitimate. Instead, in accordance with its administrative mandate, the regulator only wanted banks to "account for the risks" that they were taking in this market (Interview, French banking regulator, February 3, 2011). This focus clearly revealed itself when it was challenged in 2004 by a coalition of firms, banks, and the finance ministry, which used special procedures in the CNC to install an accounting rule that guaranteed off-balance-sheet status for multiseller conduits (Opinion No. 2004-D of the Emergency Committee of the National Accounting Board, CNC 2004). Motivated by international competitiveness concerns (CNC 2004, p. 2), this exemption contradicted the goals of the CB, which opposed it during the negotiation phase (Interview, French bank manager and accounting standard setter, March 25, 2011; Interview, French banking regulator, February 3, 2011; Interview, former French banking regulator, January 30, 2011). Following defeat on this front, in November 2005, the French banking regulator chose officially to disconnect its prudential treatment of ABCP conduits from its accounting treatment, insisting on a strict core capital regime for such conduits (Amis and Rospars 2005, p. 57f).

By decoupling their treatment of these SPEs from the accounting decisions, the CB gained back the space for discretion to impose prudence which they had lost in the prior political battle in the CNC. Instead of being bound by the accounting decision, they could apply capital charges if they estimated that no significant risk transfer had taken place. These changes did not mean a weakening but, rather, a strengthening of economic oversight, as banking regulators could still require the consolidation of an SPE in terms of core capital requirements (email, French regulator, June 4, 2012; PwC 2006). Conversely, if no consolidation had occurred it could still request core capital for the assets inside of the SPE if it deemed them to be substantially part of the conglomerate. This move then continued a tradition at the CB, as a former banking regulator explained:

What you said about Germany, that when it was deconsolidated in accounting terms, it was deconsolidated in prudential terms, I am not so sure that it was so automatic because we were often beating ourselves with the banks for SPEs because they did not like that we did not simply translate one into the other, the prudential did not follow the accounting. It was not automatic. (Interview, former banking regulator, January 30, 2011)

The Social Structure of Regulatory Supervision and the Prevention of Rule Evasion

These findings show that the respective supervisor's ability to control rule evasion in the ABCP market arose in part in the different relational configurations among the actors in the regulatory network. More specifically, the regulatory dialectic was influenced by the supervisor's positioning in the "interpretive community" (Black 2008; Ford 2010), i.e., the regulatory network where actors engage in conversations to interpret the meaning of regulation and compliance. As ABCP-related regulatory costs were determined by both accounting and banking regulation, when supervisors were embedded in the interpretive communities of both these regulatory spheres, they were more aware of rule-bending behavior and therefore better equipped to reregulate. Figure 7.1 provides a schematic overview of the differences in the regulatory network and interpretive communities in France, Germany, and the Netherlands.

In Germany, BaFin was a peripheral actor in the regulatory network and completely disembedded from the interpretive community; therefore, it lacked an awareness of specific rule-bending practices that could have triggered regulatory steps to control them. Its actions were furthermore inhibited by the Ministry of Finance's regulatory capture by bankers' interest. By contrast, in the Netherlands, the DNB was central and firmly embedded in the interpretive community for banking regulation yet was disembedded from the interpretive community for accounting regulations. The data used to assess and to debate rule compliance was produced entirely in the DNB–bank dyad, cut off from accounting discussions about how best to assess the risk exposure of ABCP conduits. Finally, in France, the CB was not only central and embedded in the interpretive communities for both accounting and banking regulation but also made sure that there was a well-organized flow of information among the CB employees involved with the respective interpretive communities.

This dense interaction between the auditors, the banks, and the regulators, which is particularly characteristic for the French system,

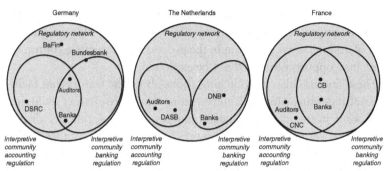

Figure 7.1 The regulatory networks governing ABCP conduits in Germany, the Netherlands, and France.

was favored by the geographic distribution of the regulatory agencies, auditing networks, and banking conglomerates, which are all situated in Paris. This is an important factor, as it permits the repeated face-to-face interactions that can create interpretive communities. In the Netherlands, regulators and banking conglomerates are also situated in the capital, and the number of relevant conglomerates is even smaller. Only the large auditing networks seem to be more geographically distributed (Besides Amsterdam, Rotterdam seems to be a center for auditing networks.). However, given the relatively small size of the Netherlands, this should not really inhibit the possibility of meetings. Instead it is the legislation for the Dutch SEC and the exclusion of the DNB from the accounting standard setting, which explicitly hinders this cooperation.

In Germany, though, the geographical distribution of regulatory actors, auditing networks as well as banking conglomerates, poses a severe problem for frequent personal interaction. While the German standard setter is situated in Berlin, the German banking regulator is situated in Bonn. The German auditing association is situated in Düsseldorf, but the German securities regulator is situated in Frankfurt. The headquarters of most private banking conglomerates are also situated in Frankfurt, whereas the large Landesbanken have their headquarters in the capitals of the different Länder. The agencies responsible for on-site supervision are situated in the different capitals, yet the off-site supervision is distributed between the Bundesbank in Frankfurt and the BaFin in Bonn. This physical distribution inhibits personal contact and might, at least in the past, have been a reason for the lack of interaction. With modern information technology, the physical distribution should increasingly lose its impact. However, if the lack of an interactive tradition in the process of compliance continues, these new opportunities will not be exploited.

These findings also provide indications about the factors that facilitate or hinder the regulator's embeddedness in the regulatory dialogues that occur in the interpretive communities, namely regulatory discretion, expertise, and sanctioning power (Thiemann and Lepoutre 2017). Embeddedness emerges when the regulator has the *sanctioning power and regulatory discretion* to interpret and to sanction, which was the case when regulators could rely more on principles-based, rather than rules-based, regulation. In addition, embeddedness in an interpretive community was more likely when the regulator had the *technical capabilities and expertise* to engage in and to contribute to the rule interpretation. For example, the German BaFin and Bundesbank were limited by legal and cultural norms to adhere to narrow rule-based interpretation of the law and were hindered by their limited resources, accounting capabilities, and expertise. Conversely, in the Netherlands and France, bank supervision was centralized in the DNB and CB respectively, both of which used their significant regulatory discretion and power to force banks into a dialogue about ABCP conduits. However, since the DNB has no regulatory or staffing capacity in the accounting realm, it effectively disembedded itself from the accounting interpretive community. The French banking regulator, by contrast, relied heavily on a diversity of inputs from a variety of sources, based on the incentives for local gatekeepers and banks to provide data about new financial innovations. The capacity of the CB to interpret and to sanction bank behavior, as well as its legal mandate to challenge auditor decisions, made it in the auditors' interest preemptively to seek dialogue with regulatory authorities. The legal capacities and expertise of the French banking regulator as well as the obligation of auditor and audited to justify their decisions allowed the regulator to be central in both spheres of the interpretive community and to be deeply involved in regulatory conversations.

In sum, legal discretion, sanctioning power, and technical expertise influenced how regulators were structurally embedded in the regulatory network determining the appropriate interpretation of accounting standards for ABCP conduits and core capital charges for liquidity lines. These aspects secured or prevented regulators' timely representation and participation in negotiations. Unlike the German and Dutch examples, the French regulator appears to have avoided cognitive capture that occurred in the Netherlands. Being embedded in two interpretive communities allowed the CB to avoid the one-sided view presented by financial engineers, to go backstage in the regulatory drama that "regulatory action at a distance" entails (Vollmer 2007), and to maintain skepticism of the final numbers provided by the regulated (Porter 1995) as well as the product itself. Critical debates with bankers and with auditors regarding the criteria for the off-balance-sheet decision for these conduits could buffer the regulators from claims of financial engineers which declared that these conduits were risks free as the debate over who bears the majority of risk and rewards, embedded in SIC 12, sensitizes the regulator to the final distribution of risk from these constructs. The logic of this debate is well summarized by a regulatory advisor reflecting upon ABCP conduits:

And, it is also a very simple truth: risks cannot disappear. And, you will always find a financial engineer that claims that afterwards there is no more risk; and that cannot work, not according to commercial law, neither to supervisory law. That means if it leaves from one, it has to arrive at the other, and if it does not arrive at the other, it has not left the first one. And, then, he has to back it up with equity. (Interview, German regulatory advisor, June 14, 2011, translation by the author)

The comparison further shows that in order to ensure that the risks to which banking conglomerates are exposed are represented more prudently and that they are not "spirited away" by financial engineers requires not only a change of rules, but also the enforcement of their prudent interpretation. Good rules are only a necessity but not a sufficient condition to deal with the problematic, as the case of the Netherlands shows. Equipped with the knowledge gained from these regulatory dialogues and legal discretion, the French regulators could maintain interpretive control and could close regulatory loopholes before the practices became so widespread that the political opposition to change became insurmountable.

Conclusions

The delegation of the implementation of rules to the regulated themselves represents a new form of regulation, one that emphasizes the "multitude of actors which constitute a regulatory regime in a particular domain" (Black 2008, p. 8). This hybridization of regulation is, on the one hand, drawing in external expertise but, on the other hand, requires many regulatory conversations between the regulator and the regulated as to the meaning of the principles (Black 2008, p. 9). This need for both mutual exchange (regulatory conversations) and the drawing in of external expertise requires the existence of regulatory networks, which include all actors engaged in the compliance exercise, and their linkage to the financial and banking regulator in order for tacit knowledge to flow from practitioners to regulators and to transmit interpretations from regulators to practitioners.

Holding finance accountable as a process means to hold bankers and the local compliance officers (e.g., auditors) to account for their compliance actions in front of the regulator, to have them explain how what they are doing is compliant with the rules. If these two agents cannot do so, regulatory circumvention is detected. For such dialogues, a principles- rather than a rules-based approach is advantageous, for in a rules-based approach, it is much more difficult to have an inquiry-based conversation of that kind, as it is replaced by a check-list approach. In the realm of compliance in general and accounting in particular, these dialogues need to be backed by the legal capacities of the banking regulator to doubt compliance decisions. This increases the incentive for bankers to interact with the regulator beforehand and to verify that the structures they have developed are indeed compliant. Lawyers and regulatory advisors of corporations favor a legal form approach, so that their structuring activity becomes easier and more certain. In order to be able to enforce regulation in the spirit of the law, rather than the letter, regulators can and should deny that. Local compliance officers (such as auditors) which operate on a principles-based approach are much easier to influence by a regulatory voice, in particular if the latter is backed up by sanctioning power. In this respect, the powers of the regulator to blame and to shame auditors are important, but effective regulation requires more. It requires the capacity to harm corporations for imprudent accounting practices, as resides, for example, in the capacity of French banking regulators to issue rectifications to banks' financial statements. Given this latitude, a quarrel with the supervisor becomes a serious threat to the corporation and the regulator can through this channel impose his views.

In such a regulatory regime, auditors are paid by the company to keep the books not only to save money on taxes and to optimize the representation of the conglomerate in financial markets, but also in order to avoid trouble with authorities. For banking regulation, this impetus toward regulatory dialogues raises the question of costs of regulation and the capacity of regulators to supervise a large amount of institutions. To these concerns, there are two answers: first, regulatory circumvention can cause large-scale negative social externalities, and, from this perspective, close supervision is worth the costs. Second, it is not necessary to supervise all financial institutions as intensely, as the social externalities caused by failure increase by size. These cost-reduction measures can also include the co-optation of the technical departments of auditing networks, as shown in the case of France.

Good regulation is the outcome of intensive regulatory dialogues that permits tight control by the regulator over a quickly innovating sector. The differential development of the ABCP market segment in different countries, based on regulatory arbitrage, is, I argue, a consequence of the variation of these dialogues, which went on for years. The qualitative difference of these dialogues was suddenly revealed by the crisis. This view was also expressed by a manager of the French Financial Regulator AMF, noting the difficulty of justifying the costs of regulation in normal times:

And, the problem with the good control is that it shows itself at a specific moment. It does not show itself today. It shows itself in ten years. It shows after something has not happened in your place, but somewhere else, which takes time. (Interview, French Financial Market Regulator, April 19, 2011)

The fact that French banks saw their space of maneuver in the off-balance-sheet realm massively constrained by the banking regulator is a very important reason why the impact of the ABCP market on French banks was so small, why "something has not happened in your place, but somewhere else."

8 | The Fate of the Bank-Based Shadow Banking System Postcrisis

What happened to the ABCP market postcrisis? How were its main features, the regulatory exemptions as well as opportunities for regulatory arbitrage, affected by the liquidity crunch and the ensuing reregulation? And, what happened to the money market mutual funds (MMMF) industry, which due to its specific regulatory constraints fueled the demand for it? Inquiring into the fate of the ABCP market and its regulation from the liquidity crisis of 2007 onward as well as the regulation of the MMMF industry that underlay its growth, the chapter shows how, despite the shifts in the regulatory outlook on financial markets, the problems that beset the regulation of shadow banking precrisis continue postcrisis.

The Liquidity Crises of 2007–2008 and Government Back Stops in the United States and EU

Once the money market refinancing collapsed in summer 2007, a crisis dynamic was set-off with the ABCP market at the center of the storm. As investors distrusted the underlying asset-backed securities warehoused in ABCP conduits, they refused to buy ABCPs. In the summer of 2007, the ABCP market collapsed, falling by $411 billion from June 30, 2007 to June 2008 (Nersisyan 2015, p. 11). To stem the outflows, the biggest players in the market sought to put together private initiatives that would salvage the imploding structured investment vehicle (SIV) segment of the market. Trying to stem the decline of ABCP financing for these conduits, JP Morgan, Citibank, and Bank of America, the three banks most engaged in the market, announced on the October 15, 2007 plans to create a "Master Liquidity Enhancement Conduit (MLEC) designed to be a 400 billion dollar entity. The construct never got off the ground, as industry events were unfolding faster than the new conduit structure could be developed" (Interview, Wall Street lawyer, March 23, 2016).

Instead, individual sponsors decided to take the assets of SIVs on their balance sheets in order to avoid reputational damage, as investors would have been forced to take losses and might refuse to engage in business with those banks again. Similar incidents occurred for all kinds of other conduits, in particular securities arbitrage conduits and hybrid conduits whose volume fell by more than 60 percent in the first year of the crisis (Moody's 2010). As a group of regulators and supervisors in spring 2008 put it,

> In other cases, firms under no contractual obligations still provided voluntary support to these and other off-balance-sheet financing vehicles, including structured investment vehicles (SIVs), because of concerns about the potential damage to their reputations and to their future ability to sell investments in such vehicles if they failed to provide support during the period of market distress. (SSG 2008, p. 2)

As a Wall Street lawyer involved in the setup of conduits pointed out, banks decided to preserve their reputation in order to maintain business contacts (Interview, March 23, 2016).

These actions revealed the implicit support banks had granted to these vehicles ex ante. It also pointed to the mutual interdependence of large banks and capital market actors. Capital market actors depended on banks to guarantee the safety of short-term private assets and, in return, capital market actors supplied liquidity to both the off-balance-sheet conduits and the banks themselves. This mutual dependency becomes even more intricate once we focus on the triadic link between banks, ABCP conduits, and those MMMFs that bought many of these ABCPs. Banks did not only step in to buy ABCP in order to prevent losses for MMMFs; they also directly supported those MMMFs, which they had sponsored, when they were at risk of imposing losses on investors (Baba et al. 2009; McCabe 2010, p. 29; Moody's 2010).[1] This problem would motivate and animate regulatory action over the course of the next eight years.

But, before any regulatory action was taken on these issues, the crisis first grew more acute, peaking on September 15, 2008 with the

---

[1] McCabe (2010, p. 31) records thirty-nine instances of sponsor support during the ABCP crisis, with bank sponsors being "over-represented among support providers." It is peculiar to see that those MMMFs sponsored by banks had a disproportionate amount of distressed ABCPs in their portfolios.

bankruptcy of Lehman Brothers and the 'breaking of the buck'[2] of the Prime Reserve Fund on September 16, 2008. As the latter had heavily invested into short-term debt of the former, it had to report losses that made it impossible to guarantee the constant net asset value (CNAV) of funds. CNAV funds guarantee the equivalence in value of MMMF shares investors hold to the money they paid in. This allows investors to treat them like a bank deposit account with a small interest rate, facilitating cash management (ICI 2009, p. 2). This "breaking of the buck" led to massive redemption requests from that fund and other MMFs, which severely disrupted the commercial paper market and other money markets, impairing the ability of issuers to roll over their short-term liabilities (Wermers 2010).

The panic and the run brought to the fore the issue of step-in risks as bank sponsors of MMMFs supported their MMMFs in the wake of the Prime Reserve Fund breaking the buck. The practice was so widespread, that on September 17, 2008, the SEC issued a press release clarifying that sponsoring banks were required to consolidate the supported money market funds (SEC press release 2008–205). In order not to increase the panic, the SEC approved short-term sponsor support, unless the sponsor assumed the majority of future risks and rewards.[3] Nevertheless, the redemption requests continued, reaching $300 billion from prime money market mutual funds in the next days (Kacperczyk and Schnabl 2012).

Two days later, on September 19, 2008, the US Department of the Treasury announced the Temporary Guarantee Program for Money Market Funds, which insured more than $2.4 trillion in shares of money market funds and the Asset-Backed Commercial Paper Money Market Mutual Fund Liquidity Facility (AMLF) in order to support the MMMF industry. On October 16, 2008, the Commercial Paper Funding facility was added, buying both normal commercial paper as well as ABCP (Adrian et al. 2010, p. 23).[4]

---

[2] The "breaking of the buck" refers to the guarantee of these MMMFs that investors can always retrieve at least $1 for $1 paid in. When this cannot be realized, an MMMF is said to be breaking the buck.
[3] Later investigations by Moody's reported that sixty-two money market funds required sponsor support during 2007–2008.
[4] In Germany, the government was forced to take similar actions, even if the MMMFs were not even registered in Germany (Wirtschaftswoche 2008).

Just as in 1970, the Fed and other central banks backstopped the commercial paper market so as to support the MMMF industry. However, this time, intervention was not motivated by problems in the commercial paper market but mainly by the need for liquidity of MMMF themselves. MMMFs could sell their commercial papers to the Federal Reserve directly, or banks could obtain funding from the Federal Reserve in order to buy commercial papers from the MMMFs, thereby allowing MMMFs to redeem their investors (Adrian et al. 2010, p. 26f).

What the crisis clarified to anyone willing to look was the symbiotic relationship between banks and the shadow banking system, where the latter depends on the implicit support of the former. This fact holds true regarding not only the ABCP market but also MMMF's (Claessens and Ratnovski 2014). This is the fundamental lesson of these liquidity events. Credit intermediation by nonbanks depends upon bank balance sheets for its stability. Thus, there is vital link to bank holding companies in terms of sponsorship for ABCP and MMMFs. The crisis of 2008 made the reregulation of MMMFs and the ABCP market seem inevitable, both because of the private sponsor support that had been granted by banks to the ABCP conduits and the MMMFs and because of the extension of the Fed discount window, hence the public safety net to these market segments (Murau 2015). The public, wary of bailing out banks and their off-balance-sheet activities, in particular in the USA (Nersisyan 2015), was demanding action.

The Regulation of the ABCP Market Postcrisis

When the regulatory machine sprang into action in 2009, it came as no surprise that some of the earliest regulatory interventions directly impacted the ABCP market, in terms of both accounting and banking regulation. On the one hand, in July 2009, the Basel Committee issued revisions to the Basel Accords, which made resecuritizations, including those in ABCP conduits less attractive by increasing core capital requirements for them. This made the provision of liquidity lines for securities arbitrage conduits and hybrids more expensive and, thus, further lowered the incentives to set up such entities.[5] However, this

---

[5] Basel II, in force from January 1, 2008, established a credit conversion factor for liquidity lines. Increasing core capital requirements for resecuritizations

regulatory measure only cemented a shift in the ABCP market that had occurred before, as investor appetite for resecuritization had already vanished (Interview, ABCP expert, Germany, July 20, 2016; Interview former S&P employee March 21, 2016).

At about the same time, the emergency meeting of heads of state at the G20 summit 2009 in London called on the Financial Accounting Standards Board (FASB) and the International Accounting Standards Board (IASB) to "achieve a single set of high quality accounting standards for ... off-balance sheet exposures" (G20 2009). In addition, the Fed was directly putting pressure on the FASB to issue such a standard (Interview, Federal Reserve regulator, March 27, 2012). As the FASB already had the issue of revisiting the consolidation standard on its agenda and given the public pressure, it complied expediently. The board issued two new accounting standards in June 2009, notably without a prior comment period. While FAS 166 was removing the Qualifying Special-Purpose Entity exemption, FAS 167 revised FIN(R) 46 that specified the off-balance-sheet treatment of ABCP conduits. By removing the quantitative test of Fin (R) 46,[6] it based the decision on qualitative regulatory judgments (Deloitte 2014, p. 18, quoting an FASB official). FAS 167 thus made achieving the off-balance-sheet status of ABCP conduits more difficult for banks, though not impossible (Mayer and Brown 2010). Commenting on the new US rules for consolidation, a manager of the Fed stated,

I am not sure we were thrilled with the outcome; as I said, we tend to be more risk focused, so we liked the IFRS standards that had a risk-and-reward overlay. We liked that approach, and we kind of hoped the FASB would do something similar. (Interview, Fed manager responsible for accounting, March 27, 2012)

However, in its results, the new rule moved closely enough to SIC 12 so that the Federal Reserve issued a press release, the same day these

---

meant that the refinancing of securitization through ABCP conduits also required higher core capital charges.

[6] The quantitative test was the foundation for the selling of expected loss notes (ELN) to outsiders, thereby also purportedly selling the majority of rewards. The new approach, basing itself on the concept of control and not on the concept of risks and rewards, requested a qualitative assessment of the relationship between the two.

rule changes were announced.[7] The Fed signaled that it was willing to endorse these rules and asked banks to calculate their new core capital requirements accordingly. Shortly thereafter, on September 15, the Fed put out a notice of proposed rule making, where it suggested eliminating the prudential filter installed in 2004. The Federal Reserve received many comment letters through the public comment process, largely arguing that removing the filter was not necessary for multiseller conduits due to the low historical loss rates that the industry had experienced. A Federal Reserve banking regulator involved in the process recalled,

We got a lot of comments from the American securitization forum and many bank-sponsors who basically said that they didn't agree. And, they have thoughtful responses; they weren't just being greedy. In fact, the American securitization forum suggested treating different conduits differently, suggesting that customer-driven conduits should receive a preferential treatment, where securities arbitrage and SIVs and other types, could be treated more harshly using an on-balance sheet approach. (Interview, May 27, 2012)

Nevertheless, in order to end regulatory arbitrage, the Federal Reserve decided to include all ABCP conduits, consolidated in financial accounting terms, in the calculation of core capital requirements and removed the prudential filter by January 21, 2010.[8] In addition, the rule provided the agencies with the authority "to require a banking organization to treat entities that are not consolidated under GAAP as if they were consolidated for risk-based capital purposes based on the risks the banking organization has with the structure" (PWC 2010, p. 1). The outcome of these regulatory interventions was that the regulatory advantages stemming from core capital relief completely vanished for US bank sponsors. Consequently, the ABCP market never regained its previous size and attractiveness for banks in the USA. Thus, the ABCP market today is merely a funding tool for treasurers in the USA, used only for diversification and largely unattractive due to higher costs (Interview, US bank manager, March 22, 2016; Interview, former Standard & Poor's employee, March 21, 2016; Interview, German ABCP expert, July 20, 2016).

---

[7] See www.federalreserve.gov/newsevents/press/bcreg/20090612a.htm.
[8] See www.federalreserve.gov/newsevents/press/bcreg/20100121a.htm.

In contrast, European regulation of the ABCP market would take a different route. First, despite having held up rather well, the IASB in 2011 replaced SIC 12 with IAS 10. In line with the FASB, the new accounting standard was moving from a risk-and-reward approach to a control approach, opening a bit more leeway for deconsolidation (BCBS 2015, p. 4). Nevertheless, according to industry reports, while consolidation is possible under specific circumstances, no large wave of deconsolidation followed. More important for the market's development is that no prudential consolidation has been required by regulators after the crisis. There is no necessary link in terms of consolidation between financial accounting and prudential requirements in Germany, France, or the Netherlands (Interview, German banker/lobbyist, July 20, 2016). In the case of Germany, this involved an act of active regulatory exemption from prudential consolidation issued in 2010 (Interview, German bankers, July 12, 2011), which, in 2018 still has not been removed. In France as well as in the Netherlands, the tradition of independent off-balance-sheet assessment with a significant risk transfer moment continues. The prudential filter recommended by the Committee for European Banking Supervisors in 2004 hence remained in force in those jurisdictions. In a sense, this is just the continuation of the precrisis trends where the multiseller business of ABCP conduits was actively encouraged in all these countries.

The only stricter regulations are those concerning resecuritization, introduced in January 2010. The Capital Requirements Directive III and the Liquidity Coverage Ratio (LCR) to be introduced in 2018[9] do disadvantage securities arbitrage and hybrid conduits and generally impose higher regulatory costs. But, other than that, regulatory agencies have actively sought to facilitate multiseller conduits. As core capital relief is still possible for banks that refinance corporate trade receivables and other credit through multisellers, this form of credit extension is profitable and favored over credit by some banks (Interview, bank manager engaged in ABCP market, July 20, 2016). To understand the rather lenient reregulation of multiseller conduits in the EU, one has to take into account the importance of the ABCP market for European small and medium-sized enterprises (SME). Just as before the crisis, the ABCP market is still the easiest way for them

---

[9] The LCR requires bank sponsors to take liquidity lines to 100 percent into account for liquidity management.

to gain capital market access (IMMFA 2013; Interview, regulatory advisor, Germany, June 14, 2011; Interview, German expert ABCP market, July 20, 2016).

Especially in the case of Germany, these companies are often family owned, hence, not subject to IFRS accounting standards and the transparency they require. These companies prefer accessing the capital markets in this way, avoiding burdensome disclosure standards (Interview, banking manager, July 20, 2016). This link to the financing of SMEs and trade receivables, further reinforced through the refinancing of leasing contracts (Cerveny et al. 2010), becomes particularly important in the context of the EU banking crises, which, because of severely damaged balance sheets of banks, led to a credit crunch in EU peripheral countries. In this context, further cracking down on the ABCP market was neither in the interest of regulators nor politicians.

As a consequence of this rather lenient regulatory intervention, the multiseller ABCP market in Europe, which is described as highly competitive, has slowly rebounded after its low in 2008, currently operating at about 200 billion euro (EBA 2014, p. 14). This small growth is supported by an increasing demand from cash-rich corporations which invest in the ABCP market in order to generate profits in times of a low-interest-rate environment (Interview, ABCP market expert, July 20, 2016). Yet, there is no accelerating growth, which is why recent policy initiatives in the EU seek to revive the market. As part of the Capital Markets Union, a flagship project started by the European Commission in 2014, European legislative bodies are currently proposing new standards to lower the capital requirements for the ABCP market. However, owing to the high complexity of the proposed standards and the risks inherent in classifying certain ABCPs issued by multisellers as noncompliant, this initiative may hamper rather than help the growth of the market (Interview, ABCP market expert Germany, July 20, 2016).

Overall, being subject to harsher regulatory measures than before the crisis, the ABCP market today has become the backwater it once was in the early 1990s. Nevertheless, while this shrinkage of the ABCP market might be taken as a sign of a crackdown on shadow banking postcrisis, such an impression would be rather mistaken (Murau 2015). As a shadow banking expert put it during a phone conversation in 2011, the regulatory intervention regarding the ABCP market can be compared to an operation in which we have cut off the part of the body that had cancer but have not removed the conditions that led to the cancer. In his view, the demand for private, safe, short-term assets outside of banks, stemming from institutional cash pools, is the foundation of shadow banking, and this demand has not abated (see also Pozsar 2011). This view can be corroborated when we highlight the larger structural changes surrounding the ABCP market, most importantly the regulation of MMMFs, both in the USA and the EU.

The Timid Reregulation of Mutual Funds and the Unabated Demand for Safe Short-Term Assets

After the run on the MMMFs in fall 2008, reforms of this sector seemed inevitable, just as it did for the ABCP market in the fall of 2007. However, in contrast to the battered ABCP market, which in 2009 represented only $600 billion, the global MMMF industry in January 2009 was about $4 trillion (ICI 2009, p. 24). Hence, they played a fundamental role regarding the liquidity of key US financial markets, which made a similar crackdown unlikely. MMMFs are crucial providers of funding for the commercial paper market, the repo market but also municipal debt markets (Deutsche Bank Research 2015, p. 16).[10] Additionally, the interests of the MMMF industry were deeply entrenched within the SEC. These factors did have a strong impact on USA, EU, and global reform efforts.

In June 2009, the SEC proposed a first round of reforms to boost the resilience of money market fund portfolios, based on industry input (Shapiro 2012). Adopting these proposals, the SEC revised Rule 2a-7 on January 27, 2010, seeking "to make money market funds more resilient and less likely to break a buck as a result of disruptions such as those that occurred in fall of 2008" (US Securities and Exchange Commission, 2010). The reforms were shortening maturities, raising credit quality standards for investment and imposing – for the first time – liquidity requirements for money market funds. In other

---

[10] In 2014, MMMFs held 34 percent of the commercial paper outstanding. MMMFs also have a 15 percent market share for the repo market. Furthermore, tax-exempt money market funds managed $253 billion in municipal bonds, which equaled 8 percent of all municipal bonds outstanding. According to 2012 figures, money market funds in addition held 29 percent of all certificates of deposit outstanding (Deutsche Bank Research 2015).

words, they were just more of the same regulatory "medicine" which was prescribed every time that the money market fund suffered runs (e.g., in 1991), namely to increase the safety and to shorten the maturities of the short-term assets which these funds hold. However, in addition to these reforms, the SEC pursued further structural reforms, requesting feedback on the need to introduce floating net asset values which would remove the promise of MMMFs to pay out at par. These reforms focused on the bank-deposit like status of MMMFs and the implicit sponsor support which characterized their existence,[11] thus getting to the heart of the problem. Debates over further regulation of MMMFs gained full force in 2010, when both the Fed as well as Moody's intervened, pointing to the problem of bank sponsor support.

First, in August 2010, Moody's published a research piece linking MMMF stability to bank sponsor support, which it recorded for more than sixty cases for the crisis and more than 200 cases since industry existence (Moody's 2010). As a consequence, Moody's hinted at the increased role that sponsors and their capacity for support will play in future ratings of Moody's. Hence, just as for ABCP conduits, the ratings of shares in MMMFs would depend on the rating of bank sponsors. In September 2010, Moody's went further in that direction when it issued a proposal to shift its rating methodology for MMMFs and officially included sponsor support as ranking criteria for MMMFs. Despite industry resistance (e.g., TSI 2010), this proposal became part of its official rating methodology in May 2011 (Moody's 2011).

Second, the Federal Reserve published a working paper in 2010 (McCabe 2010) that not only added further evidence of instances of bank sponsor support, but also linked the latter to systemic risk. The report states that bank sponsor support has been a good predictor of distress in the 2007–2008 turmoil, related to distressed ABCP (McCabe 2010, p. 3; see also Fein 2012). Regarding this practice, the report notes,

Historically, however, sponsors with the resources to support their funds have done so ... to preserve their broader reputations. In both instances

---

[11] Contradicting this critical stance, the SEC facilitated more sponsor support in March 2010 by allowing sponsors to purchase defaulted and other portfolio securities from the funds subject to certain conditions (Fein 2012, p. 16; the rule is 75 Fed. Reg. 10060, 10105 [March 4, 2010]).

in which MMFs did break the buck, the sponsor simply lacked the where-withal to absorb the fund's losses (Eaton, 1994; U.S. Securities and Exchange Commission, 2009b) and its reputation as an investment adviser was destroyed. *Hence, sponsors have gone to such lengths to prevent passing capital losses along to MMF shareholders, and sponsor support has come to be seen as a form of "private insurance."* (McCabe 2010, p. 18, emphasis mine)

Thus, the paper points out that MMMFs are characterized by the same degree of collusion and implicit support that characterized the ABCP market. The report itself does not directly draw the conclusion that sponsor support should be prohibited, but it does raise the issue prominently. The Federal Reserve would follow up on this problematic in the President's Working Group (PWG), which for the first time in 2010 brought together the US Treasury, the Federal Reserve, the Commodities Future Trading Commission, as well as the SEC to discuss issues of financial stability. In effect, it was functioning as the forerunner of the Financial Stability Oversight Council (FSOC), which was installed by the Dodd–Frank Act that same year.

The PWG issued a report in November 2010 that laid out the different options to deal with the problem of bank support (PWG 2010). It pointed out that the uncertainty over the actual support for MMMFs of bank sponsors had a negative effect on the risk of runs, as banks are not legally bound to support MMMFs. However, it pointed out that such a support remained voluntary in order for sponsors to avoid consolidation. For the case of banks, the latter would have implied core capital charges. The ambiguity of implicit, voluntary support prevented the inclusion of bank-sponsored money market funds and at the same time "contributed substantially to the perceived safety of MMFs" (PWG 2010, p. 10). According to the report, permitting this implicit support to continue meant persistent uncertainty over the stability of the MMMF industry, while at the same time nurturing a false sense of security.

In line with its mandate to focus on systemic risks and financial stability, the report weighed different options to deal with risks. Among others, it considered the installation of special liquidity insurance which would insure MMMFs against run risks for an insurance fee, be it private or public. A second option was the installation of a special banking regime, which would require MMMFs to be subject to Federal Reserve oversight and (lighter) capital requirements. At the same time, it would facilitate access to the Fed Discount Window for these funds. Doing so would, in effect, have brought MMMFs into the regulatory perimeter of banking regulation, somewhat easing both the competitive advantages MMMFs enjoyed over banks and reducing the systemic run risks they posed. Following up, the SEC requested comments on this report and hosted a May 2011 Roundtable on Money Market Funds and Systemic Risk, inviting both other agencies and industry.

The SEC used these comments and, in close collaboration with the Federal Reserve and the Treasury economic analysis, prepared to refine its proposals (Shapiro 2012). Most importantly, in the course of its enquiry, the SEC documented more than 300 instances where MMMF sponsors had voluntarily provided support to their funds since industry existence (Fein 2012, p. 9), legitimizing further regulatory efforts. The proposals then converged on either the removal of constant net asset value (CNAV), that is the guarantee of redemption at par (just like in a bank deposit account) or the imposition of capital requirements. These regulatory proposals directly tackled the quasi-bank-deposit status of MMMFs, proposing either to eliminate the CNAV option, which underlay the deposit-like nature of MMMFs, or to draw the consequence of imposing equivalent regulatory measures to bank deposits.

Implicit sponsor support was also the topic for FASB, as it was pondering the revision of FAS 167 in the summer of 2011. The FASB considered requiring banks to recognize MMMFs on their balance sheet (FASB 2011, p. 8). However, at this point, crucial constituents, among them the Board of Governors of the Federal Reserve System, Federal Deposit Insurance Corporation, National Credit Union Administration, and the Office of the Comptroller of the Currency, stressed that the SEC is already developing a new regulatory frame for MMMFs (Four Federal Financial Institutions and Regulatory Agencies 2012, p. 11) and recommended to exclude MMMFs from its scope (Four Federal Financial Institutions and Regulatory Agencies 2012, p. 12). So, the Federal Reserve and other banking regulators actively intervened in 2012 in order to prevent the prudential consolidation of MMMFs, despite the acknowledged reputation risks (Interview, Federal Reserve regulator involved in the issue, March 27, 2012). As a consequence, the FASB no longer pursued this issue.[12] Banking

---

[12] In the end, when it sharpened the consolidation criteria for SPEs, such as ABCP conduits in 2015, it explicitly excluded money market funds from

regulators were hoping for a regulatory solution to emerge from the SEC; however, this hope would soon be diminished.

After more than a year of preparation, on August 22, 2012, SEC Chairman Mary Shapiro publicly abandoned the proposal of pursuing this twofold strategy of either eliminating the CNAV or imposing core capital requirements. Shapiro had to abandon her plans, as they were boycotted by three of the five board members of the SEC, who refused to publish the proposed rules for public comments.[13] The arguments of the opposition were that such a regime would not only address risks of runs but also eliminate the cost advantage for the MMMF industry.[14] The economic reasons for this visceral response of industry and its representative on the body of the SEC were spelled out most clearly in the analysis of different proposals by the chief economist of the SEC in 2013 (Lewis 2013), where he states, "after compensating capital buffer investors for absorbing credit risk, the returns available to money market fund shareholders are comparable to default free securities, which would significantly reduce the utility of the product to investors" (Lewis 2013, p. 1).

This analysis clarifies that it is this ambiguous status of MMMFs, providing bank-like services but not being regulated like a bank, which generates the extra yield for investors.[15] If capital buffers had been imposed, MMMFs would become as attractive as bank deposits, generating the same yield. The proposal of core capital buffers was, therefore, a direct assault on the viability of the industry as a whole, which was based on the private provision of safe short-term assets with implicit, but not explicit, sponsor support. In order to prevent the loss of this status, the three opposing board members requested a review of current initiatives and publicly doubted the finding of more than 300 incidents of sponsor support. This public quarrel was a major upset for the reform efforts.

---

consolidation (see FASB 2015, Consolidation (Topic 810) No. 2015-02, www .fasb.org/jsp/FASB/Document_C/DocumentPage?cid=1176164939022&accept edDisclaimer=true)

[13] See www.sec.gov/News/PressRelease/Detail/PressRelease/1365171484078

[14] See www.sec.gov/News/PublicStmt/Detail/PublicStmt/1365171491064

[15] It is also this ambiguous status which puts continuous competitive pressure on banks' deposit base, which cannot generate similar yields (Sissoko 2016), so in order to secure their own funding from MMFs, they engage in sponsoring MMMFs.

Evidently frustrated, Chairwoman Shapiro demanded that the FSOC step into the regulatory battle and to push these reforms through. Her call for action was followed by a letter from Treasury Secretary Geithner on September 27, 2012, demanding that the FSOC counter the inaction of the SEC. By November 2012, the FSOC followed suit and, based on the authority provided to it by the Dodd–Frank Act, recommended that the SEC proceeds with much-needed structural reforms of MMMFs (FSOC 2012, p. 15). It also published its own proposals, which notably included a (capital) buffer to allow CNAV MMMFs to deal with net asset value fluctuation (FSOC 2012, p. 39). However, already at this point, external observers such as the European Systemic Risk Board doubted whether the SEC would implement such rules (ESRB 2012, p. 6). An important signpost in this respect was Chairwoman Shapiro, seemingly exhausted and frustrated by the battle over the MMMF reforms, resigning in December 2012 (Protess and Craig 2012). Another signpost was the shift in the SEC discourse itself, which was suddenly emphasizing the risk that cash might be migrating from MMFs to nonregulated funds, which would make stiffer regulation counterproductive.

Rather than upending the ambiguous status of MMMFs and the risks generated by this ambiguity, the SEC now sought to install measures to make the system safer without changing it fundamentally, allowing investors to continue to benefit from higher yields. As the formerly dissenting board member Aguilar put it, "[t]he goal is to act in the best interests of investors and the public interest" (Aguilar 2012). On June 5, 2013, the SEC announced its own intended money market reforms, which excluded the imposition of any form of capital buffers. Instead, the capacity for fund managers to impose liquidity gates, dealing with the problems of redemption by allowing funds to control the outflows was espoused. Alternatively, variable NAV MMMFs for prime institutional funds were envisioned. The reforms were clearly aimed at maintaining the attractive status of MMFs for investors, while seeking to reduce run risks. An SEC employee said that when introducing these reform proposals, "Both alternatives are designed to address the risks of money market mutual funds while maintaining the current ability of money market mutual funds to function as an effective and efficient cash management tool for investors" (Champ 2013).

Subject to a public comment period, these proposals were endorsed by the SEC on July 23, 2014. In the end, the SEC adopted Money

Market Fund Reform rules, which abstained from any radical interventions. The new rules eliminated the constant net asset value provision for MMMFs investing in private debt and selling to institutional investors. Furthermore, it elevated industry practices to general rules, granting managers the right to impose liquidity gates that limited redemption and fees for redemption. However, these new measures were to be applied only to those MMMFs investing in private debt and selling to institutional investors, whereas MMMFs investing in public debt and those selling to retail investors could continue to report CNAVs.[16]

These timid reform efforts led the IMF in 2015 to the following rather harsh critique:

> While progress has been made, the fundamental flaws in MMMFs have not been addressed: a key element in addressing this should be the imposition of variable NAVs. The recent reform proposals by the U.S. authorities considered two tacks – to regulate them more like banks (with a capital buffer), or more like traditional mutual funds (with a variable NAV) – yet the government and retail funds have neither a capital buffer nor a variable NAV. (IMF 2015, 35)[17]

The abrupt shift in the direction of reform proposals in the USA in 2012 and the watering down of reform efforts had a major impact both on global reform efforts and those in the EU. On the global level, it was first and foremost the Financial Stability Forum which coordinated the reform efforts. Upgraded from the largely powerless Financial Stability Forum at the G20 Summit in London in April 2009, its task was to coordinate global efforts to improve the resilience of the financial system through improved regulation. In this vein, the Financial Stability Board (FSB) was assigned at the G20 meeting in Seoul in October 2010 in order to coordinate the global regulatory efforts to deal with the shadow banking system. Defining the shadow banking system as "credit intermediation involving entities

---

[16] MMMFs for retail investors make up 35 percent of total MMMF assets, making this a huge exemption (Deutsche Bank 2015, 13).

[17] Nevertheless, as a consequence of these reforms, a fundamental shift has occurred in the industry, leading to an outflow of about $1 trillion from MMMFs investing in private debt and moving into government-only funds (Bloomberg 2017). This shift clarifies the preference of institutional investors for the liquidity of MMMFs over yield.

and activities outside the regular banking system" (FSB 2011a, p. 1), the FSB unveiled in spring of 2011 five work streams to deal with the matter (FSB 2011a).[18]

The work streams with the greatest potential for disrupting the bank-based shadow banking system are those that seek to mitigate the spillover effects between banking and shadow banking activities as well as to reduce run risks from MMMFs and risks from other entities such as mutual funds.[19] These reform efforts of the FSB officially seek to limit the transgressions of bank holding companies regarding the regulatory perimeter, while at the same time pursuing the goal to transform the institutional setup of the other players in order to increase the resilience of shadow banking. All these regulatory endeavors ended in a minimal regulatory intervention that stays far below the initially announced goals. Reasons for this are both the difficulties of international coordination (FSB official, conference on macroprudential regulation, June 6, 2016) as well as the continued lobbying power of the concerned industry.[20]

In its actual regulatory activity, the FSB was soon confronted with the intricacies of a splintered regulatory network and its practically nonexistent capacity to enforce its visions, be it for the regulation of the MMMF industry or the entire mutual fund industry. Having almost no staff of its own, the FSB called in November 2011 on the International Organization of Securities Commission (IOSCO, the equivalent to the Basel Committee for Banking Supervision [BCBS] for financial market regulators) to develop recommendations that would strengthen the robustness and resilience of money market funds. In April 2012, the IOSCO published such recommendations, seeking to limit the systemic

---

[18] These five workstreams are (1) mitigating the spillover effect between the regular banking system and the shadow banking system; (2) reducing the susceptibility of money market funds (MMFs) to "runs"; (3) improving transparency and aligning incentives associated with securitization; (4) dampening pro-cyclicality and other financial stability risks associated with securities financing transactions; and (5) assessing and mitigating systemic risks posed by other shadow entities and activities.

[19] Two other aspects were the attempt to regulate the pro-cyclical effects of the repo market and incentive structures in securitization.

[20] The FSB's attempt to regulate the pro-cyclical character of repo markets has been also a dismal failure (Gabor 2016; Thiemann et al. forthcoming). The installed anticyclical measures are so minimal that they pose pretty much no constraint to market agents (Tarullo 2015; Interview, Dutch banking regulator involved in the FSB workstream, September 21, 2016).

risk that runs of money market funds may represent. In its analysis, IOSCO emphasized the bank-like character of money market funds, both in terms of their deposit like status and also in terms of their involvement in credit intermediation (IOSCO 2012a, p. 10). Despite the lack of leverage and the treatment of investors as shareholders rather than creditors, certain bank-like regulatory measures were recommended. Hence, IOSCO policy proposals included the option of capital requirements for those funds with CNAVs as a potential venue for future reform.

In October 2012, when IOSCO published its final reform proposals, this option was maintained in the form of a net asset value buffer that would allow funds to absorb short-term fluctuations. Alternatively, a commitment by the sponsor to guarantee the CNAV was proposed (IOSCO 2012b, p. 15). These reform proposals were published against the wishes of the majority of the Board members of the SEC (IOSCO 2012c), and were then endorsed by the FSB (2012b) as well as the European Systemic Risk Board (2012). Indeed, the FSB was directly supporting those regulatory measures seeking to react to the bank-like status of CNAV funds with bank-like regulation "that protect [banks] against runs on their deposits" (FSB 2012b, p. 8).

Nevertheless, as the IOSCO peer review of 2015 revealed, such proposals would not leave a final mark on the reform processes in the EU or any other major legislation globally. The report noted that in 2014 at least 65 percent of global assets under management were held in CNAV MMMFs, largely driven by the USA (IOSCO 2015, p. 9). It diagnoses further need for reform in those countries where CNAVs are allowed, including four of the five largest jurisdictions in terms of assets (IOSCO 2015, p. 24). At that moment in time, no jurisdiction had implemented a capital buffer; the only one still negotiating such a version was the EU, where the EU Commission had proposed such a measure in 2013. However, also the EU, after a long and protracted process, would dilute its own reform proposals and exclude the option of capital buffers for CNAV MMMFs.

The FSB proposals were an important source of inspiration for the measures suggested for reregulating the MMMF industry in Europe. In November 2012, the EU Parliament suggested even harsher measures for MMMFs retaining a CNAV, namely "a limited-purpose banking licence and be subject to capital and other prudential requirements" in its resolution on shadow banking (European Parliament 2012).

Proper reforms were then initiated in September 2013 by the European Commission. Referring directly to FSB proposals in its impact assessment (EC 2013, p. 53), the European Commission included a minimum 3 percent capital buffer for MMMFs in its recommendations. The industry, disappointed by the fact that the European Commission failed to take the change in the proposals of the SEC into account, now focused on the European parliament in order to avoid a "lack of consistency between regulation of MMFs in the US and Europe" which "could prove highly damaging to the $1 trillion industry" (International Financial Services Center 2013). And, indeed, the European Parliament changed its position under industry pressure.

Following the EU Commission proposal, a first response draft was issued that supported the Commission and even requested to abolish CNAV MMMFs in the EU after five years. However, due to time constraints before the 2014 European elections, the reading of the first draft was postponed (Fry 2014). The elections reshuffled the responsible Economic and Monetary Affairs committee of the parliament, where industry finally succeeded in imposing its view. In January 2015, the chief EU parliament negotiator suggested dropping the buffer requirements, a decision approved by the European Parliament on April 29, 2015.[21] Thus, the European Parliament, which initially suggested eliminating all CNAV MMMFs, now proposed "to remove the obligation to hold a 3% capital buffer for constant net asset value (CNAV) MMFs" (European Parliament 2015).

While mindful of possible competitive disadvantages of EU MMMFs as compared to their US counterparts European legislators oriented themselves toward US reforms. Therefore, the final reform proposals are markedly similar to those of the SEC in 2014 (liquidity gates and fees, CNAV for private debt MMMFs). However, seeking to prevent the large-scale changes that occurred in the US market after the reforms (Crane Data 2017), the European lawmakers agreed in 2015 to add a third alternative to the Constant Net Asset Value Government Fund and the Flexible Net Asset Value Private Debt Fund. Called a low-volatility flexible NAV (LVNAV), these funds can publish a CNAV

---

[21] See www.europarl.europa.eu/legislative-train/theme-deeper-and-fairer-internal-market-with-a-strengthened-industrial-base-financial-services/file-money-market-funds.

because their assets have a low volatility. This form of MMMFs can guarantee withdrawal at par, unless the volatility of the assets rises too much. This reform is in effect instituting a hybrid between these two forms of MMMFs. They will be allowed to invest 20 percent of their holdings into ABCPs, subject to the condition that the latter finance the real economy (European Parliament 2015).[22] In November 2016, a compromise solution between the EU Parliament, the European Commission, and the European Council was achieved that approved all requested changes (European Council 2016).

The final compromise text furthermore contains the provision that bank support of MMMFs should be forbidden (European Council 2016, p. 19), but it is not yet clear whether this provision will survive final legislation.[23]

Overall, what we can observe are legislators treading very carefully with respect to MMMFs, invoking the necessity to maintain the real economy funding these nonbanks provide (European Council 2016, p. 1). Whatever the final outcome in the EU, it is clear that MMMFs themselves will not officially be included in the regulatory perimeter of banking or be subjected to bank-like regulation. Therefore, they will not have regular access to the discount window of the central bank, making them prone to future runs. It also means that the competition for banking conglomerates on their liability side still prevails (Sissoko 2016).

And this is not the only failure to achieve meaningful regulatory interventions by the FSB. Another remarkable example regarding the failure of the regulatory agenda of the FSB regarding shadow banking is the attempt to reduce the run risks emerging from open-ended mutual funds. Just like MMMFs, open-ended mutual funds offer their investors the possibility for redemption at short notice. However, in contrast to MMMFs, they are allowed to invest in longer term illiquid assets such as emerging market bonds, thereby engaging in much larger maturity transformation than MMMFs. As of the end of 2013, at about $33 trillion (IMF 2015), these funds are thus much more like

---

[22] This rule can be interpreted as part of the endeavor to rejuvenate the ABCP market.

[23] If it does, we would have, on the one hand, an MMMF system, which is dependent on bank support but does not invest in private debt and, on the other hand, an MMMF system, which does invest in private debt but is not backed by the banks.

banks than MMMFs and pose a severe systemic risk. If large-scale requests for redemptions occur, they will be forced to sell (nonliquid) assets in order to satisfy these redemption requests (IMF 2015, p. 95). In this way, they might produce spillover effects or fire sales, thereby initiating downward spirals of funding and market liquidity in the system as a whole (Brunnermeier and Pedersen 2009). Having grown by more than 8% annually since 2008 (FSB 2015), the FSB started an attempt to deal with these entities in 2012.

As part of its work stream assessing the extent to which nonbank financial entities other than MMMFs are involved in shadow banking (FSB 2012b), the FSB initially considered extending the framework of systemically important financial institutions and including these funds and other asset managers (FSB 2014c). Such an extension would impose core capital charges for systemically important mutual funds and reduce the dangers of runs by allowing these funds to deal with credit risks. For the industry, just as in the case of MMMFs, such a move would imply a large reduction of profits due to higher core capital expenditures. As a reaction to these proposals, the industry was pointing to its character as a mere fiduciary for investors, arguing that the industry simply distributes losses to shareholders when redemptions occur, hence making core capital unnecessary (Investment Company Institute 2014).

Unimpressed by these arguments, the FSB, together with IOSCO, proceeded to develop measures for designating such funds. It published consultation documents for appropriate methodologies both in 2014 and 2015 (FSB–IOSCO 2014, 2015). However, despite being much advanced, the entire approach was finally abandoned in June 2015. Large-asset managers, such as Blackrock or Pimco, managed to convince the FSB that such measures would be inappropriate, pointing instead to concrete liquidity risks in individual markets (*Financial Times* 2015). In this way, the focus of the FSB shifted to individual market activity and market liquidity (FSB 2015).

In the next two years, this new approach produced a list of policy options, culminating in January 2017 with the "Policy Recommendations to Address Structural Vulnerabilities from Asset Management Activities" (FSB 2017b). None of the proposed measures contains the request for core capital charges. Instead, they all focus on individual risk management practices of investment funds, seeking to impose redemption gates and other means so as to reduce the outflow of funds. These measures are doing little more than improving industry practices, where the suggestion to undertake appropriate stress testing can be seen as the most radical step among these proposals. However, stress testing and other such measures are likely to increase further the demand of these open-ended mutual funds for short-term safe assets.

Already investing about $5 trillion in the money market, such measures will hence only increase demand for safe and liquid short-term assets, which banks, if given the chance, will be happy to produce by using techniques of securitization. Hence, credit intermediation, outside and beyond the banking perimeter continues to drive a global shadow banking system that successfully manages to avoid radical regulatory interference. The existing regulatory interference, which does not target the bank-like nature of these entities, stands the risk of only increasing the demand for private short-term assets, just like in the case of MMMFs.

A last attempt to deal with the problematic of reputation risk and implicit sponsor support of MMMFs and open-ended mutual funds was undertaken by the Basel Committee in December 2015. It issued a consultation paper on the issue of step-in risks of banks, the fact that banks might step in to support entities to which they are not contractually obliged. The BCBS did so in the context of the work stream of the FSB that seeks to limit the links between shadow banking and banking. The paper suggests that the implicit support which banks grant to MMMFs, mutual funds generally but also ABCP conduits, should lead to core capital charges when such support is seen as likely due to reputation risks (BCBS 2015). The report notes critically the sponsor support by MMFs and suggests dealing with it through either qualitative prudential supervision or rules (BCBS 2015, p. 12). In addition, it points to the ambiguous status of reputation risk in accounting standards as a reason for action.[24] Primary and secondary indicators are provided for regulators to evaluate step-in risks, clearly aiming at special-purpose vehicles and all kinds of entities that directly depend on banks. Still, it also proposes to evaluate the dependence of a bank on a certain market, thereby getting at the source of step-in risks.

---

[24] Recognized both in IASB and in FASB as a secondary indicator for consolidation, its presence alone does not force the banking conglomerate to consolidate (BCBS 2015, p. 4).

In the comment period ending March 2016, American regulators supported this initiative, while the overall feedback (mainly by industry) was negative and requested the proposal to be halted.[25] Nevertheless, on March 15, 2017, the BCBS issued a second consultative document on the guidelines for the identification and management of step-in risk (BCBS 2017). In reaction to the criticism of industry, banks are now asked to self-assess their exposure to step in risks, which is to be evaluated by the regulator. No additional core capital charges are envisioned in this approach. Instead, banks are tasked to include entities to which a large step-in risk exists in their scope of consolidation, or, if inappropriate to apply a risk factor to assess the degree of exposure (BCBS 2017, 12f).

In the evolution of this text, several developments are noteworthy. First, there is no longer any general core capital charge envisioned for this kind of risk. Instead, through a dialogue between banks and regulators a "tailored rather than a standardized approach" (BCBS 2017, p. 3) to the problem is to be generated. While the criteria for the assessment of such step-in risks remain clearly specified, their use in assessing step-in risks is now handed over to the banks themselves, with the task of regulators being the assessment of their application. This shifts the dynamic in favor of banks, with regulators having to criticize banks' self-assessment, rather than being immediately in charge of the assessment themselves. In a world where there would be only one regulator having to make this decision repeatedly, such a shift might not be that detrimental, as a firm regulatory opinion could settle contentious issues rather quickly. However, as Chapter 5 has shown, decisions regarding the perimeter of consolidation are heavily charged with international competitiveness considerations. Hence, placing the assessment of step-in risks with banks, which then has to be challenged by regulators, puts not only a further argumentative burden on regulators but also forces them to weigh the international effects of their action. In this respect, a standardized approach applicable the world-over would have been more advantageous to deal with this problem.

This rather timid version of the regulation of step-in risks fits well within the current regulatory climate, which insists that the work of

---

[25] This opposition was most forcefully expressed by the Institute of International Finance and International Banking Federation Comment (IIF–IBF 2016).

regulation postcrisis is completed (Carney 2015). Hence, the window of opportunity to reregulate the relationship between MMMFs and banks, a vital relationship within the shadow banking system has closed without bringing about fundamental regulatory change. The current regulatory climate, which seeks to reduce what is perceived as a too-high regulatory burden is not adductive to any further changes to MMMFs, neither in the EU nor in the USA. In the EU, the project of capital markets union, started in 2014 by the new EU Commission, is a move toward deregulation with European Commissioner Hill calling for regulators to tread carefully when regulating markets (Hill 2016).[26] Regulatory competition is again a major trope in the EU, where national regulators seek to prevent harm imposed on national champions wherever possible (Interview, Bundesbank official, January 14, 2017). On the other side of the Atlantic, the USA is moving toward deregulation under the presidency of Donald Trump, calling for the (partial) dismantling of the Dodd–Frank Act (*New York Times* 2017). Are we hence observing the beginning of a new cycle of deregulation that will allow banks to reengage with capital markets in an unfettered way and thereby sow the seeds for future crises? Did nothing in the (global) regulatory architecture change after all? We will turn to this question in the final chapter.

[26] Since Brexit occurred in the summer of 2016, Lord Hill has been replaced as Commissioner by Mister Dombrovski. Nevertheless, the rhetoric of a too high regulatory burden has not changed.

9 | Conclusion: Changing the Façade, but Not the Structure: The Continuing Threat of Shadow Banking

This book documents how, as a central part of the shadow banking system, the ABCP market blossomed in the precrisis regulatory architecture and how it collapsed during the crisis. It traces how it was born in the USA as a result of competitive pressure exerted upon the US banks from nonbank credit intermediaries and how it grew there amidst internal regulatory struggle regarding its regulation. It then traces how it blossomed in a global financial architecture that encouraged laissez-faire and hindered national regulatory action. Honing in on its regulation in three EU countries, it traces how this particular constellation of national and transnational governance systems influenced regulatory dynamics. It details the evolution of the regulatory regime for this market and the role that the banking regulator played in its evolution, both in terms of rule making as well as its supervision, while paying attention to the national banking systems' positioning within the emerging European banking system. It tries to show how the direct insertion of regulators in terms of the compliance and accounting standards making, coupled with the necessary discretion and expertise, allowed some regulators to detect rule evasion, whereas others failed. Furthermore, it points out that such recognition was also coupled with political economy considerations regarding the fate of national champions within a liberalizing market for banking services, particularly in the EU.

Looking at the lack of regulation of banks' shadow banking activities precrisis, one can identify a strong belief in the market's ability to self-regulate and always provide sufficient liquidity as a proximate cause. This ideology is best encapsulated in an influential paper by Goodfriend and King (1988), where they state,

> If information were freely available about such assets, then private markets would stand ready to lend any bank the present value of the expected income streams from its assets, discounted at a rate appropriate for the risk. Thus, any bank would always be fully liquid, able to pay all claimants, as long as it was also solvent. (Goodfriend and King 1988, p. 14)

In this view, markets always provide financially solvent banks with sufficient liquidity if they have sufficient information on the true state of the bank in question. Thus, regulators only have to ensure the availability of information through transparency and let the markets discipline bank behavior.

However, this embrace of self-regulation by leading regulators, especially in the USA and the UK, was widely endorsed but not universally shared, as the case of France shows. Even in the USA, as this book has documented, this ideology was not all-encompassing, with a critical faction emerging within the Fed concerned about the lack of regulation of short-term liquidity lines granted by the banks to nonbank actors. Postcrisis, this ideology of ever-liquid self-regulating and self-disciplining markets has been destroyed by the events unfolding in financial markets since 2007. Looking at the regulation of shadow banking postcrisis, then, allows us to test certain propositions entailed in the analysis of this book regarding the role of ideology.

Beyond this facilitating ideology, this book argues that there was an underlying driver for the development of shadow banking, one that extends beyond technological change. There was a shift in the regulatory dialectic that favored regulatory inaction following rule evasion. This shift was caused by three structural factors.

First, there was an increasing competition for banks from nonbanks, in particular in the USA. Nonbanks took over bank-like functions, while having cost advantages because of lower regulatory costs. Their existence was linked to a fractured domestic governance framework of different regulatory agencies that largely did not communicate with each other and failed to engage in a shared problem perspective. Such a fractured governance network had the effect that market regulators were pursuing transparency and fraud prevention as their primary goals, while ignoring the systemic risks emerging from these new players, thereby leading to a competitive disadvantage for banks (Sissoko 2016).

This had a tremendously negative effect on banking regulators. This effect is beautifully explained in this lengthy passage by Federal Reserve Governor Tarullo:

If regulators with responsibility for one sector believe that the failure of regulators with responsibility for another sector to act on financial stability concerns is creating debilitating disadvantages for firms in the first sector, they might be tempted to relax regulation on their firms, even though they might agree that the best outcome would be to retain their existing regulations but have the other sector subject to some constraints as well. This seems to me not a bad description of what happened in banking for a good part of the three decades beginning in the mid-1970s, when the banking agencies pursued a variety of deregulatory measures in part because they believed that the franchise of commercial banking was being eroded by various capital market activities that were not subject to appropriate prudential requirements. (Tarullo 2015, p. 7)

As the analysis of Chapter 4 has shown, it was exactly this concern from the late 1970s onwards, which led the Fed to support the expansion of bank holding companies into capital market activities.

Second, the growth of those nonbank entities, which – just like banks – promise redemption on demand, led to an increasing demand for safe short-term assets. As they do not have bank deposit insurance, actors such as money market mutual funds (MMMFs) need to invest in safe short-term assets that carry few to no credit risks so that they can pay out quickly. Asset-backed commercial paper was such an instrument, as it effectively carried no credit risk. Banks absorbed this risk through liquidity lines. This fact made ABCPs very attractive to investors while rating agencies included the sponsor support as an explicit part of their ranking. When seeking to intervene in this delicate web of relationships based on private risk management systems and the implicit collusion to transfer risks toward bank balance sheets, regulators were faced with the question of where these nonbank entities should place their money were the ABCP market to disappear. Hence, the growth of shadow banking had a self-affirming effect in that once created, regulation had to pursue carefully.

Third, there was a fractured global governance network at the same time that liberalization increased competition for domestic banks from foreign banks. While operating also in the USA, this was most clearly the case for the EU, where the EU passport for banks meant increasing competition, while banks were subject to different regulatory regimes based on the intersection of national and transnational laws. Postcrisis, have these three structural changes been amended? Is there today less of a fractured governance network domestically, on the European level, as well as globally?

Inquiring into the fate of the ABCP market and its regulation from the liquidity crisis of 2007 onwards as well as the regulation of the MMMFs industry that underlay its growth, the most recent chapter provides important insights in this respect. It shows how postcrisis regulation ended the special status of the ABCP market as a venue for regulatory arbitrage but nonetheless maintained the underlying pressure on banking systems emanating from bank-like nonbanks. Hence, it suggests that the problems that impeded the regulation of shadow banking continue postcrisis, despite the shifts in the regulatory outlook on financial markets. Focusing on these timid regulatory changes reveals the shortcomings of domestic and global reforms of the regulatory governance architecture that occurred postcrisis.

Assessing the Changes in the Postcrisis Governance Architecture

These sobering results for the regulation of MMMFs should not lead to the conclusion that nothing has changed; instead, it allows us to put these changes into perspective. Indeed, on the domestic level, there have been changes both in the USA and in the EU. The most remarkable change has been the move in the EU to banking union at the height of the eurozone crisis in 2012 which brought a common banking supervision by the European Central Bank (ECB). This common supervision was indeed a response to the perceived protection of national champions by domestic supervisors (Veron 2015, pp. 20ff). The outcome of astute political maneuvering by the ECB (De Rynck 2016), supervision is organized today by joint European teams, including both ECB and national supervisors. In this way, a crucial limiting feature of the precrisis governance architecture is supposed to be overcome. Together with this change, we can observe a move toward European regulations, reducing the leeway of national banking regulators when implementing these rules. Unquestionably, this change is an important structural readjustment postcrisis.

However, to date, the question of which nonbank entities should be included in banking supervision remains to be answered on the national level. This means that the perimeter problem of banking regulation, the continuous expansion of aspects of banking regulation to nonbanks continues to be decided on the national, not the EU, level. Furthermore, the supervision of nonbank financial institutions is still operating at the national level, thus remaining fragmented and giving rise to regulatory competition (Maijoor 2017). The European Securities and Markets Authority (ESMA) has no legal authority over domestic regulations and no real power in terms of supervision or rule making. Instead, its function is mostly to aggregate national supervisors in fora, where they monitor and comment their mutual actions. This lack of common European jurisdiction has gained increasing salience with Brexit on the horizon, as ESMA fears to have no control over national regulators engaging in regulatory competition. The best example for this problematic is the supervision of central counterparties (CCPs) postcrisis.

Having risen to prominence due to postcrisis attempts at ending the too-big-to-fail problematic (Interview, Bundesbank regulator, July 25, 2016), these nonbank entities are supervised by national financial market regulators. However, as their business model is based on high volume and low margins, regulatory costs again become a major competitive factor (Krahnen and Pelizzon 2016). As such, there are great incentives for national supervisors to be lenient in the interpretation of rules in order to foster the competitiveness of domestic industries (Interview, ECB supervisor, October 11, 2016), with all attendant financial stability risks. This intra-EU problem is aggravated by a comparison to US regulation, which is perceived as less stringent and less demanding (Interview, German banking regulator, July 25, 2016). Thus, it seems that the problem of international regulatory competition regarding financial services might have just migrated from one segment of financial markets to others.

One might argue that the newly installed macroprudential supervisory authorities, which bring together market and banking regulators could attenuate the consequences of such a fragmented governance network. Applying a systemic perspective on credit growth and liquidity risks, these bodies are supposed to warn of impending dangers and to request harsher regulation. And, indeed, today, there is a Financial Stability Oversight Council (FSOC) in the USA, which brings together the different regulatory agencies,[1] while there is also a European Systemic Risk Board (ESRB) in the EU that unites national

[1] The most important of which are the SEC, Federal Reserve, Comptroller of the Currency, the FDIC, the Consumer Protection Bureau, as well as the Commodities Future Trading Commission.

and European regulators both for markets and banks. Lastly, there is the Financial Stability Board (FSB), which is supposed to address these issues on the global level. However, academic research shows that their installation was driven by the logic of symbolic politics, which provided those institutions with very limited regulatory enforcement power (Helleiner 2014; Lombardi and Moschella 2017).

In the case of the USA, the FSOC has the capacity to request stricter regulation for nonbanks as well as bank holding companies supervised by the Federal Reserve. However, just like its counterpart, the ESRB, it only has the capacity to release recommendations; it cannot issue binding decisions. Regulators who are affected by such recommendations can explain why they choose to not comply. This is an important caveat for regulatory dynamics, as we saw in the case of the regulation of MMMFs. The SEC simply refused to abide or to follow up on FSOC recommendations. Another issue is that these bodies only operate on the level of rule making, but are not engaged in supervision directly. However, as the previous chapters illustrate, there is an important link between the two. This means that concerned banking regulators would have to raise alarm over developments for nonbanks, while the expertise and data mostly reside with the market regulator, leading to clashes both in terms of expertise as well as regulatory turf (Thiemann et al. 2018). How such a dynamic plays out can be seen for the case of the reregulation of MMMFs detailed in Chapter 8.

On the level of the EU, the ESRB is even less powerful than FSOC. Its main task is the collection of data and issuance of warnings and recommendations. It consists of thirty-eight voting members, including the twenty-eight national central banks and the three European Supervisory Authorities,[2] and it is chaired by the head of the ECB, which also supports the body logistically (Lombardi and Moschella 2017, p. 96). In addition, the relevant financial authorities of member states attend the boards as nonvoting members. Given this large size of voting members and the limited degree of decision-making power, the process has been described as "cumbersome" by those involved (Interview, Dutch banking regulator, member ESRB,

[2] Namely, these are the European Banking Authority, the European Market Authority as well as the European Pension and Insurance Fund authority.

September 21, 2016). While the recent unification of banking supervisory powers in the ECB in 2012 has given this joint supervision of the system a stronger institutional foundation and more impetus than initially envisioned (Lombardi and Moschella 2017; Interview, German banking regulator, July 21, 2016; Interview, ECB regulator, May 11, 2016), the ESRB remains weak and necessitates the formation of consensus among market and banking regulator, a consensus notably missing regarding CCPs (Thiemann et al. forthcoming). At best, what we can observe is an incremental buildup of macroprudential powers at the level of the ECB, which will take years to come to fruition.

On the global level, we can observe similar dynamics with the FSB as a body coordinating the work of market regulators and banking regulators globally. The most potent capacity that the FSB was given is to request peer reviews and installing a "comply or explain" procedure for international standards it agrees upon. This and the monitoring exercise are important contributions to global governance. Undoubtedly, the FSB, on behalf of the G20 has taken up important reform projects postcrisis, initiating regulatory reform efforts on the global level (Gadinis 2013, pp. 166–167). And, still, this umbrella body, which comprises government representatives as well as international standard setters (such as the Basel Committee or the International Organization of Securities Commissions [IOSCO]), has no rule-making power by itself. Instead, it can only issue recommendations, based on consensus of all members participating (with a total of more than seventy members, a cumbersome task (Pagliari 2013).

This lack of both rule-making power and enforcement capabilities is a severe problem for global governance, as the analysis conducted in this book suggests. As shown earlier, it was not only a lack of knowledge about the rule evasion occurring in the ABCP market, which was a problem, but also a lack of follow-up in terms of rule changes and enforcement once the problem was detected. Arguably, different regulators with different capabilities will spot rule evasion at different points in time. However, as shown in this book, such knowledge does not immediately translate into action, hindered by exactly such a dysfunctional global governance architecture.

Instead of rule making and enforcement, the FSB's role is about coordinating the efforts of existing transnational regulatory bodies, with the Basel Committee occupying center stage (Helleiner 2011).[3] As a recent article puts it,

The Board remains in this sense focused on communication, consensus-building, coordination and puzzling about the right way to prevent another global crisis, not about handing out instructions to the ISSBs. .... The FSB is the arena in which this takes place, rather than a central authority per se. (Donnelly 2012, p. 268)

Hence the FSB should merely be seen as an additional coordinating body, one with no capacity to enforce its views. Arguably, however, such a view on the FSB still remains too benign with respect to the effects this global body has on reform dynamics, as it downplays the effect of discursive interventions by this body. Unable to bring about substantial change, the FSB might even contribute to a conciliatory regulatory discourse which changes the outlook on phenomena rather than the phenomenon itself. This was the case, I argue, with respect to the global coordinated efforts by the FSB regarding the regulation of shadow banking.

At the same time that the FSB failed to achieve the regulatory goals that it set out for itself in 2011, it engaged in an important discursive rebranding of shadow banking during its reform efforts. Starting from its second report in 2012, the FSB pointed to the positive effects of the shadow banking system for the economy as a whole (FSB 2012a, p. 1). It argued that the shadow banking system contributes to economic growth by diversifying and cheapening the supply of credit through gains from specialization. Therefore, it became a concern of the FSB to regulate shadow banking "while not inhibiting sustainable and resilient non-bank financing models" (FSB 2012b). This discursive attempt reached its peak in 2014, when the FSB announced its intention to transform shadow banking into "resilient market-based financing" (FSB 2014b; Engelen 2015), as such rebranding the negatively connoted term into something positive. The trend toward a growing segment of shadow banking is greeted with cautious optimism by the FSB, as it extols some further efforts to deal with the liquidity risks inherent in this new system.

---

[3] Given this lack of regulatory powers, the FSB has been derided as just another global coordinative body, a place of communication with no enforcement power (Helleiner 2014).

The combination of this stance when coupled with a self-congratulatory language of the FSB, language that announces that the global fault lines revealed by the financial crisis have been addressed (letter by FSB president Carney to the G20 in November 2015), does not bode well for the future. It is as if a new ideology is emerging that believes in the possibility of managing liquidity risks (FSB 2017b). Such a mind-set covers up the failures of a fragmented governance architecture, assuaging concerns over shadow banking without resolving them. As a result of these minimal reforms, neither the competition for banks has been lowered, nor is there any attempt to include those bank-like actors within the banking perimeter. "Prudential market regulation," desired by banking regulators (Tarullo 2015), is still an unrealized dream. Instead, banking regulators keep a watchful eye on an industry that they cannot control, much like before the crisis (Tarullo 2015).

The Future of the Shadow Banking System

Since Kapstein's early work on the Basel standards (1989), research in the international political economy of financial regulation has mostly focused on the growth and the increasing importance of international standards (see Macey 2003; Simmons 2004; Drezner 2007; Singer 2007; Helleiner and Pagliari 2011, p. 170). The shortcomings and deficiencies of these international standards, however, have remained less analyzed (but see Scott and Iwahara 1994; Tarullo 2008; Lall 2012). This book casts doubt on the belief that global regulations for financial markets might be able to solve the problem of competitive inequity concerns and, thus, overly lenient regulation (Kapstein 1991). Given the difficulty of inventing a complete global legal framework from the basic terms upward, it is likely that competition among national jurisdictions will continue to play a crucial role.

As a Federal Reserve employee put it when asked about how often he encountered the argument of the level playing field postcrisis,

It is very frequent, and since the crisis, it has been almost on a daily basis … The problem is that it doesn't do any good, really for Basel III to be so consistent … if the accounting differs from jurisdiction to jurisdiction, … if you look at any of my presentations that I have given over the last two years, they are all about the interaction effects between accounting and regulatory capital, and they all have that underlying theme that there is going to be a *competitive issue if we don't get the accounting converged at the same time* *that we are seeking trying to ensure that we have a consistent regulatory* *capital treatment.* (March 27, 2012, emphasis mine)

Unfortunately, the two standard setters International Accounting Standards Board (IASB) and Financial Accounting Standards Board (FASB) have halted the convergence process without achieving substantial improvements, and further progress is, therefore, very unlikely (Baudot 2014). This means that one of the main structural preconditions of shadow banking activities of banks, different accounting frames, are still operating.

These findings support on a normative level those voices arguing for principled minimalism (Rodrik 2009; Warwick Commission 2009; Pistor 2010; Griffith-Jones et al. 2011; Sohn 2012). Such an approach would allow host-country regulators to impose regulation above and beyond global rules on domestic as well as foreign banks. And, indeed, scholars in International Political Economy have identified the emergence of normatively fragmented international regulation as an increasingly likely outcome for the postcrisis world (see Helleiner 2009; Germain 2010, 2012; Mosley 2010), with "co-existence of divergent national or regional standards" (Helleiner and Pagliari 2011, p. 190). On the level of research, this book, then, adds further weight to Helleiner and Pagliari's suggestion (2011) that research in IPE should reorient itself toward the question of which institutional setup is needed to make such normative fragmentation work (see Sohn 2012) for an investigation for the East Asia region). However, it also points to the fact that the shadow banking system, the intertwinement of banks and certain nonbank actors, is unconstrained by regional boundaries and is, thus, difficult to control within a regional approach.

Making matters even worse, access to liquidity in global capital markets is seen as highly valuable. The amount of money flowing into global capital markets is growing as high net worth Individuals and corporations place their savings into financial markets other than banks (Pozsar 2015). The large amounts of cash held by corporate conglomerates fuels the demand for safe short-term assets characterizing shadow banking (Mehrling et al. 2013). What happens if this capital market liquidity is denied was on full display in the summer of 2011, when US MMMFs withdrew from European banks because of the fears over the eurozone crisis (ESRB 2012, p. 20f). These fears led to large-scale outflows from MMMFs invested in eurozone banks, fueling the eurozone crisis (Chernenko and Sunderam 2014). To the great relief of EU banks and regulators, liquidity provided by US MMMFs returned in the summer of 2014 (FT 2014), once more showing the dependency of banks' business models on capital market actors.

The structural factors supporting the expansion of shadow banking activities are most pronounced in the EU, which is bound together by treaties guaranteeing the free movement of capital and that seeks to install one consistent European financial market. At the same time, the EU is not a coherent Institution and has different national supervisory structures for nonbank financial institutions. The EU is, thus, caught in between, encouraging competition on the European level while simultaneously engaging in national supervision and regulation. This book argues that the global financial crisis had such a large impact on continental European banking systems and that its vulnerability emerged from the shadow banking activities of European banks is not coincidental.

While other explanations mostly point to banks as agents of change and to their choices about business activities as crucial factors explaining this impact (Hardie and Howarth 2013b, p. 51; Hardie et al. 2013b, p. 1; Bell and Hindmoor 2015a), this book points to (lacking) regulatory agency as a decisive factor. The ABCP market was one of the main markets for precrisis shadow banking activities (Pozsar et al. 2010), which largely transmitted the crisis to Europe (Shin 2011), and it could thrive only if excluded from costly banking regulation. Regulatory agency was, thus, an important factor in constraining or facilitating these activities. I argue here that the regulatory agency of European banking regulators was influenced by regulatory concerns over the fate of "national champions." In the project of producing large national champions, EU financial market integration, which occurred stepwise from 1988 onward, aligned the interests of national regulators and banks. Where this project ran into difficulties, there was a particular pressure to allow banks to engage in shadow banking activities in wholesale markets in order to grow their fee income and to make them more competitive.

Today, this form of regulatory competition is no longer operating, as there is a common EU banking supervision. However, it seems that regulatory competition has merely shifted, now operating on the grounds of critical financial market infrastructures as central counterparties (CCPs). Clearing houses again operate based on low margins and the incentives for regulatory leniency. Securing the short-term economic success of these entities in national space is high on the agenda. As national policymakers seek to attract employment in financial industries, the problematic of regulatory competition is by no means eliminated.

But, even if normative fragmentation could be made to work or a truly global regulation could be imposed, thus removing structural constraints from regulatory action,[4] regulators would still have to pick up acts of harmful regulatory arbitrage and to intervene. The second question that this book has sought to analyze is how regulatory dialogues should be shaped in order for regulators to overcome cognitive capture and to gain an independent picture of the risk taking of banks. Here the analysis of this book provides more concrete answers by understanding how the French and US banking regulators picked up the rule circumventions in the accounting and banking realm, while the Dutch and Germans did not or only did so belatedly. When comparing the four cases from an integrated systems perspective, it becomes apparent that the diversity of views, regulatory discretion, and legal incentives to make compliance officers interact proactively with the regulator concerning financial innovations are all crucial for the early detection of potential forms of regulatory arbitrage. These legal capacities to challenge compliance decisions need to be supported by information gathering and monitoring activities of regulators, which differed markedly between the four cases.

On the one hand, French regulation is characterized both by diversity, with its strong linkage to the auditing community and the power of its regulators to impose their more prudent interpretation of standards, at least temporarily. They changed the regulatory dialectic of regulation and subsequent rule evasion by changing the rules of the game: forcing regulatory uncertainty on the financial engineers. The regulated were never granted the security of regulatory bright lines and a legal framework approach but, instead, had to defend their compliance decisions in front of the regulator in terms of economic substance. The auditors, acting as gatekeepers, were forced to take into

---

[4] While some current reforms go in that direction, the sheer complexity of the task cast a doubt on it.

account not only the interests of their clients but also those of state regulators. This interactive regulatory regime, centered on the regulator and economic substance, finds its expression in the toughest prudential regime for ABCP conduits.

The US system is close behind, where on- and off-site supervision is closely coordinated and where a degree of communication between accounting regulator and the banking regulator exists. What hindered action there was an accounting standard setter, which did not dare to effectively challenge the off-balance-sheet practices of banks, but rather remained wedded to bright lines, allowing financial engineers to circumvent accounting rules. This seems to be an outcome, on the one hand, of regulatory capture[5] and, on the other hand, of a legalistic culture that threatened the accounting standard setter with lawsuits in case of lacking legal clarity. With respect to banking regulation, it was not local, on-the-ground supervision but, rather, an ideological embrace of market disciplines at the higher echelons of power that prevented stronger reregulation. As Chapter 4 demonstrates, there was a continuous battle on the supervisory frontlines regarding attempts of banks to evade core capital requirements while assuming credit risks. This battle fed concerns into the higher, rule-making level of the regulator, who, however, refused to regulate up until 2004. This refusal was partially caused by a belief in self-regulation and partially by the numbers provided by the regulated, showing very low historical loss rates.

French as well as US banking regulators were included in the networks of accounting governance in such a way that they were capable of gathering independent information and were monitoring the accounting activities of their banks. For this reason, it was easier for them to detect ABCP conduits as a risky technique of regulatory circumvention.[6] Diversity of views was strong in the Information gathering and monitoring activities in France, where the different regulators collaborated and sought to gain information from the technical departments of large auditing networks and banks. In the

---

[5] The reader shall be reminded that the SEC in 1989 considered the introduction of harsh rules limiting off-balance-sheet financing, but then abstained. This left off-balance-sheet financing techniques largely unconstrained. Even in 2003, when reregulation occurred and the FASB showed an awareness of rule circumvention, the FASB left intact a quantitative test that allowed the regulated to continue off-balance-sheet financing.
[6] This also holds for the Spanish regulator (Thiemann 2012).

USA as well, given that on-site supervision includes the control of the application of these rules, the banking regulator and the banks are in close contact where compliance decisions, including accounting, are concerned. Furthermore, in France and the USA, the banking regulator had the necessary regulatory discretion to define what was acceptable within the framework of the law, which allowed a regulator to push through more prudent interpretations of the rules. If a banking regulator has the capacity to define right and wrong in the application of rules, he or she can limit self-interested interpretations of regulatees and install a second line of control in form of the application of standards. In addition, these enforcement activities contribute to the monitoring capabilities of the regulator.

If the regulator was disembedded from this circuit of information, there was the danger of "cognitive closure" regarding the acts of creative compliance in securitization (Aalbers et al. 2011, p. 1790), as can be seen in the cases of the Netherlands and Germany. In Germany and the Netherlands, the banking regulators were rather blind to developments in accounting, did not have a strong linkage to the accounting standard setter and – in the case of the Netherlands – were suffering from cognitive closure due to lacking diversity in the regulatory dialogues. Being largely excluded from the field of compliance supervision, the German regulator BaFin lacked the institutional linkages as well as the capabilities for an expedient regulatory dialogue. These structural weaknesses in the supervision of this sector were amplified in Germany by the pro-securitization stance of the ministry of finance, which had control over the banking regulator. In the Netherlands, regulatory dialogues, information gathering, and monitoring were intense but were lacking the focus on accounting decisions, whereby the critical stance on the rewards of banking conglomerates, garnered from ABCP conduits, was excluded from these conversations.

Postcrisis, several reports have pointed to the advantages for banking regulators stemming from increased engagement with auditors (Masciandaro 2015; World Bank 2015) and several policy initiatives are under way. For example, in the EU, banking supervisors and auditors shall establish an effective dialogue.[7] Most helpfully, the regulation clarifies that in the context of such a dialogue, any information provided by external auditors does not constitute a breach

---

[7] As set out in Article 12 of the Regulation (EU) No 537/2014.

of any contractual or legal restriction on disclosure of information (European Parliament 2016, p. 2). However, much still remains to be done. A report by the World Bank notes that the majority of banking regulators has limited expertise in matters of accounting (World Bank 2015, p. 74) and that contacts between regulators and auditors are infrequent (World Bank 2015, p. 75). However, without expertise and continuous encounters, banking regulators risk being too distant from processes of compliance. Hence, much depends on regulators actively engaging auditors through these new institutional linkages and continuously challenging their bent toward the interests of the regulated. Auditors, left alone, will most likely bend the rules in favor of the regulated. As a consequence, only the active engagement of regulators with them will be able to stem this trend.

As this book shows, the growth of the bank-based shadow banking system is no natural or inevitable process, but, instead, it is one that is shaped by human volition and institutional setup. In this vein, this book seeks to enlighten what has driven this process and what currently drives it. In closing, I would like to point out that the structural factors that facilitated the growth of the bank based shadow banking system still operate today. The philosopher Santayana among others has pointed out that those who do not remember the past are condemned to repeat it. However, I am afraid that remembering alone will be insufficient. What we need to do is to change not only the intellectual outlook on financial markets at a time when the most radical challenges to the orthodox outlook on financial markets are already receding but also the structural conditions that inhibit decisive regulatory action. One without the other will just lead to a revelation that has befallen many observers after the last financial crisis: that regulators were aware of most of the problems precrisis; it was just regulatory action that was lacking.

Appendix A: Interview Data

The interviews were semistructured in order to deal with the information asymmetry between me as an interviewer and the experts I interviewed regarding the highly complex matter of ABCP conduits and their regulation. Being semistructures, these interviews allowed me to learn during the interviews as well as asking specific questions generated from the regulatory texts that I analyzed beforehand.[1] Given the complexity of the regulation, the participation of several interviewees (up to three) was often helpful, because uncertainties on the part of interviewees could be cross-checked in the moment of interviewing. As some of the events of interest were a decade or more in the past, I used regulatory texts and pronouncements from this period during these semistructured interviews in order to help actors remember. Going over the events chronologically served the function of refreshing the memory of those involved.

I tried with considerable success to gain interview partners from all important players in the regulatory networks in these four countries, which includes the central banks, the financial supervisors, the auditing associations, banking associations, bankers concerned with accounting decisions, accounting and law professors involved in the accounting standard setting, accounting standard setters and state officials concerned with accounting standard setting, external auditors as well as regulatory service provider for the big auditing networks (see Table A.1). In addition to these actors, I interviewed academics and politicians involved in governmental research on the causes of the crisis (Germany), an economic advisor to the president (France), analysts for banking stocks (France, Germany), as well as members of the rating agencies (Standard and Poor's, France; Moody's, USA) to

---

[1] To overcome this asymmetry I also attended a one-day seminar at the True Sale Initiative (a German think tank/lobbying group for securitization) on May 15, 2011, focusing on the international and German regulation of securitization markets, which thanks to the generosity of the TSI I could attend free of charge.

Table A.1 *Categories and number of interviewees*

Function of Interviewee/ Country	Germany	Netherlands	France	USA	Total
Central banks/ banking supervisor	4	6	10	3	23
Financial market regulators	2	2	1	1	6
Auditing association	3	2	2	1	8
Banking association	0	0	1	0	1
Senior bank managers concerned with accounting decisions regarding SPEs	5	3	5	1	14
Accounting and law professors involved in accounting standard setting	3	3	4	0	10
Accounting standard setters and state officials concerned with accounting standard setting	3	2	5	1	11
External auditors from the big four auditing networks	2	2	3	1	8
Rating agencies	0	0	1	4	5
Regulatory services big auditing networks	1	1	0	0	2
Total	23	21	31	12	88[a]

[a] The numbers add up to more than eighty-five, as some interviews held different functions over the course of their careers.

better understand the developments in the banking sector before the crisis.[2]

The entrance into the regulatory networks in the different countries was different, in line with the different structures and processes in these networks, and thus provided itself important information. In Germany, where the regulatory elite is much more splintered geographically (Frankfurt, Düsseldorf, Berlin) and the standard setter is not inclusive but exclusive, interviews had to be more often organized by email requests and involved substantial travel. The same held for the USA, where such structural separation also exists, with a distinct split between Washington (the regulatory center) and New York, the hub for both rating agencies as well as bankers. In the Netherlands, which in terms of geographic location of the elite provides a middle ground, the collection of interviewees was a mixture of email requests and recommendations of former interviewees and acquaintances. In France, because of the location of the regulatory elite in one city (Paris) and the high frequency of meetings in the inclusive standard-setting body, interview collection by referral proved to be the predominant way.[3]

[2] In particular, the interviews with the researchers in Germany proved to be enlightening, as certain issues were only written between the lines in the final government reports.

[3] At the end, a warning specification: Process tracing and the comparative method cannot provide us with certainty about the degree of impact a specific variable has on an outcome, knowledge that is produced by large n statistics. In the end, using this method a researcher will be able to present a causal model for how the different configurations in the cases explain different outcomes, but he or she will not be able to specify which of the variables had exactly which kind of effect. In this respect, case studies are much better in identifying the scope conditions under which a causal mechanism holds, not the degree of impact single variables have (George and Bennett 2005, p. 25).

Appendix B

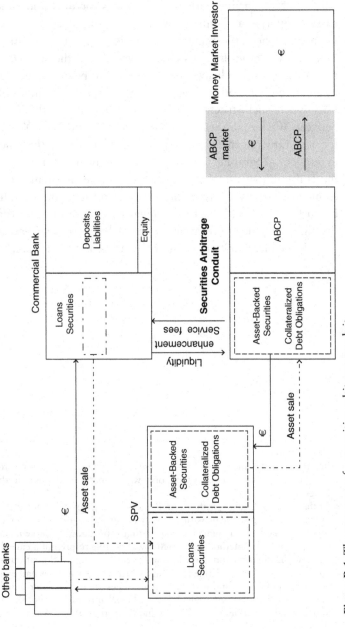

Figure B.1 The structure of a securities arbitrage conduit.

References

Aalbers, M., E. Engelen, and A. Glasmacher (2011). "Cognitive Closure" in the Netherlands: Mortgage Securitization in a Hybrid European Political Economy. *Environment and Planning A* 43(8), 1779–1795.

Abbott, K., and D. Snidal (2009). The Governance Triangle: Regulatory Standards, Institutions and the Shadow of the State: Regulatory Standards, Institutions and the Shadow of the State. In W. Mattli and N. Woods (eds.), *The Politics of Global Regulation*, pp. 44–88. Princeton, NJ: Princeton University Press.

Abken, P. A. (1981). Commercial Paper. *Economic Review* (March/April), 11–21.

Acharya, V., and P. Schnabl (2009). Do Global Banks Spread Global Imbalances? The Case of Asset-Backed Commercial Paper during the Financial Crisis of 2007–2009. Paper presented at the 10th Jacques Polak Annual Research Conference, the International Monetary Fund Washington, DC, November 5–6, 2009.

Acharya, V. V., and P. Schnabl (2010). Do Global Banks Spread Global Imbalances? Asset-Backed Commercial Paper during the Financial Crisis of 2007–2009. *IMF Economic Review* 58(1), 37–73. www.imf .org/external/np/res/seminars/2009/arc/pdf/acharya.pdf

Acharya, V., P. Schnabl, and G. Suarez (2009). *Securitization without Risk Transfer.* http://richmondfed.org/conferences_and_events/research/2009/ pdf suarez_paper.pdf

Acharya, V. V., P. Schnabl, and G. Suarez (2013). Securitization without Risk Transfer. *Journal of Financial Economics* 107(3), 515–536.

Adams, J. A. (1982). Money Market Mutual Funds: Has Glass–Steagall Been Cracked. *Banking and Law Journal* 99(4), 4–54.

Adelson, M. (2003a). *Off-Balance Sheet Update (March 2003).* Nomura Fixed Income Research, March 11, 2003.

(2003b). *Off-Balance Sheet Update (November 2003).* Nomura Fixed Income Research, November 24, 2003.

Adelson, M., and T. Cho (2002). *Accounting vs. Reality: Can We Handle the Truth?* Nomura Fixed Income Research, April 16, 2002. www .markadelson.com/pubs/Accounting_vs_Reality.pdf

Adhikari, A., and L. Betancourt (2008). Accounting for Securitizations: A Comparison of SFAS 140 and IASB 39. *Journal of International Financial Management & Accounting* 19(1), 73–105.

Adrian, T., and A. Ashcraft (April 2012). Shadow Banking Regulation. Staff Report No. 559, Federal Reserve Bank of New York.

Adrian, T., P. de Fontnouvelle, E. Yang, and A. Zlate (2015). Macroprudential Policy: Case Study from a Tabletop Exercise. Staff Report No. 742, Federal Reserve Bank of New York.

Adrian, T., K. Kimbrough, and D. Marchioni (2010). The Federal Reserve's Commercial Paper Funding Facility. Staff Report No. 423, Federal Reserve Bank of New York.

Adrian, T., and H. S. Shin (2009). The Shadow Banking System: Implications for Financial Regulation. Staff Report No. 382, Federal Reserve Bank of New York.

Aguilar, L. A. (2012). *Public Statement: Statement on Money Market Funds as to Recent Developments*, December 5, 2012. www.sec.gov/news/public-statement/2012-spch120512laahtm

Allen, F., B. Bartiloro, and O. Kowalewski (2005). The Financial System of the EU 25. MPRA Paper No. 652. http://mpra.ub.uni-muenchen.de/652/

Allen, F., and D. Gale (2000). *Comparing Financial Systems*. Cambridge, MA: MIT Press.

American Banker (1985a). *Capital Guidelines Revision Foreseen*. March 29.

(1985b). *Fed Staff Eyes Funding Unit Reserve Rules; Changes Would Affect 'Orphan' Finance Companies of Banks*. December 3.

(1986). *Big Banks to Feel Brunt of Risk-Based Capital Plan; Fed Would Apply Capital Rules to Off-Balance-Sheet Activities*. January 16.

(1987). *Off-Balance-Sheet Items Are Piling Up Total Commitments Exceed $1 Trillion at Top Five Banks*. May 1, Series 1.

(1988a). *More Banks Gear Up to Issue Asset-Backed Commercial Paper*. September 8.

(1988b). *Citicorp Broadens Paper Market*. November 11.

(1989). *Surge Seen in Asset-Backed Paper*. July 11.

(1991a). *Capital Rules Are Pressuring Funding Units*. December 13, Series 5, 156 (239).

(1991b). *Regulators Examine Risk of Asset-Backed Paper*. March 12, Series 11, 156 (48).

(1991c). *Citicorp Is Trying to Restructure as Much as $20 Billion in Paper*. February 19, Series 5, 156 (33).

(1992). *Citi Innovates in Funding Card Balances*. May 11, 157 (090).

(1993). Capital Rules Spur Foreign Banks into Asset-Backed Commercial Paper. May 20, Series 10, 158 (96).

(2000). *Rule Would Close Capital Loophole on Securitization.* February 18, 165, 34.

Americans for Financial Reform (AFR) (2017). Letter to Congress on the Hearing of HFSC 10–11; October 11, 2017.

Amis, P., and E. Rospars (2005). Prudential Supervision and the Evolution of Accounting Standards: The Stakes for Financial Stability. *Banque de France, Financial Stability Review* 7, 47–58.

Andrews, D. M. (1994). Capital Mobility and State Autonomy: Toward a Structural Theory of International Monetary Relations. *International Studies Quarterly* 38(2), 193–218.

Arestis, P., and E. Karakitsos (2013). *Financial Stability in the Aftermath of the 'Great Recession.'* London: Palgrave.

Arrow, K. J., and G. Debreu (1954). Existence of an Equilibrium for a Competitive Economy. *Econometrica* 22(3), 265–290.

Arteta, C., M. Carey, R. Correa, and J. Kotter (2013). Revenge of the Steamroller: ABCP as a Window on Risk Choices. Federal Reserve Board International Finance Discussion Papers.

Asmussen, J. (2006). Verbriefungen aus Sicht des Bundesfinanzministeriums. *Zeitschrift für das gesamte Kreditwesen* 19(1), 1016–1019.

Awrey, D. (2013). Toward a Supply-Side Theory of Financial Innovation. *Journal of Comparative Economics* 41(2), 401–419.

Ayres, I., and J. Braithwaite (1992). *Responsive Regulation: Transcending the Deregulation Debate.* Oxford: Oxford University Press.

Baba, N., R. N. McCauley, and S. Ramaswamy (2009). US Dollar Money Market Funds and Non-US Banks. *BIS Quarterly Review* March, 65–81.

Baker, A. (2010). Restraining Regulatory Capture? Anglo-America, Crisis Politics and Trajectories of Change in Global Financial Governance. *International Affairs* 86(3), 647–663.

Baker, C. R., and E. M. Barbu (2007). Evolution of Research on International Accounting Harmonization: A Historical and Institutional Perspective. *Socio-Economic Review* 5(4), 603–632.

Ballwieser, W. (2010). Germany. In G. J. Previts, P. J. Walton, and P. Wolnizer (eds.), *A Global History of Accounting, Financial Reporting and Public Policy: Europe. Studies in the Development of Accounting Thought*, pp. 59–88. Sydney: Emerald.

Balthazar, L. (2006). *From Basel 1 to Basel 2: The Integration of State of the Art Risk Modelling in Banking Regulation.* London: Palgrave Macmillan.

Banco de Espana (2008). *Circular 3/2008, de 22 de mayo a entidades de crédito: Sobre determinación y control de los recursos propios mínimos.* www.bde.es/f/webbde/SJU/normativa/circulares/c200803.pdf

Bank of England (2007). *Financial Stability Report*. October, Issue No. 22. www.bankofengland.co.uk/publications/Documents/fsr/2007/ fsrfull0710.pdf

Bannier, C., and D. Haensel (2006). *Determinants of Banks' Engagement in Loan Securitization*. www.frankfurt-school.de/dms/Arbeitsberichte/ Arbeits85.pdf

Barendregt, J., and H. Visser (1997). Towards a New Maturity, 1940–1990. In M. Hart, J. Jonker, and L. van Zanden (eds.), *A Financial History of the Netherlands*, pp. 152–194. Cambridge: Cambridge University Press.

Barth, J. R., G. Caprio, Jr., and R. Levine (2012). *Guardians of Finance – Making Regulator Work for Us*. Cambridge, MA: MIT Press.

Basel Committee for Banking Supervision (BCBS) (1986). *Recent Innovations in International Banking*, April 1986. www.bis.org/publ/ecsc01a.pdf

(1988). *International Convergence of Capital Measurement and Capital Standards*, July 1988. www.bis.org/publ/bcbs04a.pdf

(1999a). *Enhancements to the Basel II Framework*, July 2009. www.bis .org/publ/bcbs157.pdf

(1999b). *A New Capital Adequacy Framework: Consultative Paper Issued by the Basel Committee on Banking Supervision*. Issued for Comment by March 31, 2000, Basel June 1999. www.bis.org/publ/ bcbs50.pdf

(1999c). Capital Requirements and Bank Behaviour: The Impact of the Basel Accord. Working Papers 1, April. www.bis.org/publ/bcbs_wp01 .pdf

(2004). *International Convergence of Capital Measurement and Capital Standards: A Revised Framework*. www.bis.org/publ/bcbs107.pdf

(2009a). *Report on Special Purpose Entities*.

(2009b). *Risk Management Lessons from the Global Banking Crisis in 2008*.

(2015). *Identification and Measurement of Step-in Risk*. Consultative Document.

(2017). *Guidelines for Identification and Management of Step-in Risk*. Consultative Document. www.bis.org/bcbs/publ/d398.pdf

Battilossi, S. (2002). Introduction: International Banking and the American Challenge in Historical Perspective. In S. Battilossi and Y. Cassis (eds.), *European Banks and the American Challenge: Competition and Cooperation in International Banking under Bretton Woods*, pp. 1–35. Oxford: Oxford University Press.

Battilossi, S., and Y. Cassis (2002). *European Banks and the American Challenge: Competition and Cooperation in International Banking under Bretton Woods*. Oxford: Oxford University Press.

Baud, C. (2013). Le crédit sous Bâle II-un dispositif néolibéral de financiarisation en pratiques. Doctoral dissertation, Jouy-en Josas, HEC. www.theses.fr/2013EHEC0007.pdf

Baud, C., and E. Chiapello (2014). Disciplining the Neoliberal Bank: Credit Risk Regulation and the Financialization of Loan Management. https://ssrn.com/abstract=2417396

Baudot, L. (2014). GAAP Convergence or Convergence Gap: Unfolding Ten Years of Accounting Change. *Accounting, Auditing & Accountability Journal* 27(6), 956–994.

BDO (2011). *IFRS versus BE GAAP: A Comprehensive Comparison.* www.kmocockpit.be/media/docs/boekhouding/vergelijkingIFRSvs BEGAAP_07 102011_RGB.pdf

Becker, G. S. (1983). A Theory of Competition among Pressure Groups for Political Influence. *The Quarterly Journal of Economics* 98(3), 371–400.

Bell, S., and A. Hindmoor (2015a). Masters of the Universe, but Slaves of the Market: Bankers and the Great Financial Meltdown. *British Journal of Politics and International Relations* 17(1), 1–22.

(2015b). Taming the City? Ideas, Structural Power and the Evolution of British Banking Policy Amidst the Great Financial Meltdown. *New Political Economy* 20(3), 454–474.

Bens, S., and D. Monahan (2008). Altering Investment Decisions to Manage Financial Reporting Outcomes: Asset-Backed Commercial Paper Conduits and FIN 46. *Journal of Accounting Research* 46(5), 1017–1055.

Benston, G. J., M. Bromwich, R. E. Litan, and A. Wagenhofer (2006). *Worldwide Financial Reporting: The Development and Future of Financial Reporting.* Oxford: Oxford University Press.

Berger, A. N. (2007). Obstacles to a Global Banking System: "Old Europe" versus "New Europe." *Journal of Banking & Finance* 31(7), 1955–1973.

Bernanke, B. (2007). The Subprime Mortgage Market. Speech at the Federal Reserve Bank of Chicago's 43rd Annual Conference on Bank Structure and Competition, Chicago, IL, May 17, 2007. www.federalreserve.gov/newsevents/speech/bernanke20070517a.htm

Bernanke, B. S. (2013). The Crisis as a Classic Financial Panic. Remarks by Chairman Board of Governors of the Federal Reserve System at Fourteenth Jacques Polak Annual Research Conference Sponsored by the International Monetary Fund, Washington, DC. https://www.federalreserve.gov/newsevents/speech/bernanke20131108a.pdf

Bezemer, D. J. (2009). "No One Saw This Coming": Understanding Financial Crisis through Accounting Models. MPRA Paper No. 15892, June

16, 2009. http://izvor-denarja.si/wp-content/uploads/2012/08/Study-Bezemer-No-one-saw-this-coming.pdf

Bhattacharya, S., A. W. A. Boot, and A. V. Thakor (1998). The Economics of Bank Regulation. *Journal of Money, Credit and Banking* 30(4), 745–770.

Bhidé, A. (2011). An Accident Waiting to Happen: Securities Regulation and Financial Deregulation. In J. Friedman (ed.), *What Caused the Financial Crisis?*, pp. 69–106. Oxford: University of Pennsylvania Press.

Biener, H. (2000). Das DRSC: Aufgaben und Perspektiven. In D. Kleindiek and W. Oehler (eds.), pp. 55–70. *Die Zukunft des deutschen Bilanzrechts im Zeichen internationaler Rechnungslegung und privater Standardsetzung*. Cologne: Dr. Otto Schmidt.

Black, J. (1997). *Rules and Regulators*. Oxford Socio-Legal Studies. Oxford: Oxford University Press.

    (2002). Regulatory Conversations. *Journal of Law and Society* 29(1), 163–196.

    (2003). Enrolling Actors in Regulatory Systems: Examples from UK Financial Services Regulation. *Public Law* 2003 (Spring), 63–91.

    (2008). Forms and Paradoxes of Principles-Based Regulation. *Capital Markets Law Journal* 3(4), 425–458.

    (2012). Paradoxes and Failures: "New Governance" Techniques and the Financial Crisis. *The Modern Law Review* 75(6), 1037–1063.

    (2013). Seeing, Knowing and Regulating Financial Markets. LSE Law, Society and Economy Working Papers 24, pp. 1–47.

Block, F. (2010). The Future of Economics, New Circuits for Capital, and Re-envisioning the Relation of State and Market. In M. Lounsboury and P. M. Hirsch (eds.), *Markets on Trial: Toward a Policy Oriented Economic Sociology*, pp. 309–330. Research in the Sociology of Organizations, Vol. 28, Part B. Bingley: Emerald.

Bloomberg (2017). *Almost a Decade Later, U.S. Money Markets Are Yet to Recover.* https://www.bloomberg.com/news/articles/2017-04-02/money-funds-overhaul-spurs-shakeup-of-dollar-financing-markets

Blundell-Wignall, A., and P. Atkinson (2010). Thinking beyond Basel 3. OECD. *Financial Market Trends* 2010(1), 9–33.

Blyth, M. (2014). *Austerity: The History of a Dangerous Idea.* Oxford: Oxford University Press.

Board of Governors of the Federal Reserve System (1992). SR 92-11 to the Officer in Charge of Supervision at Each Federal Reserve Bank. Subject: Asset-Backed Commercial Paper Programs.

Bocqueraz, C. (2010). France. In G. J. Previts, P. J. Walton, and P. Wolnizer (eds.), *A Global History of Accounting, Financial Reporting and Public Policy: Europe*, pp. 37–58. Studies in the Development of Accounting Thought. Sydney: Emerald.

Boot, W. A. (1999). European Lessons on Consolidation in Banking. *Journal of Banking & Finance* 23(2), 609–613.

Borio, C. E. V., and K. Tsatsaronis (2005). Accounting, Prudential Regulation and Financial Stability: Elements of a Synthesis. BIS Working Paper 180, 1–32.

Botzem, S. (2012). *The Politics of Accounting Regulation: Organizing Transnational Standard Setting in Financial Reporting*. Cheltenham: Edward Elgar.

Botzem, S., and L. Dobusch (2012). Standardization Cycles: A Process Perspective on the Formation and Diffusion of Transnational Standards. *Organization Studies* 33(5–6), 737–762.

Botzem, S., and S. Quack (2006). International Standard-Setting in Accounting. In M.-L. Djelic and K. Sahlin-Andersson (eds.), *Transnational Governance: Institutional Dynamics of Regulation*, pp. 266–286. Cambridge: Cambridge University Press,

(2009). (No) Limits to Anglo-American Accounting? Reconstructing the History of the International Accounting Standards Committee: A Review Article. *Accounting, Organization and Society* 34(8), 988–998.

Brimmer, A. F. (1989). Distinguished Lecture on Economics in Government: Central Banking and Systemic Risks in Capital Markets. *Journal of Economic Perspectives* 3(2), 3–16.

Brinkhuis, D., and R. van Eldonk (2008). Still Going Strong: The Netherlands Remains the Jurisdiction of Choice for Structured Finance Transactions. In Deutsche Bank Services (ed.), *Global Securitisation and Structured Finance*, pp. 215–220. London: Globe White Page.

Brunnermeier, M. K., and L. H. Pedersen (2009). Market Liquidity and Funding Liquidity. *Review of Financial Studies* 22(6), 2201–2238.

Buethe, T. (2010a). Private Regulation in the Global Economy: A (P) Review. *Business and Politics* 12(3), 1–40.

(2010b). Engineering Uncontestedness? The Origins and Institutional Development of the International Electrotechnical Commission (IEC). *Business and Politics* 12(3), 1–62.

Buethe, T., and W. Mattli (2011). *The New Global Rulers: The Privatization of Regulation in the World Economy*. Princeton, NJ: Princeton University Press.

Buiter, W. H. (2008). Central Banks and Financial Crises. Paper presented at the Federal Reserve Bank's Symposium at Jackson Hole, Wyoming, August 21–23, 2008, pp. 1–147.

(2012). The Role of Central Banks in Financial Stability: How Has It Changed? CEPR Discussion Paper No. 8780.

Bundesaufsichtsamt für das Kreditwesen (BaKred) (1997a). *Anschreiben zum Rundschreiben 4/1997 – Veräusserung von Kundenforderungen im Rahmen von Asset-Backed Securities-Transaktionen durch deutsche Kreditinstitute.* Frankfurt am Main: Bundesaufsichtsamt für das Kreditwesen.

(1997b). *Veräusserung von Kundenforderungen im Rahmen von Asset-Backed Securities-Transaktionen durch deutsche Kreditinstitute.* Frankfurt am Main: Bundesaufsichtsamt für das Kreditwesen.

(2002). *Stellungnahme an das Bundesministerium für Justiz. Entwurf eines DRS 16 (10 alt): Aufstellung des Konzernabschlusses und Konsolidierungskreis,* pp. 1–2.

Burger, A. E. (1969). A Historical Analysis of the Credit Crunch of 1966. *Federal Reserve Bank of St. Louis Review* (September), 13–30.

Burlaud, A., and B. Colasse (2010). Normalisation comptable internationale: Le retour du politique? *Comptabilité Contrôle Audit* 16(3), 153–175.

Calomiris, C. W., and G. Gorton (1991). The Origins of Banking Panics: Models, Facts, and Bank Regulation. In R. G. Hubbard (ed.), *Financial Markets and Financial Crises,* pp. 109–174. Chicago, IL: University of Chicago Press.

Camffermann, K., and S. Zeff (2007). *Financial Reporting and Global Capital Markets.* Oxford: Oxford University Press.

Carletti, E. (2008). Competition and Regulation in Banking. In A. V. Thakor and W. A. Boot (eds.), *Handbook of Financial Intermediation and Banking,* pp. 449–482. Amsterdam: North Holland.

Carletti, E., P. Hartmann, and S. Ongena (2006). Cross-Border Banking and Competition Policy. *European Central Bank Research Bulletin* 4, 7–10.

Carney, M. (2014). The Future of Financial Reform. Speech given at the Monetary Authority of Singapore. www.bankofengland.co.uk/publications/Pages/speeches/default.aspx

(2015). *To G20 Leaders: Financial Reforms – Achieving and Sustaining Resilience for All,* November 9, 2015. www.fsb.org/wp-content/uploads/FSB-Chairs-letter-to-G20-Leaders-9-Nov.pdf

(2017). Ten Years On: Fixing the Fault Lines of the Global Financial Crisis. *Banque de France Financial Stability Review* (21), April 2017, 13–20.

Carpenter, D., and D. A. Moss (2013). Introduction. In D. Carpenter and D. A. Moss (eds.), *Preventing Regulatory Capture: Special Interest Influence and How to Limit It,* pp. 1–22. New York, NY: Cambridge University Press.

Cerveny, F., T. Lange, R. Raebel, and T. Stumpf (2010). ABS & Structured Credits: Eine Research Publication der DZ Bank AG, Asset-basierte Finanzierungen "Made in Germany." Teil 2. *Eine Research-Publikation der DZ BANK AG.*

Champ, N. (2013). Speech: Money Market Mutual Fund Reform: Opening Statement at the SEC Open Meeting, Washington, DC, June 5, 2013. www.sec.gov/news/speech/2013-spch060513nchtm

Chang, M., and E. Jones (2013). Belgium and the Netherlands: Impatient Capital. In I. Hardie and D. Howarth (eds.), *Market-Based Banking and the International Financial Crisis*, pp. 79–102. Oxford: Oxford University Press.

Chant, J. (2009). *The ABCP Crisis in Canada: The Implications for the Regulation of Financial Markets, A Research Study Prepared for the Expert Panel on Securities Regulation.* http://investisseurautonome .info/PDF-Downloads/COMMENT-INVESTIR-RENDEMENT-INDEX/doc.1495-%20Chant%202009%20ABCP%20report%20.pdf

Chantiri-Chaudemanche, R. (2009). Organismes de Normalisation. In Bernard Colasse (ed.), *Encyclopédie de Comptabilité, contrôle de gestion et audit*, Vol. II, pp. 1109–1120. Paris: Economica.

Chantiri-Chaudemanche, R., and C. Pochet (2012). La normalisation comptable: L'expert, le politique et la mondialisation. In M. Nikitin and C. Richard (eds.), *Comptabilité, Société, Politique*, pp. 143–156. Paris: Economica.

Chernenko, S., and A. Sunderam (2014). Frictions in Shadow Banking: Evidence from the Lending Behavior of Money Market Mutual Funds. *Review of Financial Studies* 27(6), 1717–1750.

Chiapello, E. (2009). Die Konstruktion der Wirtschaft durch das Rechnungswesen. In R. Diaz-Bone and G. Krell (eds.), *Diskurs und Ökonomie*, pp. 125–149. Wiesbaden: VS Verlag für Sozialwissenschaften.

Choi, F., and G. K. Meek (2005). *International Accounting*, Vol. 5. Upper Saddle River, NJ: Pearson Education.

Christophers, B. (2011). Making Finance Productive. *Economy and Society* 40(1), 112–140.

(2013). *Banking across Boundaries: Placing Finance in Capitalism.* Hoboken, NJ: John Wiley & Sons.

Claessens, S., and L. Ratnovski (2014). What Is Shadow Banking? IMF Working Paper 14/25.

Claessens, S., and G. R. D. Underhill (2010). The Political Economy of Basel II in the International Financial Architecture. In G. R. D. Underhill, J. Blom, and D. Mügge (eds.), *Global Financial Integration Thirty Years on, from Reform to Crisis*, pp. 113–133. Cambridge: Cambridge University Press.

Clift, B., and C. Woll (2012). Economic Patriotism: Reinventing Control over Open Markets. *Journal of European Public Policy* 19(3), 307–323.

(2013). *Economic Patriotism in Open Economies.* Abingdon: Routledge.

Coffee, J. C., Jr. (2006). *Gatekeepers.* Oxford: Oxford University Press.

Colasse, B., and C. Pochet (2009). The Genesis of the 2007 Conseil National de la Comptabilite: A Case of Institutional Isomorphism? *Accounting in Europe* 6(1), 25–55.

Coleman, W. D. (1996). *Financial Services, Globalization and Domestic Policy Change*. London: Macmillan.

(2001). Governing French Banking: Regulatory Reform and the Credit Lyonnais Fiasco. In M. Bovens, M. Hart, and B. G. Peters (eds.), *Success and Failure in Public Governance*, pp. 326–342. Cheltenham: Edward Elgar.

Commission Bancaire (CB) (2002). *Bulletin de la Commission Bancaire No. 27 – November. 2002.* https://acpr.banque-france.fr/fileadmin/user_upload/banque_de_france/archipel/publications/cb_bul/cb_bu l_2002/cb_bul_27.pdf

(CB) (2003). *Modalités de calcul du ratio internatinoal de solvabilité au 01/01/2003.* Paris: Commission Bancaire.

Committee of European Banking Supervisors (CEBS) (2004). *Guidelines on Prudential Filters for Regulatory Capital.* http://eba.europa.eu/getdoc/dcb751c89d21-4cf585b7-d0d6d5f5985/prudential_filters-21-Dec-2004.aspx

Committee on Global Financial System (2009). The Role of Valuation and Leverage in Procyclicality. CGFS Papers No. 34. www.bis.org/publ/cgfs34.pdf?noframes=1

Conseil National de la Comptabilité (2004). *Note de Présentation – Avis N_2004-D du Comité d'Urgence relatif aux dispositions particulirés concernant la consolidation des fonds communs de créances et des organismes étrangers.*

Cook, T. Q., and J. G. Duffield (1993). Money Market Mutual Funds and Other Short-Term Investment Pools. In T. Q. Cook and R. K. LaRoche (eds.), *Instruments of the Money Market*, pp. 156–172. Richmond, VA: Federal Reserve Bank of Richmond.

Cooper, D., and K. Robson (2006). Accounting, Professions and Regulation: Locating the Sites of Professionalization. *Accounting, Organizations and Society* 31(4/5), 415–444.

Council of the European Union (2016). *Proposal for a Regulation of the European Parliament and of the Council on Money Market Funds [first reading], Brussels*, November 30, 2016. http://data.consilium.europa.eu/doc/document/ST-14939-2016-INIT/en/pdf

Crane Data (2017). *Fitch's Sewell and Gkeka on Timing of European Money Fund Reforms.* https://cranedata.com/archives/all-articles/6476/

Crouch, C. (2009). Privatised Keynesianism: An Unacknowledged Policy Regime. *The British Journal of Politics & International Relations* 11(3), 382–399.

Culpepper, P. D. (2011). *Quiet Politics and Business Power: Corporate Control in Europe and Japan.* New York, NY: Cambridge University Press.

D'Arista, J. W. (1994). *The Evolution of US Finance: Restructuring Institutions and Markets,* Vol. II. Armonk, NY: M.E. Sharpe.

De Goede, M. (2004). Repoliticizing Financial Risk. *Economy and Society* 33(2), 197–217.

De Nederlandsche Bank (DNB) (1979). *De herziene Wet Toezicht Kredietwezen (The Revised Act on Supervision of the Credit System).* Amsterdam: De Nederlandsche Bank.

(1997). *Memorandum inzake securitisatie en toezicht,* pp. 1–14. Amsterdam: De Nederlandsche Bank.

(2005). *Handboek Wet Toezicht Kredietwezen.* Amsterdam: De Nederlandsche Bank.

De Rynck, S. (2016). Banking on a Union: The Politics of Changing Eurozone Banking Supervision. *Journal of European Public Policy* 23(1), 119–135.

Deeg, R. (2012). Liberal Economic Nationalism and Europeanization: The Rise of Spanish and Italian Banks. Paper presented at the American Political Science Association.

Deeg, R. E. (2010). Institutional Change in Financial Systems. In G. Morgan J. L. Campbell, C. Crouch, O. K. Pedersen and R. Whitley (eds.), *Oxford Handbook of Comparative Institutional Analysis,* pp. 438–452. Oxford: Oxford University Press.

Delloite (2014). *Securitization Accounting.* www2.deloitte.com/content/dam/Deloitte/global/Documents/Financial-Services/dttl-us-aers-favs-securitization-accounting-edition9-2014-01-20.pdf

Delpeuch, T., C. Bessy, and J. Pélisse (2011). *Droit et régulations des activités économiques: Perspectives sociologiques et institutionnalistes.*

Deutsche Bank Research (2015). *Money Market Funds: An Economic Perspective: Matching Short-Term Investment and Funding Needs.* EU Monitor Global Financial Markets. www.dbresearch.com/PROD/DBR_INTERNET_EN-PROD/PROD0000000000351452/Money_market_funds_%E2%80%93_an_economicperspective%3A_Matc.pdf

Deutsche Bundesbank (1995). Verbriefungstendenzen im deutschen Finanzsystem und ihre geldpolitische Bedeutung. *Monatsbericht April* 47(4), 19–33.

Deutsches Institut fuer Wirtschaftsforschung (DIW) (2006). *Evaluierungsuntersuchungen zur Bewertung der Aufsicht der Kreditwirtschaft und Erstellung eines Erfahrungsberichts (Erfahrungsbericht Bankenaufsicht),* pp. 1–8. Berlin: Deutsches Institut für Wirtschaftsforschung.

Dexia (2009). *Risk Report 2008: Pillar III of Basel II.* www.dexia.com/
EN/shareholder_investor/individual_shareholders/publications/
Documents/risk_repport_2008_UK.pdf

Dharan, B. G., and W. R. Bufkins (2008). *Red Flags in Enron's Reporting
of Revenues & Key Financial Measures.* http://baladharan.com/files/
dharan-bufkins_enron_red_flags.pdf

Diamond, D. W., and G. R. Rajan (2009). The Credit Crisis: Conjectures
about Causes and Remedies. *American Economic Review: Papers and
Proceedings* 99(2), 606–610.

Diaz-Alejandro, C. F., P. R. Krugman, and J. D. Sachs (1984). Latin American
Debt: I Don't Think We Are in Kansas Anymore. *Brookings Papers on
Economic Activity* 1984 (2), 335–340.

DiMaggio, P., and W. Powell (1983). The Iron Cage Revisited. *American
Sociological Review* 48(2), 147–160.

Djelic, M.-L. (1998). *Exporting the American Model: The Postwar
Transformation of Business.* Oxford: Oxford University Press.

   (2007). Overcoming Path Dependency: Path Generation in Open Systems.
   Theory and Society 36(2), 161–186.

   (2011). The Power of Limited Liability: Transnational Communities
   and Cross-Border Governance. In C. Marquis, M. Lounsbury,
   and R. Greenwood (eds.), *Communities and Organizations*, pp.
   73–109. Research in the Sociology of Organizations, Vol. 33.
   Bingley: Emerald Books.

Djelic, M.-L., and S. Quack (2003). Introduction: Governing Globalization –
Bringing Institutions Back In. In M.-L. Djelic and S. Quack (eds.),
*Globalizations and Institutions: Redefining the Rules of the Economic
Game*, pp. 1–14. Cheltenham: Edward Elgar.

   (2007). Overcoming Path Dependency: Path Generation in Open Systems.
   Theory and Society 36(2), 161–186.

   (2008). Institutions and Transnationalization. In R. Greenwood, C.
   Oliver, K. Sahlin, and R. Suddaby (eds.), *The SAGE Handbook of
   Organizational Institutionalism*, pp. 299–323. London: SAGE.

   (2011). The Power of "Limited Liability": Transnational Communities
   and Cross-Border Governance. In C. Marquis, M. Lounsbury,
   and R. Greenwood (eds.), *Communities and Organizations*, pp.
   73–109. Research in the Sociology of Organizations, Vol. 33.
   Bingley: Emerald.

Donnelly, S. (2012). Institutional Change at the Top: From the Financial
Stability Forum to the Financial Stability Board. In R. Mayntz (ed.), *Crisis
and Control: Institutional Change in Financial Market Regulation*, pp.
261–275. Frankfurt am Main: Campus Verlag; Chicago, IL: Chicago
University Press.

Dowd, K. (1992). Models of Banking Instability: A Partial Review of the Literature. *Journal of Economic Surveys* 6(2), 107–132.

Drezner, D. (2007). *All Politics Is Global*. Princeton, NJ: Princeton University Press.

Drezner, D. W. (2010). Afterword: Is Historical Institutionalism Bunk? *Review of International Political Economy* 17(4), 791–804.

Eaton, S. (2005). Crisis and the Consolidation of International Accounting Standards: Enron, the IASB, and America. *Business and Politics* 7(3), 1–20.

Ebbinghaus, B. (2005). When Less Is More: Selection Problems in Large-N and Small-N Cross-National Comparisons. *International Sociology* 20(2), 133–152.

Edelman, L. (1990). Legal Environments and Organizational Governance: The Expansion of Due Process in the American Workplace. *American Journal of Sociology* 95(6), 1401–1440.

Edelman, L., L. Krieger, S. R. Eliason, C. R. Albiston, and V. Mellema (2011). When Organizations Rule: Judicial Deference to Institutionalized Employment Structures. *American Journal of Sociology* 117(3), 888–954.

Edelman, L., and T. Shauhin (2011). To Comply or Not to Comply – That Isn't the Question: How Organizations Construct the Meaning of Compliance. In C. Parker and V. Nielsen (eds.), *Explaining Compliance-Business Responses to Regulation*, pp. 103–122. Cheltenham: Edward Elgar.

Edelman, L., and R. Stryker (2005). A Sociological Approach to Law and the Economy. In N. J. Smelser and R. Swedberg (eds.), *Handbook of Economic Sociology*, pp. 527–551. Princeton, NJ: Princeton University Press.

Edwards, F., and F. Mishkin (1995). The Decline of Traditional Banking: Implications for Financial Stability and Regulatory Policy. *Federal Reserve Bank of New York Economic Policy Review* 1, 27–45.

Ehrlich, M., A. Anandarajan, and B. Chou (2009). Structured Investment Vehicles: The Unintended Consequences of Financial Innovation. *Bank Accounting and Finance* October–November, 22 (6), 29–37.

Eichengreen, B. (2003). Governing Global Financial Markets. International Responses to the Hedge Fund Problem. In M. Kahler and D. Lake (eds.), *Governance in a Global Economy: Political Authority in Transition*, pp. 168–198. Princeton, NJ: Princeton University Press.

Ekkenga, J. (2011). Sachverhaltsgestaltung durch Window-dressing: Der Fall "Lehman Bros" aus europäischer Sicht. *Der Konzern* 9, pp. 321–330.

Engelen, E. (2017). Shadow Banking after the Crisis: The Dutch Case. *Theory, Culture and Society* 34(5–6), 53–75.

Enria, A., and P. G. Teixeira (2011). A New Institutional Framework for Financial Regulation and Supervision. In F. Cannata and M. Quagliariello (eds.), *Basel III and Beyond: A Guide to Banking Regulation after the Crisis*, pp. 421–468. London: RiskBooks.

Epstein, G. A. (eds.) (2005). *Financialization and the World Economy*. Northampton, MA: Edward Elgar.

Espeland, W., and M. Sauder (2007). Rankings and Reactivity: How Public Measures Recreate Social Worlds. *American Journal of Sociology* 113(1), 1–40.

European Banking Authority (EBA) (2014). *EBA Report on Qualifying Securitization: Response to the Commission's Call for Advice of January 2014 on Long-Term Financing*. www.eba.europa.eu/documents/10180/ 950548/EBA+report+on+qualifying+securitisation.pdf

European Central Bank (ECB) (2001). *Le role des banques centrales en matiere de controle prudential*. www.ecb.de/pub/pdf/other/prudential supcbrole_fr.pdf

European Commission (EC) (1995). Accounting Harmonization: A New Strategy vis-à-vis International Harmonization. Commission Communication COM 95 (508).

(1999). Financial Services – Implementing the Framework for Financial Markets: Action Plan. Commission Communication of 11.05.1999 COM (1999) 232.

(2000a). EU Financial Reporting Strategy: The Way Forward. Commission Communication (2000) 359.

(2000b). *Implementation of the Seventh Directive in EU Member States. Summary of Findings from a Study on the Implementation of Seventh Directive 83/349/EEC in the Member States of the European Union.* http://ec.europa.eu/internal_market/accounting/docs/studies/1998- seventh-dir_en.pdf

(2005). Cross-Border Consolidation in the EU Financial Sector. Commission Staff Working Document. Brussels: Commission of the European Communities.

(2009). *SIC Interpretation 12 Consolidation – Special Purpose Entities*. Consolidated Version. http://ec.europa.eu/internal_market/accounting/ docs/consolidated/sic12_en.pdf

(2013). *Commission Staff Working Dokument: Impact Assesement. Proposal for a Regulation of the European Parliament and of the Council on Money Market Funds, Brussels, 4.9.2013.* http://eur-lex .europa.eu/legal-content/EN/TXT/PDF/?uri=CELEX:52013SC0315&f rom=EN

European Council (2016). *Proposal for a Regulation of the European Parliament and of the Council on Money Market Funds.* http://data .consilium.europa.eu/doc/document/ST-14939-2016-INIT/en/pdf

European Financial Markets Lawyers Group (EFMLG) (2007a). *Obstacles to Cross-Borders Securitization*, pp. 1–102.

(2007b). *Obstacles to Cross-Border Securitization: Annex*, pp. 1–183.

European Financial Stability Board (ESRB) (2012). Money Market Funds in Europe and Financial Stability. Occasional Paper Series No. 1/ June 2012.

European Parliament (EP) (2002). *Regulation (EC) No. 1606/2002 of the European Parliament and of the Council of 19 July 2002 on the Application of International Accounting Standards.* http://eur-lex.europa .eu/LexUriserv/LexUriServ.do?uri=OJ:L:2002:243:0001:0004:en:PDF

(2012). *European Parliament Resolution of 20 November 2012 on Shadow Banking (2012/2115(INI)).* www.europarl.europa.eu/sides/ getDoc.do?pubRef=-//EP//TEXT+TA+P7-TA-2012-0427+0+DOC+ XML+V0//EN

(2015). *Legislative Train Schedule Deeper and Fairer Internal Market with a Strengthened Industrial Base / Financial Service.* www.europarl.europa .eu/legislative-train/theme-deeper-and-fairer-internal-market-with-a-strengthened-industrial-base-financial-services/file-money-market-funds

(2016). *Briefing: The Relationship between Banking Supervisors and Banks' External Auditors.* www.europarl.europa.eu/RegData/etudes/ BRIE/2015/542685/IPOL_BRI(2015) 542685_EN.pdf

European Parliament: Committee on Economic and Monetary Affairs (2015). *Amendments 472–800, 9.1.2015.* www.europarl.europa .eu/sides/getDoc.do?pubRef=-//EP//NONSGML+COMPARL+PE-546.610+02+DOC+PDF+V0//EN&language=EN

European Securitization Forum. (2002). *Letter to IASB Re: Consolidation and SIC 12.* Accessible at: www.sifma.org/workarea/downloadasset .aspx?id=1022; last accessed April 21, 2012.

European Systemic Risk Board (ESRB) (2012). *Annex to the ESRB Recommendation on Money Market Funds.* www.esrb.europa.eu/pub/ pdf/recommendations/2012/ESRB_2012_1_annex.en.pdf?bb7dbe5446 aa3f8f3e14bc80060f2569

Evans, P. B. (1995). *Embedded Autonomy: States and Industrial Transformation.* Princeton, NJ: Princeton University Press.

Farrell, H., and A. L. Newman (2010). Making Global Markets: Historical Institutionalism in International Political Economy. *Review of International Political Economy* 17(4), 609–638.

(2014). Domestic Institutions beyond the Nation-State: Charting the New Interdependence Approach. *World Politics* 66(2), 331–363.

Federal Reserve (1990). *To the Officer in Charge of Supervision at Each Federal Reserve Bank: Subject: Implementation of Examination Guidelines for the Review of Asset Securitization Activities.* Board

of Governors of the Federal Reserve System, Washington, DC. www
.federalreserve.gov/boarddocs/srletters/1990/SR9016.HTM

(1997). *84th Annual Report 1997*. Board of Governors of the Federal
Reserve System, Washington, DC, May 29, 1998. www.federalreserve
.gov/boarddocs/rptcongress/annual97/ann97.pdf

(2002). *Letter of Comment No: 137*. Board of Governors of the Federal
Reserve System, Washington, DC, September 24, 2002.

(2009). *Press Release, Release Date: June 12, 2009*. www.federalreserve
.gov/newsevents/press/bcreg/20090612a.htm

(2010). *Joint Press Release: Agencies Issue Final Rule for Regulatory
Capital Standards Related to Statements of Financial Accounting
Standards Nos. 166 and 167*, January 21. www.federalreserve.gov/
newsevents/press/bcreg/20100121a.htm

(2014). *Press Release: Release Date: February 18, 2014*. www
.federalreserve.gov/newsevents/press/bcreg/20140218a.htm

Fein, M. L. (2012). Money Market Funds, Systemic Risk and the Dodd–
Frank Act. Paper presented the American Enterprise Institute,
June 28.

Financial Accounting Standards Board (FASB) (2006). *FASB Responds to SEC
Study on Off-Balance Sheet Arrangements, Reaffirming Commitment to
Address and Improve Outdated, Complex Standards: Priority Remains
on Improving Transparency, Usefulness of Financial Reporting for
Investors and Capital Markets*/News Release 02/16/06. www.fasb.org/
news/nr021606a.shtml

(2011). *Exposure Draft: Proposed Accounting Standards Update.
Consolidation (Topic 810). Principal versus Agent Analysis*. http://fasb
.org/jsp/FASB/Document_C/DocumentPage?cid=1176159223847&ac
cepte dDisclaimer=true

Financial Crisis Inquiry Commission (FCIC) (2011). *The Financial Crisis
Inquiry Report: Final Report of the National Commission on the on
the Causes of the Financial and Economic Crisis in the United States*.
http://fcic-static.law.stanford.edu/cdn_media/fcic-reports/fcic_final_
report_full.pdf

Financial Stability Board (FSB) (2011a). *Shadow Banking: Scoping the
Issues. A Background Note of the Financial Stability Board*. Available
at www.fsb.org/wp-content/uploads/r_110412a.pdf, last accessed
March 20, 2018.

(2011b). *Shadow Banking: Strengthening Oversight and Regulation.
Recommendations of the Financial Stability Board*. Available at
www.fsb.org/wp-content/uploads/r_111027a.pdf?page_moved=1, last
accessed March 20, 2018.

(2012a). *Strengthening the Oversight and Regulation of Shadow Banking: Progress Report to G20 Ministers and Governors.* Available at www.fsb.org/wp-content/uploads/r_120420c.pdf?page_moved=1, last accessed March 20, 2018.

(2012b). *Letter of the Chairman: To the G20 Finance Ministers and Central Bank Governors.* Available at www.fsb.org/wp-content/uploads/r_121105.pdf, last accessed March 20, 2018.

(2014a). *Strengthening Oversight and Regulation of Shadow Banking Regulatory Framework for Haircuts on Non-centrally Cleared Securities Financing Transactions.* Available at www.fsb.org/wp-content/uploads/r_141013a.pdf, last accessed March 20, 2018.

(2014b). *Global Shadow Banking Monitoring Report 2014.* Available at www.fsb.org/wp-content/uploads/r_141030.pdf, last accessed March 20, 2018.

(2014c). *Assessment Methodologies for Identifying Non-Bank Non-Insurer Global Systemically Important Financial Institutions.* Consultative Document. www.fsb.org/wp-content/uploads/r_140108 .pdf

(2015). *Letter of the Chairman to G20 Leaders: Financial Reforms – Achieving and Sustaining Resilience for All.* Available at www.fsb .org/2015/11/chairs-letter-to-the-g20-financial-reforms-achieving-and-sustaining-resilience-for-all/, last accessed March 20, 2018.

(2017a). *Third Annual Report to the G20: Implementation and Effects of the G20 Financial Regulatory Reforms.* Available at www .fsb.org/2017/07/implementation-and-effects-of-the-g20-financial-regulatory-reforms-third-annual-report/, last accessed March 20, 2018.

(2017b). *Policy Recommendations to Address Structural Vulnerabilities from Asset Management Activities, Policy Recommendations to Address Structural Vulnerabilities from Asset Management Activities.* Available at www.fsb.org/2017/01/policy-recommendations-to-address-structural-vulnerabilities-from-asset-management-activities/, last accessed March 20, 2018.

Financial Stability Board and International Organization of Securities Commissions (FSB–IOSCO) (2014). *Consultative Document: Assessment Methodologies for Identifying Non-Bank Non-Insurer Global Systemically Important Financial Institutions. Proposed High-Level Framework and Specific Methodologies,* January 8. www.fsb.org/wp-content/uploads/r_140108.pdf

(2015). *Consultative Document (2nd): Assessment Methodologies for Identifying Non-Bank Non-Insurer Global Systemically Important Financial Institutions. Proposed High-Level Framework and Specific*

Methodologies, March 4. www.fsb.org/wp-content/uploads/2nd-Con-Doc-on-NBNI-G-SIFI-methodologies.pdf

Financial Stability Oversight Council (FSOC) (2012). *Proposed Recommendations Regarding Money Market Mutual Funds.* www.treasury .gov/initiatives/fsoc/Documents/Proposed%20Recommendations %20Regarding%20Money%20Market%20Mutual%20Fund%20 Reform%20- %20November%2013,%202012.pdf

Financial Times (FT) (2014). *EU Banks Win Backing of US Money Market Funds,* April 13, 2014. www.ft.com/content/a10dc4a2-c184-11e3-97b2-00144feabdc0

   (2015). *Fund Managers to Escape 'Systemic' Label,* July 14, 2015. https:// www.ft.com/content/4e9d566e-2999-11e5-8613-e7aedbb7bdb7

Fiss, P. C. (2009). Case Studies and the Configurational Analysis of Organizational Phenomena. In D. Byrne and C. Ragin (eds.), *The SAGE Handbook of Case Based Methods,* pp. 424–440. London: SAGE.

Fitch Ratings (2007). *Asset-Back Commercial Paper & Global Banks.* Slides for the Teleconference, August 23, 2007.

Fleischer, V. (2010). Regulatory Arbitrage. *Texas Law Review* 89(2), 227–275.

Fligstein, N. (1996). Markets as Politics: A Political-Cultural Approach to Market Institutions. *American Sociological Review* 61(4), 656–673.

Fligstein, N., and A. Goldstein (2010). The Anatomy of the Mortgage Securitization Crisis. In M. Lounsboury and P. M. Hirsch (eds.), *Markets on Trial: Toward a Policy Oriented Economic Sociology,* pp. 29–70. Research in the Sociology of Organizations, Vol. 28 Part A. Bradford: Emerald.

   (2012). A Long Strange Trip: The State and Mortgage Securitization, 1968–2010. In K. Knorr-Cetina and A. Preda (eds.), *The Oxford Handbook of the Sociology of Finance,* pp. 339–356. Oxford: Oxford University Press.

Fligstein, N., and J. Habinek (2014). Sucker Punched by the Invisible Hand: The World Financial Markets and the Globalization of the US Mortgage Crisis. *Socio-Economic Review* 12(4), 637–665.

Florstedt, T. (2013). Finanzkrise als Krise der Normbehauptung. *Zeitschrift für Bankrecht und Bankwirtschaft* 25(2), 81–92.

Fooks, G. (2003). Auditors and the Permissive Society: Market Failure, Globalisation and Financial Regulation in the US. *Risk Management: An International Journal* 5(2), 17–26.

Ford, C. (2008). New Governance, Compliance, and Principles-Based Securities Regulation. *American Business Law Journal* 45(1), 1–60.

   (2010). Principles Based Securities Regulation in the Wake of the Global Financial Crisis. *McGill Law Journal* 55, 1–50.

Four Federal Financial Institutions and Regulatory Agencies (2012). *Re: File Reference 2011-220: Proposed Accounting Standards Update to Topic 810 – Consolidation: Principal versus Agent Analysis. Comment Letter No. 67.* March 6, 2012. www.fasb.org/cs/BlobServer?blobkey=id&blobnocache=true&blobwhere=1175 823783341&blobheader=application%2Fpdf&blobheadername2=Content-Length&blobheadername1=Content- Disposition&blobheadervalue2=260853&blobheadervalue1=filename%3DCONPP.E D.0067.FOUR_FEDERAL_FINANCIAL_ INSTITUTION_REGULATORY_AGENCIES_STEVEN_P._ MERRIETT.pdf&blobcol=urldata&blobtable=MungoBlobs

Fourcade, M. (2006). The Construction of a Global Profession: The Transnationalization of Economics. *American Journal of Sociology* 112(1), 145–194.

Fredman, A. J. (1997). A Closer Look at Money Market Funds: Bank CD Alternatives. *All American Institutional Investor Journal* (February), 22 (2), 22–27.

Fuchs, D., and A. Kalfagianni (2010). The Causes and Consequences of Private Food Governance. *Business and Politics* 12(3), 1–34.

Funk, R., and D. Hirschmann (2014). Derivatives and Deregulation: Financial Innovation and the Demise of Glass-Steagall. *Administrative Science Quarterly* 59(4), 669–704.

G20 (2009). *Declaration on Strengthening the Financial System: London Summit.* https://www.iasplus.com/en/binary/resource/0904g20comm unique2.pdf

Gabor, D. (2016). A Step Too Far? The European Financial Transactions Tax on Shadow Banking. *Journal of European Public Policy* 23(6), 925–945.

Gabor, D., and C. Ban (2015). Banking on Bonds: The New Links between States and Markets. *Journal of Common Market Studies* 54(3), 617–635.

Gadinis, S. (2013). The Financial Stability Board: The New Politics of International Financial Regulation. *Texas International Law Journal* 48(2), 157–175.

Galati, G., and K. Tsatsaronis (2003). The Impact of the Euro on Europe's Financial Markets. *Financial Markets, Institutions & Instruments* 12(3), 165–222.

Gallagher, D. M., and T. A. Paredes (2012). *Public Statement: Statement on the Regulation of Money Market Funds,* August 28. www.sec.gov/ news/public-statement/2012-spch082812dmgtaphtm

Gart, A. (1994). *Regulation, Deregulation, and Reregulation: The Future of the Banking, Insurance, and the Securities Industries.* New York, NY: John Wiley & Sons.

George, A. L., and A. Bennett. (2005). *Case Studies and Theory Development in the Social Sciences.* Cambridge, MA: MIT Press.

Germain, R. (2010). *Global Politics and Financial Governance*. London: Palgrave.

(2012). Governing Global Finance and Banking. *Review of International Political Economy* 19(4), 530–535.

Gill, M. (2009). *Accountants' Truth-Knowledge and Ethics in the Financial World*. Oxford: Oxford University Press.

Gilliam, L. (2005). Accounting Consolidation vs. Capital Calculation: The Conflict over Asset-Backed Commercial Paper Programs. *North Carolina Banking Institute 9*, 291–315.

Goldbach, R. (2015). *Global Governance and Regulatory Failure: The Political Economy of Banking*. London: Palgrave Macmillan.

Goodfriend, M., and R. G. King (1988). Financial Deregulation, Monetary Policy, and Central Banking. *Economic Review* (May/June), 3–22.

Goodhart, C. (2011). *The Basel Committee on Banking Supervision: A History of the Early Years 1974–1997*. Cambridge: Cambridge University Press.

(2016). *Central Bank Evolution: Lessons Learnt from the Sub-prime Crisis*. *LSE Research Online*. http://eprints.lse.ac.uk/67348/1/ Goodhart_Central_Bank_Evolution.pdf

Goodstadt, L. F. (2011). *Reluctant Regulators: How the West Created and How China Survived the Global Financial Crisis*. Hong Kong: Hong Kong University Press.

Gorton, G. B. (2010). *Slapped by the Invisible Hand: The Panic of 2007*. New York, NY: Oxford University Press.

Gorton, G. B., and A. Metrick (2010). *Regulating the Shadow Banking System* (October 18, 2010). http://ssrn.com/abstract=1676947

Gorton, G. B., and N. S. Souleles (2007). Special Purpose Vehicles and Securitization, NBER Chapters. In M. Carey and R. M. Stulz (eds.), *The Risks of Financial Institutions*, pp. 549–602. Boston: NBER Press.

Green, J. F. (2010). Private Standards in the Climate Regime: The Greenhouse Gas Protocol. *Business and Politics* 12(3), 1–37.

Greenlaw, D., J. Hatzius, A. Kashyap, and H. S. Shing (2008). Leveraged Losses: Lessons from the Mortgage Market Meltdown. *U.S. Monetary Policy Forum 2008*. http://vladyslavsushko.com/docs/presentation3.pdf

Greenspan, A. (1998). The Role of Capital in Optimal Banking Supervision and Regulation. *Federal Reserve Bank of New York Economic Policy Review* 4(3), 163–168.

(2008). *We Will Never Have a Perfect Model of Risk*. *Financial Times* (March 16). www.ft.com/content/edbdbcf6-f360-11dc-b6bc-0000779fd2ac

Griffith-Jones, S., and A. Persaud (2004). *Basel II, Its Impact on Emerging Markets and Its Political Economy*. www.researchgate.net/profile/ Stephany_Griffith-Jones/publication/265219940_BASLE_II_ITS_ IMPACT_ON_EMERGING_MARKETS_AND_ITS_POLITICAL_ ECONOMY/links/554ba09a0cf29752ee7d2942.pdf

Griffith-Jones, S., M. Thiemann, and L. Seabrooke (2011). Taming Finance by Empowering Regulators: A Survey of Policies, Politics and Possibilities. United Nations Development Programme.

Grossman, E., and P. Leblond (2011). European Financial Integration: Finally the Great Leap Forward? *Journal of Common Market Studies* 49(2), 413–435.

Guttmann, R. (2016). *Finance-Led Capitalism: Shadow Banking, Re-Regulation, and the Future of Global Markets*. London: Palgrave Macmillan.

Hackethal, A. (2004). German Banks and Banking Structure. In J. P. Krahnen and R. H. Schmidt (eds.), *The German Financial System*, pp. 71–105. Oxford: Oxford University Press.

Haensel, D., and J. P. Krahnen (2007). Does Credit Securitization Reduce Bank Risk? Evidence from the European CDO Market. SSRC Working Paper.

Hakenes, H., and I. Schnabe (2006). Braucht Deutschland eine 'private starke deutsche Bank'? Über die Notwendigkeit nationaler Champions im Bankwesen. *Kredit und Kapital* 39(2), 163–181.

Hall, P., and D. Soskice (eds.) (2001). *Varieties of Capitalism: The Institutional Foundations of Comparative Advantage*. Oxford: Oxford University Press.

Hall, P., and K. Thelen (2009). Institutional Change in Varieties of Capitalism. *Socio-Economic Review* 7(1), 7–34.

Halliday, T. C. (2009). Recursivity of Global Normmaking: A Sociolegal Agenda. *Annual Review of Law and Social Sciences* 5, 263–289.

Halliday, T. C., and B. G. Carruthers (2007). The Recursivity of Law: Global Norm Making and National Lawmaking in the Globalization of Corporate Insolvency Regimes. *American Journal of Sociology* 112(4), 1135–1202.

Hansmann, H., and U. Mattei (1998). The Functions of Trust Law: A Comparative and Economic Analysis. *NYU Law Review* 73, 434–479.

Hardie, I., and D. Howarth (2009). Die Krise but not la crise? The Financial Crisis and the Transformation of German and French Banking System. *Journal of Common Market Studies* 47(5), 1017–1039.

    (2013a). *Market-Based Banking and the International Financial Crisis*. Oxford: Oxford University Press.

    (2013b). Framing Market-Based Banking and the Financial Crisis. In I. Hardie and D. Howarth (eds.), *Market-Based Banking and the International Financial Crisis*, pp. 22–55. Oxford: Oxford University Press.

Hardie, I., D. Howarth, S. Maxfield, and A. Verdun (2013a). Banks and the False Dichotomy in the Comparative Political Economy of Finance. *World Politics* 65(4), 691–728.

    (2013b). Introduction: Towards a Political Economy of Banking. In I. Hardie and D. Howarth (eds.), *Market-Based Banking and the International Financial Crisis*, pp. 1–21. Oxford: Oxford University Press.

Harnay, S., and L. Scialom (2016). The Influence of the Economic Approaches to Regulation on Banking Regulations: A Short History of Banking Regulations. *Cambridge Journal of Economics* 40(2), 401–426.

Hartgraves, A. L., and G. J. Benston (2002). The Evolving Accounting Standards for Special Purpose Entities and Consolidations. *Accounting Horizons* 16(3), 245–258.

Hartmann-Wendels, T., M. Hellwig, and M. Jaeger (2009). *Arbeitsweise der Bankenaufsicht vor dem Hintergrund der Finanzmarktkrise.* Köln: Institut der deutschen Wirtschaft Köln Medien GmbH.

Harvey, D. L. (2009). Complexity and Case. In D. Byrne and C. Ragin (eds.), *The SAGE Handbook of Case Based Methods*, pp. 16–38. Los Angeles, CA: SAGE.

Hatherly, D., D. Leung, and D. MacKenzie (2008). The Finitist Accountant. In T. Pinch and R. Swedberg (eds.), *Living in a Material World: Economic Sociology Meets Science and Technology Studies*, pp. 131–160. Boston, MA: MIT Press.

Hayek, F. A. (1945). The Use of Knowledge in Society. *The American Economic Review* 35(4), 519–530.

Heinemann, F., and M. Schueler (2004). A Stiglerian View on Banking Supervision. *Public Choice* 121(1–2), 99–130.

Helleiner, E. (1994). *States and the Reemergence of Global Finance: From Bretton Woods to the 1990s.* Ithaca, NY: Cornell University Press.

(2009). Reregulation and Fragmentation in International Financial Governance. *Global Governance* 16(1) (January–March 2009), 16–22.

(2011). The Limits of Incrementalism: The G20, the FSB, and the International Regulatory Agenda. *Journal of Globalization and Development* 2(2), Article 11.

(2014). *The Status Quo Crisis: Global Financial Governance after the 2008 Meltdown.* Oxford: Oxford University Press.

Helleiner, E., and S. Pagliari (2011). The End of an Era in International Financial Regulation? A Postcrisis Research Agenda. *International Organization* 65(Winter), 169–200.

Hellwig, M. (2010). Finanzmarktregulierung – Welche Regelungen empfehlen sich für den deutschen und europäischen Finanzsektor? Gutachten zum 68. Deutschen Juristentag Berlin 2010. In M. Hellwig, W. Höfling, and D. Zimmer (eds.), *Verhandlungen des 68. Deutschen Juristentages*, Vol. 1, pp. E5–E57. Munich: Verlag C. H. Beck.

Herring, R. J. (2007). Conflicts between Home and Host Country Prudential Supervision. In D. D. Evanoff, G. G. Kaufman, and J. R. LaBrosse (eds.), *International Financial Instability: Global Banking and National Regulation*, pp. 179–239. Hackensack, NJ: World Scientific.

Hill, J. (2016). *European Commission – Speech: Speech by Commissioner Jonathan Hill at the Public Hearing on the 'Call for Evidence' – A Review of the EU Regulatory Framework for Financial Services, Brussels*, May 17, 2016. http://europa.eu/rapid/press-release_SPEECH-16-1788_en.htm

Hines, R. D. (1988). Financial Accounting: In Communicating Reality, We Construct Reality. *Accounting, Organizations and Society* 13(3), 251–261.

Hoarau, C. (2010). La nouvelle gouvernance du normalisateur comptable Français. In Jean-Luc Rossignol (ed.), *La gouvernance juridique et fiscale des organisations*, pp. 25–43. Paris: Editions Lavoisier.

Hofer, S. (2007). Das Aktiengesetz von 1884- ein Lehrstueck fuer prinzipielle Schutzkonzeptionen. In M. Habersack and W. Bayer (eds.), *Aktienrecht im Wandel: 1807–2007*, Vol. I, pp. 388–414. Entwicklung des Aktienrechts. Munich: Mohr-Siebeck Verlag.

Horsfield-Bradbury, J. (2008). *Hedge Fund Self-Regulation in the US and the UK*. www.law.harvard.edu/programs/corp_gov/papers/Brudney2008_Horsfield- Bradbury.pdf

Howarth, D. (2013). France and the International Financial Crisis: The Legacy of State-led Finance. *Governance* 26(3), 369–395.

Hutchins, E. (1995). *Cognition in the Wild*. Cambridge, MA: MIT Press.

IASB (2002). *Consolidation and Special Purpose Entities*. IASB Board Meeting October 23–25. https://www.iasplus.com/en/meetingnotes/iasb/2002/agenda_0210/agenda177

IIF-IBFED (2016). *Identification and Measurement of Step-in Risk*. Consultative Document. https://www.iif.com/system/files/32370132_iif_ibfed_bcbs_step-in-risk_submission.pdf

Ingham, G. (2004). *The Nature of Money*. Cambridge: Polity.

Institutional Money Market Funds Association (IMMFA) (2013). *The Institutional Money Market Funds Association's (IMMFA) Views on The European Commission's Proposed Regulation on Money Market Funds (MMFR)*. www.citibank.com/transactionservices/home/oli/files/immfa_summary_reform_ 1013.pdf

International Accounting Standards Committee (IASC) (1989). *Framework for the Preparation and Presentation of Financial Statements*. International Accounting Standards Committee.

International Financial Services Center (IFSC) (2013). *EC Proposes Regulation on Money Market Funds*. www.ifsc.ie/feature.aspx?id feature=167417

International Monetary Fund (IMF) (2009a). *France: 2009 Article IV Consultation- Staff Report; Public Information Notice on the Executive Board Discussion; and Statement by the Executive Director for France*. Washington, DC: IMF Press.

(2009b). *Germany: 2008 Article IV Consultation – Staff Report; Staff Supplement; Public Information Notice on the Executive Board Discussion; and Statement by the Executive Director for Germany*, January. www.imf.org/external/pubs/ft/scr/2009/cr0915.pdf

(2009c). *IMF Global Financial Stability Report* April 2009. www.imf.org/external/pubs/ft/gfsr/2009/01/pdf/text.pdf

(2011). *Kingdom of the Netherlands: Netherlands: Financial System Stability Assessment.* Washington, DC: IMF Press.

(2015). *United States: Financial Sector Assessment Program. Systemic Risk Oversight and Management – Technical Note.* IMF Country Report No. 15/172. www.imf.org/external/pubs/ft/scr/2015/cr15172.pdf

(2017a). *World Economic Outlook.* www.imf.org/en/Publications/WEO/Issues/2017/09/19/world-economic-outlook-o ctober-2017

(2017b). *Global Financial Stability Report.* www.imf.org/en/Publications/GFSR/Issues/2017/09/27/global-financial-stability-report-october-2017

International Organization of Securities Commissions (IOSCO) (2012a). *Money Market Fund Systemic Risk Analysis and Reform Options: Consultation Report,* April 27. www.iosco.org/library/pubdocs/pdf/IOSCOPD379.pdf

(2012b). *Policy Recommendations for Money Market Funds: Final Report,* October. www.csrc.gov.cn/pub/csrc_en/affairs/AffairsIOSCO/201210/P02012101050013 8903810.pdf

(2012c). *IOSCO Publishes Policy Recommendations for Money Market Funds, Madrid,* October 9. www.iosco.org/news/pdf/IOSCONEWS255.pdf

(2015). *Peer Review of Regulation of Money Market Funds: Final Report,* September 2015. www.iosco.org/library/pubdocs/pdf/IOSCOPD502.pdf

Investment Company Institute (ICI) (2009). *Report of the Money Market Working Group: Submitted to the Board of Governors of the Investment Company Institute,* March 17, 2009. www.law.berkeley.edu/files/bclbe/ICI_MMWG_Report.pdf

(2014). *Comment Letter Re: Assessment Methodologies for Identifying Non-Bank Non-Insurer Global Systemically Important Financial Institutions: Proposed High-Level Framework and Specific Methodologies,* April 7, 2014. www.fsb.org/wp-content/uploads/r_140423af.pdf

Jabko, N. (2006). *Playing the Market: A Political Strategy for Uniting Europe 1985–2005.* London: Cornell University Press.

Jabko, N., and E. Massoc (2012). French Capitalism under Stress: How Nicolas Sarkozy Rescued the Banks. *Review of International Political Economy* 19(4), 562–585.

Jablecki, J., and M. Machaj (2009). The Regulated Meltdown of 2008. *Critical Review* 21(2–3), 301–328.

Jasanoff, S. (2012). *Science and Public Reason.* London: Routledge.

Jean-Pierre, T. (1997). *Credit lyonnais: L'enquête*. Paris: Fixot.

Jeffrey, P. (2002). International Harmonization of Accounting Standards, and the Question of Off-Balance Sheet Treatment. *Duke Journal of Comparative & International Law* 12(2), 341–351.

Jennen, B., and N. van de Vijver (2010). *Banking and Securities Regulation in the Netherlands*. Amsterdam: Wolters Kluwer.

Jepperson, R. L. (1991). Institutions, Institutional Effects, and Institutionalism. In W. Powell and P. DiMaggio (eds.), *The New Institutionalism in Organizational Analysis*, pp. 143–163. Chicago, IL: University of Chicago Press.

Johnson, M. (2017). Yield-Hungry Investors Are Driving Demand for Leveraged Loans and High-Yield Bonds. *Financial Times*, October 13.

Joint Bank Regulators (2005). *Office of the Comptroller of the Currency Board of Governors of the Federal Reserve System Federal Deposit Insurance Corporation Office of Thrift Supervision.* Supervisory guidance to assist in the determination of the appropriate risk-based capital treatment to be applied to direct credit substitutes issued in connection with asset-backed commercial paper programs. www.fdic .gov/news/news/inactivefinancial/2005/fil2605a.pdf

Jones, D. (2000). Emerging Problems with the Basel Capital Accord: Regulatory Capital Arbitrage and Related Issues. *Journal of Banking and Finance* 24(1), 35–58.

Kacperczyk, M., and P. Schnabl (2012). *How Safe Are Money Market Funds?* Draft: April 2012. http://pages.stern.nyu.edu/~sternfin/mkacperc/ public_html/mmfs.pdf

Kahler, M., and D. A. Lake (2003). Globalization and Governance. In M. Kahler and D. Lake (eds.), *Governance in a Global Economy: Political Authority in Transition*, pp. 1–32. Princeton, NJ: Princeton University Press.

Kane, E. (1987). Competitive Financial Reregulation: An International Perspective. In R. Portes and A. K. Swoboda (eds.), *Threats to International Financial Stability*, pp. 111–145. Cambridge: Cambridge University Press.

(1988). Interaction of Financial and Regulatory Innovation. *The American Economic Review*, 78(2), *Papers and Proceedings of the One-Hundredth Annual Meeting of the American Economic Association* (May 1988), 328–334.

(2008). Regulation and Supervision: An Ethical Perspective. Paper presented at the Conference on Principles vs. Rules in Financial Regulation. www2.bc.edu/~kaneeb/

Kapstein, E. B. (1991). Supervising International Banks: Origins and Implications of Basle Accord. *Essays in International Finance* 185, pp. 1–40.

Kavanagh, B., T. R. Boemio, and G. A. Edwards, Jr. (1992). Asset-Backed Commercial Paper Programs. *Federal Reserve Bulletin* 78, 107.

King, M. (2009). *Speech to British Bankers' Association*. London: Mansion House, Bank of England, June 17. www.bankofengland.co.uk/archive/ Documents/historicpubs/speeches/2009/spee ch394.pdf

Kleindiek, D. (2000). Gestaltungsaufgaben der Bilanzrechtsreform. In D. Kleindiek and W. Oehler (eds.), *Die Zukunft des deutschen Bilanzrechts im Zeichen internationaler Rechnungslegung und privater Standardsetzung*, pp. 1–13. Cologne: Dr. Otto Schmidt.

Koehler, M. (2007). Merger Control as Barrier to EU Banking Market Integration. ZEW Discussion Paper No. 07-082.

 (2009). Transparency of Regulation and Cross-Border Bank Mergers. *International Journal of Central Banking* 5(1), 39–74.

Konings, M. (2008). The Institutional Foundations of US Structural Power in International Finance: From the Re-emergence of Global Finance to the Monetarist Turn. *Review of International Political Economy* 15(1), 35–61.

 (2011). *The Development of American Finance*. Cambridge: Cambridge University Press.

Krahnen, J.-P., and L. Pelizzon (2016). "Predatory" Margins and the Regulation and Supervision of Central Counterparty Clearing Houses (CCPs). SAFE White Paper No. 41.

Krippner, G. R. (2011). *Capitalizing on Crisis*. Cambridge, MA: Harvard University Press.

Kwak, J. (2013). Cultural Capture and the Financial Crisis. In D. Carpenter and D. A. Moss (eds.), *Preventing Regulatory Capture: Special Interest Influence and How to Limit It*, pp. 71–98. New York, NY: Cambridge University Press.

Lall, R. (2012). From Failure to Failure: The Politics of International Banking Regulation. *Review of International Political Economy* 19(4), 609–638.

Langfield, S., and M. Pagano (2016). Bank Bias in Europe: Effects on Systemic Risk and Growth. *Economic Policy* 31(85), 51–106.

Larsson, R. K. (2008). Examination of Comment Letters Submitted to the IASC: Special Purpose Entities. *Research in Accounting Regulation* 20, 27–47.

Lewis, C. M. (2013). *The Economic Implications of Money Market Fund Capital Buffers*. Vanderbilt Owen Graduate School of Management Research Paper, 2388676. www.sec.gov/divisions/riskfin/ workingpapers/rsfi-wp2014-01.pdf

Lockwood, E. (2015). Predicting the Unpredictable: Value-at-Risk, Performativity, and the Politics of Financial Uncertainty. *Review of International Political Economy* 22(4), 719–756.

Lombardi, D., and M. Moschella (2017). The Symbolic Politics of Delegation: Macroprudential Policy and Independent Regulatory Authorities. *New Political Economy* 22(1), 92–108.

Macey, J. (2003). Regulatory Globalization as a Response to Regulatory Competition. *Faculty Scholarship Series*, Paper 1418.

(2011). Reducing Systemic Risk: The Role of Money Market Mutual Funds as Substitutes for Federally Insured Bank Deposits. *Stanford Journal of Law, Business & Finance* 17(1), 131–174.

MacKenzie, D. (2008). Producing Accounts: Finitism, Technology and Rule Following. In M. Mazzotti (ed.), *Knowledge as Social Order-Rethinking the Sociology of Barry Barnes*, pp. 99–117. Hampshire: Ashgate,

(2009). *Material Markets: How Economic Agents Are Constructed.* Oxford: Oxford University Press.

Maes, I., and E. Buyst (2009). Financial Crisis and Regulation: An Overview of the Belgian Experience. In Banca D'Italia (ed.), *Financial Market Regulation in the Wake of Financial Crises: The Historical Experience*, pp. 95–117. Rome: Printing Office of the Banca d'Italia.

Mahoney, J. (2003). Strategies of Causal Assessment in Comparative Historical Analysis. In James Mahoney and Dietrich Rueschemeyer (eds.), *Comparative Historical Analysis in the Social Sciences*, pp. 337–372. Cambridge: Cambridge University Press.

Mahoney, J., and K. Thelen (2010). A Theory of Gradual Institutional Change. In J. Mahoney and K. Thelen (eds.), *Explaining Institutional Change: Ambiguity, Agency and Power*, pp. 1–37. Oxford: Oxford University Press.

Maijoor, S. (2017). *Steven Maijoor's Address to ALDE Seminar on the Review of the European Supervisory Authorities.* www.esma.europa .eu/press-news/esma-news/steven-maijoors-address-alde-seminar-review-european-supervisory-authorities

Major, A. (2012). Neoliberalism and the New International Financial Architecture. *Review of International Political Economy* 19(4), 536–561.

Malets, O. (2013). The Translation of Transnational Voluntary Standards into Practices: Civil Society and the Forest Stewardship Council in Russia. *Journal of Civil Society* 9(3), 300–324.

Mallaby, S. (2016). *The Man Who Knew.* New York, NY: Penguin Press.

Martinez-Diaz, L. (2005). Strategic Experts and Improvising Regulators: Explaining the IASC's Rise to Global Influence, 1973–2001. *Business and Politics* 7(3), 1–22.

Masciandaro, D. (2015). *Study: Banking Supervision and External Auditors in the European Union Economics, Institutions and Policies.* www .europarl.europa.eu/RegData/etudes/STUD/2015/542673/IPOL_STU(2015)542673_EN.pdf

Mason, J. R. (2009). Regulating for Financial System Development, Financial Institutions Stability, and Financial Innovation. In A. Gigliobianco and G. Toniolo (eds.), *Financial Market Regulation in the Wake of Financial Crises: The Historical Experience*, pp. 225–242. Seminari e convegni: Workshops and Conferences,

Mathérat, S., and P. Troussard (2000). La titrisation et le système financier. *Revue d'économie financière* 59, 25–39.

Mattli, W., and T. Buethe (2005). Global Private Governance: Lessons from a National Model of Setting Standards. *Accounting, Law and Contemporary Problems* 68(3/4), 225–262.

Mattli, W., and N. Woods (2009). In Whose Benefit? Explaining Regulatory Change in Global Politics. In W. Mattli and N. Woods (eds.), *The Politics of Global Regulation*, pp. 1–43. Princeton, NJ: Princeton University Press.

Mayer Brown (2009). *Big Changes to Securitization Accounting*. Securitization Update, June 22, 2009. www.mayerbrown.com/files/Publication/fab3ec91-d064-4740-89b2-a9c42d373dc1/Presentation/PublicationAttachment/6a14e039-2b95-4246-85b8-bde2733bb7fb/UPDATE_Securitization_FASB_0609_V2.pdf

(2010). *Basel II Modified in Response to Market Crisis*. https://www.mayerbrown.com/public_docs/0406fin-BaselII_Article.pdf

Mayntz, R. (2009). *Über Governance: Institutionen und Prozesse politischer Regelung*. Frankfurt am Main: Campus-Verlag.

(2010). Die transnationale Ordnung globalisierter Finanzmärkte Was lehrt uns die Krise? MPIfG Working Paper 10/8.

McCabe, P. E. (2010). The Cross Section of Money Market Fund Risks and Financial Crises. FEDS Working Paper No. 2010–51.

McLeay, S., D. Ordelheide, and S. Young (2000). Constituent Lobbying and Its Impact on the Development of Financial Reporting Regulations Evidence from Germany. *Accounting, Organization and Society* 25(1), 79–102.

Mediobanca (2009). *Sintesi dei principali piani di stabilizzazione finanziaria in Europe e negli Stati Uniti, Aggiornamento al 5 giugno 2009. Ricerche e Studi*. Available at https://www.mbres.it/sites/default/files/resources/download_it/rs_Piani%20di%20stabilizzazione%20finanziaria.pdf; last accessed September 5, 2012.

Mehrling, P., Z. Pozsar, J. Sweeney, and D. H. Neilson. (2013). *Bagehot Was a Shadow Banker: Shadow Banking, Central Banking, and the Future of Global Finance*. (November 5, 2013). Available at SSRN: https://ssrn.com/abstract=2232016 or http://dx.doi.org/10.2139/ssrn.2232016

Meyer, J., and B. Rowan (1977). Institutionalized Organizations: Formal Structure as Myth and Ceremony. *American Journal of Sociology* 83(2), 340–363.

Millenium BCP (2011). *Market Discipline Report 2010*. www .millenniumbcp.pt/multimedia/archive/00437/2010_Market_Discipl_ 437955a.pdf

Miller, P. (2001). Governing by Numbers: Why Calculative Practices Matter. *Social Research* 68(2), 379–396.

Minsky, H. P. (1986). *Stabilization in Unstable Economy*. New Haven, CT: Yale University Press.

Montagne, S. (2011). *Investir avec prudence: Histoire de la construction d'un standard juridique*. Paris: Paris Dauphine University.

Moody's (1993). *Asset-Backed Commercial Paper: Understanding the Risks*. Structured Finance: Special Report. www.kisrating.com/ report/moody's_report/%ED%8F%89%EA%B0%80%EB% B0%A9%EB%B2%95%EB%A1%A0/risks.pdf

(1997). *Understanding Structured Liquidity Facilities in Asset-Backed Commercial Paper Programs*. *Structured Finance*. Special Report, pp. 1–6.

(1998). *The ABCP Market in the Third Quarter of 1998: A Whole New Ball Game*. Structured Finance: Special Report. https://cybercemetery .unt.edu/archive/fcic/20110310210457/http://c0181567.cdn1.clo udfiles.rackspacecloud.com/1999-02-02%20The%20ABCP%20 Market%20in%20the%20Third%20Quarter%20of%201998%20 (Moody's%20Special%20Report).pdf

(2002). *ABCP 2002 Year in Review: Maturity and a Pause in the U.S., Youth and Rapid Growth in Europe*. Structured Finance: Special Report.

(2003a). PhDs of ABCP. *Moody's Investors Service*. Presented at the Union League Club, New York, NY, October 30, 2003.

(2003b). *ABCP Market Overview: First Quarter 2004, All Talk and No Action*. Structured Finance: Special Report.

(2005). Review and 2006 Outlook: *U.S. Asset-Backed Commercial Paper Will 2006 Issuance Hit the $1 Trillion Milestone?* Structured Finance: Special Report.

(1999–2010). ABCP-Program Index CP Outstanding as of July.

(2010). *Sponsor Support Key to Money Market Funds*. August 9, 2010. www.alston.com/files/docs/Moody's_Report.pdf

(2011). *Announcement: Moody's Updates Money Market Fund Ratings Based on Revised Methodology*. Global Credit Research – 23 May 2011. www.moodys.com/research/Moodys-updates-money-market-fund-ratings-based-on-revised-methodology–PR_218030

Morgan, G. (2005). Institutional Complementarities, Path Dependency and the Dynamics of Firms. In G. Morgan, R. Whitley, and E. Moen (eds.), *Changing Capitalisms? Internationalization, Institutional Change and*

Systems of Economic Organization, pp. 415–446. Oxford: Oxford University Press.

(2012). Supporting the City: Economic Patriotism in Financial Markets. *Journal of European Public Policy* 19(3), 373–387.

Morgan, G., and S. Quack (2000). Confidence and Confidentiality: The Social Construction of Performance Standards in Banking. In S. Quack, G. Morgan, and R. Whitley (eds.), *National Capitalisms, Global Competition and Economic Performance*, pp. 131–158. Amsterdam: John Benjamins.

Morgan Stanley (2003). *Comment Letter to FASB on Fin 46. Exposure Draft on Consolidation of Variable Interest Entities, a Modification of FASB Interpretation No. 46 (the "Exposure Draft")*. December 1, Letter of Comment No: 03, File Reference: 1082–300. www.fasb .org/cs/BlobServer?blobkey=id&blobnocache=true&blobwhere=1175 817973972&blobheader=application%2Fpdf&blobheadername2=Co ntent- Length&blobheadername1=Content- Disposition&blobheaderv alue2=340910&blobheadervalue1=filename%3D18760.pdf &blobcol =urldata&blobtable=MungoBlobs

Moschella, M., and E. Tsingou, (eds). (2013). *Great Expectations, Slow Transformations: Incremental Change in Post-Crisis Regulation*. Colchester: ECPR Press.

Mosley, L. (2010). Regulating Globally, Implementing Locally: The Financial Codes and Standards Effort. *Review of International Political Economy* 17(4), 724–761.

Mosley, L., and D. A. Singer (2009). The Global Financial Crisis: Lessons and Opportunities for International Political Economy. *International Interactions* 35(4), 420–429.

Mügge, D. (2010). *Widen the Market, Narrow the Competition: Banker Interests and the Making of a European Capital Market*. Colchester: ECPR Monographs.

Mügge, D. K. (2006). Reordering the Market Place: Competition Politics in European Finance. *Journal of Common Market Studies* 44(5), 991–1022.

Mügge, D., and J. Perry (2014). The Flaws of Fragmented Financial Standard Setting: Why Substantive Economic Debates Matter for the Architecture of Global Governance. *Politics & Society* 42(2), 194–222.

Murau, S. (2015). *Private Credit Money Accommodation in the 2008 Financial Crisis: A Study of Money Market Fund Shares, Repurchase Agreements and Assetbacked Commercial Papers, Conference Presentation EAEPE Genoa*. September 19, 2015.

Murphy, D. (2004). *Structure of Regulatory Competition: Corporations and Public Policies*. Oxford: Oxford University Press.

Nersisyan, Y. (2015). The Repeal of the Glass-Steagall Act and the Federal Reserve's Extraordinary Intervention during the Global Financial Crisis. Levy Economics Institute Working Paper Collection, Working Paper No. 829.

Nesvetailova, A. (2010). *Financial Alchemy in Crisis: The Great Liquidity Illusion*. London: Pluto Press.

New York Times (NYT) (2012). *Rebuilding Wall St.'s Watchdog*. https://dealbook.nytimes.com/2012/11/26/schapiro-head-of-s-e-c-to-announce- departure/?_r=2

(2017). *Trump Moves to Roll Back Obama-Era Financial Regulations*. www.nytimes.com/2017/02/03/business/dealbook/trump-congress-financial-regulations.html?_r=1

Noelke, A. (2005). Introduction to the Special Issue: The Globalization of Accounting Standards. *Business and Politics* 7(3), 1–7.

Noelke, A., and J. Perry (2007). The Power of Transnational Private Governance: Financialization and the IASB. *Business and Politics* 9(3), 1–25.

Office of the Federal Register (2001). Risk-Based Capital Guidelines; Capital Adequacy Guidelines; Capital Maintenance: Capital Treatment of Recourse, Direct Credit Substitutes and Residual Interests in Asset Securitizations. Rules and Regulations. *Federal Register* 66(230), 59614–59667.

(2003). Risk-Based Capital Guidelines; Capital Adequacy Guidelines; Capital Maintenance: Asset-Backed Commercial Paper Programs and Early Amortization Provisions. Proposed Rules. *Federal Register* 68(190), 56568–56586.

(2010). Money Market Fund Reform; Final Rule. *Federal Register* 75(42), 10060–10120.

Omarova, S. T. (2012). *Bankers, Bureaucrats, and Guardians: Toward Tripartism in Financial Services Regulation*. Cornell Law Faculty Publications. 1010. http://scholarship.law.cornell.edu/facpub/1010

Onaran, Y. (2008). *Banks' Subprime Losses Top $500 bn on Writedowns-Update 1*. Bloomberg, August 12, 2008.

O'Sullivan, M. (2007). Acting Out Institutional Change: Understanding the Recent Transformation of the French Financial System. *Socio-Economic Review* 5(3), 389–436.

Pagliari, S. (2013). Governing Financial Stability: The Financial Stability Board as the Emerging Pillar in Global Economic Governance. In M. Moschella and C. Weaver (eds.), *Handbook of Global Economic Governance*, pp. 143–155. New York, NY: Routledge.

Peltzman, S. (1976). Toward a More General Theory of Regulation. *Journal of Law and Economics* 19(2), 211–240.

Peltzman, S., M. E. Levine, and R. G. Noll (1989). The Economic Theory of Regulation after a Decade of Deregulation. *Brookings Papers on Economic Activity. Microeconomics* 1989, 1–59.

Perez, S. (1997). *Banking on Privilege: The Politics of Spanish Financial Reform*. Ithaca, NY: Cornell University Press.

Pistor, K. (2002). The Standardization of Law and Its Effect on Developing Economies. *American Journal of Comparative Law* 50(1), 97–130.

(2010). Host's Dilemma: Rethinking EU Banking Regulation in Light of the Global Crisis. ECGI – Finance Working Paper No. 286/2010.

Porter, T. M. (1995). *Trust in Numbers: The Pursuit of Objectivity in Science and Public Life*. Princeton, NJ: Princeton University Press.

Posner, E. (2010). Sequence as Explanation: The International Politics of Accounting Standards. *Review of International Political Economy* 17(4), 639–664.

Pozsar, Z. (2008). The Rise and Fall of the Shadow Banking System, Moody's Economy.com. *Regional Financial Review* 44, 1–14.

(2011). Institutional Cash Pools and the Triffin Dilemma of the US Banking System. IMF Working Paper WP/11/190.

(2015). *A Macro View of Shadow Banking. Levered Betas and Wholesale Funding in the Context of Secular Stagnation*. Draft (as of January 31, 2015).

Pozsar, Z., T. Adrian, A. Ashcraft, and H. Boesky (2010). Shadow Banking. Federal Reserve Bank of New York Staff Reports. Staff Report No. 458, July 2010.

Pozsar, Z., and M. Singh (2011). The Nonbank-Bank Nexus and the Shadow Banking System. IMF Working Papers No. 11/289, pp. 1–18.

President's Working Group on Financial Markets (PWG) (2010). *Report of the President's Working Group on Financial Markets Money Market Fund Reform Options. October 2010.* www.treasury.gov/press-center/press-releases/Documents/10.21%20PWG%20Report%20 Final.pdf

PricewaterhouseCoopers (PWC) (2003). *Comment Letter to FASB on Fin 46. Proposed Interpretation, Consolidation of Variable Interest Entities – a Modification of FASB Interpretation No. 46*. November 30, Letter of Comment No: 100, File Reference: 1082–300. www.fasb.org/cs/BlobServer?blobkey=id&blobnocache=true&blobwh ere=1175 817979689&blobheader=application%2Fpdf&blobheader name2=Content- Length&blobheadername1=Content- Disposition& blobheadervalue2=1798676&blobheadervalue1=filename%3D18833 .pdf &blobcol=urldata&blobtable=MungoBlobs

(2004). *SIC 12 and Fin 46R: The Substance of Control*. London: PwC Press.

(2005). *Structuring Securitization in Belgium*. Brussels: PwC Press.

(2006). *The Great Debate: Conduits- On- or Off-Balance Sheet.* London: PwC Press.

(2010). *Capital Markets Accounting Developments Advisory. Financial Instruments and Credit Group (FICG): Regulatory Impact of Consolidated Variable Interest Entities.* www.pwc.com/us/en/financial-instruments-and-credit/assets/cmada-2010–2.pdf

Quaglia, L. (2010). Completing the Single Market in Financial Services: The Politics of Competing Advocacy Coalitions. *Journal of European Public Policy* 17(7), 1007–1023.

Quintyn, M., S. Ramirez, and M. W. Taylor (2007). The Fear of Freedom: Politicians and the Independence and Accountability of Financial Sector Supervisors. IMF Working Paper 07/25.

Rajan, R. R. and L. Zingales (2003). *Saving Capitalism from the Capitalists.* New York, NY: Random House.

Ramirez, C. (2010). Promoting Transnational Professionalism: Forays of the 'Big Firm' Accounting Community in France. In M.-L. Djelic and S. . Quack (eds.), *Transnational Communities*, pp. 271–302. Cambridge: Cambridge University Press.

Reinicke, W. H. (1995). *Banking, Politics and Global Finance.* Aldershot: Edward Elgar.

Richerche e Studi Sp. A. (2009). *Major International Banks: Financial Aggregates.* www.mbres.it/eng/download/banche_int_08.pdf

Richardson, A. J., and B. Eberlein (2011). Legitimating Transnational Standard- Setting: The Case of the International Accounting Standards Board. *Journal of Business Ethics* 98(2), 217–245.

Riles, A. (2011). *Collateral Knowledge: Legal Reasoning in the Global Financial Markets.* Chicago, IL: University of Chicago Press.

Ring, H. (2009). *Bericht über die Durchführung der Sonderprüfung bei der IKB Deutsche Industriebank AG, Düsseldorf, gemäss Beschluss des Landgerichts Düsseldorf vom 14.08.2009*, pp. 1–998.

Robé, J.-P. (2011). The Legal Structure of the Firm. *Accounting, Economics, and Law* 1(1), 1–88.

Robson, K. (1992). Accounting Numbers as "Inscription": Action at a Distance and the Development of Accounting. *Accounting, Organizations and Society* 17(7), 685–708.

Rodrik, D. (2009). A Plan B for Global Finance. *The Economist* March 12.

Rose, N., and P. Miller (1992). Political Power beyond the State: Problematics of Government. *British Journal of Sociology* 43(2), 173–205.

Rousseau, P., and R. Sylla (2003). Financial Systems, Economic Growth and Globalization. In D. M. Bordo, A. M. Taylor, and J. G. Williamson (eds.), *Globalization in Historical Perspective*, pp. 132–156. Chicago, IL: Chicago University Press.

Royal Bank of Scotland (RBS) (2009). Annual Report Pillar 3 Disclosure 2008. Available at https://investors.rbs.com/~/media/Files/R/RBS-IR/annual-reports/rbs-group-accounts-2008.pdf

Royo, S. (2013). How Did the Spanish Financial System Survive the First Stage of the Global Crisis? *Governance* 26(4), 631–656.

Sassen, S. (1996). *Losing Control? Sovereignty in an Age of Globalization.* New York, NY: Columbia University Press.

Schadrack, F., and F. Breimyer (1970). Recent Developments in the Commercial Paper Market. *Federal Reserve Monthly Review* 57 (December), 280–291.

Schiavello, G., and M. Mimun (2007). *The International Comparative Legal Guide to Securitization 2007.* Italy. London, UK: Global Legal Group.

Schmidt, V. (2003). French Capitalism Transformed, Yet Still a Third Variety of Capitalism. *Economy and Society* 32(4), 526–554.

Schoenmaker, D., and C. van Laecke (2006). Current State of Cross-Border Banking. LSE Financial Markets Group Paper Series Special Paper 168, London.

Scott, H. S., and S. Iwahara (1994). In Search of a Level Playing Field – The Implementation of the Basel Capital Accord in Japan and the United States. Group of Thirty Occasional Paper 46, Washington, DC.

Seabrooke, L., and E. Tsingou (2009). Revolving Doors and Linked Ecologies in the World Economy: Policy Locations and the Practice of International Financial Reform. CSGR Working Paper 260/09, 2009. CSGR Working Paper 260 (09), pp. 1–29.

Securities and Exchange Commission (SEC) (2010). *Money Market Fund Reform: Final Rule.* www.sec.gov/rules/final/2010/ic-29132.pdf

(2014). *Press Release: SEC Adopts Money Market Fund Reform Rules. Rules Provide Structural and Operational Reform to Address Run Risks in Money Market Funds.* www.sec.gov/news/press-release/2014–143

Seerden, R., and F. Stroink (2007). Administrative Law in the Netherlands. In R. Seerden and B. Antwerpen (eds.), *Administrative Law of the European Union, Its Member States and the United States: A Comparative Analysis,* pp. 155–219. Cambridge: Intersentia.

Seikel, D. (2014). How the European Commission Deepened Financial Market Integration: The Battle over the Liberalization of Public Banks in Germany. *Journal of European Public Policy* 21(2), 169–187.

Senior Supervisors Group (SSG) (2008). *Observations on Risk Management Practices during the Recent Market Turbulence,* March 6, 2008. www .sec.gov/news/press/2008/report030608.pdf

Shapiro, M. L. (2012). *Press Release: Statement of SEC Chairman Mary L. Schapiro on Money Market Fund Reform. Washington, DC, August 22, 2012.* www.sec.gov/news/press-release/2012-2012-166htm

Sherman, M. (2009). *A Short History of Financial Deregulation in the United States*. CEPR Working Paper. http://cepr.net/documents/publications/dereg-timeline-2009-07.pdf

Shin, H. S. (2011). Global Banking Glut and Loan Risk Premium. *Mundell-Fleming Lecture the 2011 Annual Research Conference*, November 6, 2011. www.imf.org/external/np/res/seminars/2011/arc/pdf/hss.pdf

Sikka, P., and H. Willmott (2009). All Offshore: The Sprat, the Mackerel, Accounting Firms and the State in Globalization. In C. Chapman, D. Cooper, and P. Miller (eds.), *Accounting, Organizations and Institutions*, pp. 396–414. Oxford: Oxford University Press.

Simmons, B. (2004). The International Politics of Harmonization: The Case of Capital Market Regulation. In D. Vogel and R. A. Kagan (eds.), *Dynamics of Regulatory Change: How Globalization Affects National Regulatory Policies*, pp. 42–83. London: University of California Press,

Singer, A. (2007). *Regulating Capital*. Ithaca, NY: Cornell University Press.

Sissoko, C. (2013). Is Financial Regulation Structurally Biased to Favor Deregulation? *Southern California Law Review* 86(2), 365–420.

(2016). *The Economic Consequences of 'Market-Based' Lending*. May 24. https://papers.ssrn.com/sol3/papers.cfm?abstract_id=2766693

Skocpol, T., and M. Somers (1980). The Uses of Comparative History in Macrosocial Inquiry. *Comparative Studies in Society and History* 22(2), 174–197.

Slager, A. (2004). *Banking Across Borders*. Rotterdam: Erasmus Research Institute of Management.

Slaughter, A.-M. (2003). *A New World Order*. Princeton, NJ: Princeton University Press.

Smit, J. (2009). *The Perfect Prey: The Fall of ABN Amro*. London: Quercus.

Sohn, I. (2012). Toward Normative Fragmentation: An East Asian Financial Architecture in the Post-Global Crisis World. *Review of International Political Economy* 19(4), 586–608.

Spendzharva, A. (2014). *Regulating Banks in Central and Eastern Europe: Through Crisis and Boom*. London: Palgrave Macmillan.

Standard and Poor's (2010). *European ABCP Is Showing Resilience Despite The Downturn. Global Credit Portal Ratings Direct Structured Finance Research*. London, UK: Standard and Poors Rating Services.

Stigler, G. J. (1971). The Theory of Economic Regulation. *The Bell Journal of Economics and Management Science* 2(1), 3–21.

(1974). The Optimum Enforcement of Laws. In G. S. Becker and W. M. Landes (eds.), *Essays in the Economics of Crime and Punishment*, pp. 55–67. Cambridge, MA: National Bureau of Economic Research.

Stiglitz, J. (2009). Regulation and Failure. In D. Moss and J. Cisternino (eds.), *New Perspectives on Regulation*, pp. 11–23. Cambridge, MA: Tobin Project.

(2010). *Freefall*. New York, NY: W. W. Norton.

Stojanovic, D., and M. D. Vaughan (1998). The Commercial Paper Market: Who's Minding the Shop? St Louis Fed. *The Regional Economist* 17 (April), 5–9.

Story, J., and I. Walter (1997). *Political Economy of Financial Integration in Europe: The Battle of the Systems*. Manchester: Manchester University Press.

Strasser, K., and P. Blumberg (2011). Legal Form and Economic Substance of Enterprise Groups: Implications for Legal Policy. *Accounting, Economics and the Law* 1(4), 1–30.

Streeck, W., and K. Thelen (2005). *Beyond Continuity: Institutional Change in Advanced Political Economies*. Oxford: Oxford University Press.

Streeck, W., and K. Thelen (eds.) (2005). Introduction: Institutional Changes in Advanced Political Economies. In *Beyond Continuity: Institutional Change in Advanced Political Economies*, pp. 1–39. New York, NY: Oxford University Press.

Stryker, R. (2003). Mind the Gap: Law, Institutional Analysis and Socio-economics. *Socio-Economic Review* 1(3), 335–367.

Swedberg, R. (2010). The Structure of Confidence and the Collapse of Lehman Brothers. In M. Lounsboury and P. M. Hirsch (eds.), *Markets on Trial: Toward a Policy Oriented Economic Sociology*. Research in the Sociology of Organizations, Vol. 28 Part A, pp. 71–114. Bingley: Emerald.

Sylla, R. (2002). Financial Systems and Economic Modernization. *Journal of Economic History* 62(2), 277–292.

Synthetic Assets (2009). *The Parallel Banking System: The Regulation of ABCP*. http://syntheticassets.wordpress.com/2009/06/23/the-parallel-banking-system-2-of-3/

Tabe, H. (2010). *The Unravelling of Structured Investment Vehicles: How Liquidity Leaked through SIVs. Lessons in Risk Management and Regulatory Oversight*. London: Thoth Capital LLP.

Tamm Hallström, K. (2004). *Organizing International Standardization. ISO and the IASC in Quest of Authority*. Cheltenham: Edward Elgar.

Tarullo, D. K. (2008). *Banking on Basel: The Future of International Banking*. Washington, DC: Peterson Institute for International Economics.

(2015). *Thinking Critically about Nonbank Financial Intermediation: A Speech at the Brookings Institution, Washington, DC, November 17, 2015* (No. 879). www.federalreserve.gov/newsevents/speech/tarullo20151117a.htm

Tett, G. (2017). Ham-Fisted Banking Rules Spark the Creativity of Lenders Real Credit Growth and Innovation Occur in the World of Private Capital. *Financial Times* October 12.

Thatcher, M. (2007). Regulatory Agencies, the State and Markets: A Franco-British Comparison. *Journal of European Public Policy* 14(7), 1028–1047.

Thiemann, M. (2012). Out of the Shadows: Accounting for Special Purpose Entities in European Banking Systems. *Competition and Change* 16(1), 37–55.

(2014a). The Impact of Meta-Standardization upon Standards Convergence: The Case of the International Accounting Standard for Off-Balance-Sheet Financing. *Business and Politics* 16(1), 79–112.

(2014b). In the Shadow of Basel: How Competitive Politics Bred the Crisis. *Review of International Political Economy* 21(6), 1203–1239.

Thiemann, M., M. Birk, and J. Friedrich (Forthcoming). Much Ado about Nothing? Macro-Prudential Ideas and the Post-Crisis Regulation of Shadow Banking. *Koelner Zeitschrift für Soziologie und Sozialpsychologie.*

Thiemann, M., and J. Lepoutre (2017). Stitching on the Edge: Regulatory Arbitrage, Shadow Banks and Negative Externalization. *American Journal of Sociology* 122(6), 1775–1821.

Timmermans, S., and S. Epstein (2010). A World of Standards but Not a Standard World: Toward a Sociology of Standards and Standardization. *Annual Review of Sociology* 36, 69–89.

Treasury Strategies (TSI) (2010). *Re: Request For Comment: Moody's Proposes New Money Market Fund Rating Methodology and Symbols (Report Number 126642).* November 5, 2010. www.treasurystrategies .com/wp- content/uploads/TSI_MMF_Ratings_11052010.pdf

Tsingou, E. (2004). Policy Preferences in Financial Governance: Public-Private Dynamics and the Prevalence of Market-Based Arrangements in the Banking Industry. CSGR Working Paper No. 131/04.

(2008). Transnational Private Governance and the Basel Process: Banking Regulation and Supervision, Private Interests and Basel II. In J.-C. Graz and A. Nölke (eds.), *Transnational Private Governance and Its Limits*, pp. 58–68. London: Routledge.

Turner, A. (2010). Interview with Financial Crisis Inquiry Commission Staff. November 30, audiotape. http://fcic.law.stanford.edu/interviews/view/102

(2011). *Reforming Finance: Are We Being Radical Enough? 2011 Clare Distinguished Lecture in Economics and Public Policy.* www.fsa .gov.uk/pubs/speeches/0218_at_clare_college.pdf

(2012). *Economics after the Crisis.* Boston, MA: MIT Press.

(2015). *Between Debt and the Devil: Money, Credit, and Fixing Global Finance.* Princeton, NJ: Princeton University Press.

Underhill, G. R. D. (1997a). Introduction. In G. Underhill (ed.), *The New World Order in International Finance*, pp. 1–16. New York, NY: Saint Martin's Press.

(1997b). Private Markets and Public Responsibility. In G. Underhill (ed.), *The New World Order in International Finance*, pp. 17–49. New York, NY: Saint Martin's Press.

(2007). Markets, Institutions, and Transaction Costs: The Endogeneity of Governance. World Economy and Finance Research-Working Paper Series No. 0025. London: Birkbeck College, University of London.

Van Hulle, K. (1993). Harmonization of Accounting Standards in the EC. Is It the Beginning or Is It the End? *European Accounting Review* 2(2), 387–396.

Véron, N. (2015). *Europe's Radical Banking Union*. Bruegel Essay and Lecture Series 6. Available at http://bruegel.org/2015/05/europes-radical-banking-union/, last accessed March 20, 2018.

Vojtech, Cindy (2017). Post-Crisis Lending by Large Bank Holding Companies. FEDS Notes. Washington: Board of Governors of the Federal Reserve System, July 6, 2017. https://doi.org/10.17016/2380-7172.1985.

Vollmer, H. (2007). How to Do More with Numbers: Elementary Stakes, Framing, Keying, and the Three-Dimensional Character of Numerical Signs. *Accounting, Organizations and Society* 32(6), 577–600.

Wainwright, T. (2009). Laying the Foundations for a Crisis: Mapping the Historico-Geographical Construction of Residential Mortgage Backed Securitization in the UK. *International Journal of Urban and Regional Research* 33(2), 372–388.

(2011). Elite Knowledges: Framing Risk and the Geographies of Credit. *Environment and Planning A* 43(3), 650–665.

Wall Street Journal (1998). *Travelers and Citicorp to Merge in Megadeal Valued at $83 Billion.* https://www.wsj.com/articles/SB891818705198998500

(2008). *U.S. Agrees to Rescue Struggling Citigroup Plan Injects $20 Billion in Fresh Capital, Guarantees $306 Billion in Toxic Assets.* www.wsj.com/articles/SB122747680752551447

Walter, I. (1999). Financial Services Strategies in the Euro-Zone. *European Investment Bank Conference on European Banking after EMU*, Luxembourg, January 21, 1999.

(2004). *Mergers and Acquisitions in Banking and Finance.* Oxford: Oxford University Press.

Walton, P. (2008). *La comptabilité anglo-saxon.* Paris: La Découverte.

Warwick Commission on International Financial Reform (2009). *In Praise of Unlevel Playing Fields.* Coventry: University of Warwick.

Wermers, R. (2010). *Money Fund Runs*, September 2010. www.uts.edu.au/sites/default/files/Wermers.pdf

Whitley, R. (1986). The Transformation of Business Finance into Financial Economics: The Roles of Academic Expansion and Changes in US Capital Markets. *Accounting, Organizations and Society* 11(2), 171–192.

William Fry (2014). *ECON Publishes New Report on Proposed EU Money Market Fund Regulation.* http://hb.betterregulation.com/external/ECON%20Publishes%20New%20Report%20on%20Proposed%20EU%20Money%20Market%20Fund%20Regulation.pdf

WirtschaftsWoche (2008). *Finanzkrise: Geldmarktfonds gerettet,* October 15. www.wiwo.de/finanzen/finanzkrise-geldmarktfonds-gerettet/5475440.html

Woll, C. (2014). *The Power of Inaction: Bank Bailouts in Comparison.* Ithaca, NY: Cornell University Press.

World Bank (2008). Bank Regulation and Supervision: Extended Database. http://econ.worldbank.org/WBSITE/EXTERNAL/EXTDEC/EXTRESEARCH/0,contentMDK:20345037~pagePK:64214825~piPK:64214943~theSitePK:469382,00.html# Survey_III

(2015). Banking Supervision and External Auditors. Building a Constructive Relationship: Supervisors' Insights. https://openknowledge.worldbank.org/bitstream/handle/10986/25074/Banking0superv0supervisors0insights.pdf?sequence=1&isAllowed=y

Xiao, Y. (2009). French Banks Amid the Global Financial Crisis. IMF Working Paper. European Department, September 2009.

Young, K. (2012). Transnational Regulatory Capture? An Empirical Examination of the Transnational Lobbying of the Basel Committee on Banking Supervision. *Review of International Political Economy* 19(4), 663–688.

Zeff, S., A. F. Van der Wel, and K. Camfferman (2002). A Reflection on Company Financial Reporting After 10 Years. *Externe Verslaggeving* November, 513–519.

Zimmermann, J., J. R. Werner, and P. B. Volmer (2008). *Global Governance in Accounting- Rebalancing Public Power and Private Commitment.* London: Palgrave Macmillan.

Zingales, L. (2013). Preventing Economists' Capture. In D. Carpenter and D. A. Moss (eds.), *Preventing Regulatory Capture: Special Interest Influence and How to Limit It,* pp. 124–151. New York, NY: Cambridge University Press.

Index

accounting standards
    Dutch banks and, 154–56
    French banks and, 158–60
    German banks and, 161–63
Asset-Backed Commercial Paper market,
    4, 5. *See also* hybrid conduits;
    multiseller conduits; securities
    arbitrage conduits; shadow banking
    system; single-seller conduits;
    special-purpose entities; structured
    investment vehicles
    Basel Accords as furthering growth
        of and limiting national regulation
        of, 113–16
    Citibank and emergence of in
        1983, 86–88
    differential engagement and
        exposure to in U.S. vs. European
        countries, 16–19, 35–38
    European and U.S. bank exposure to
        in 2007, 42–43
    evolution of market segments of
        pre and postcrisis, 40–41, 225
    fall of during financial crisis,
        32–35, 202
    financial turbulence and core
        capital requirements in 1980s
        and, 84–86
    lack of regulation of in U.S. until
        1992, 88
    methodological methods used in
        study of, 18–19
    regulatory impact of sponsoring
        ABCP conduits on U.S. and
        European banks, 44–48
    regulatory intervention in
        postcrisis, 205–10
    regulatory loopholes and, 20–21
Asset-Backed Commercial Paper
    market (U.S.)

changes and regulatory unease in
    during 1990s, 96–100
Fin 46 rule and, 104–8
first regulatory dialogues on in
    1980s, 89–90
first regulatory framework on from
    1988–92, 90–96
uncertainty in after Enron, 102–3

Bank of America, 202
Bank Holding Company Act (1956,
    U.S.), 77, 79
Banking Act (1933, U.S.), 77
Basel Accords, 7, 53, 64, 110
    ABCP market growth and national
        regulation and, 113–16
    as leveling international
        competitiveness, 71–73
    revisions to postcrisis, 205
Basel Committee for Banking
    Supervision (BCBS), 11
Basel I
    first regulatory dialogues on ABCP
        market in 1980s and, 90
Basel II, 6
    negotiations from U.S.
        perspective, 100–2
Big Four auditing companies, 15, 18
Black, Julia, 16, 67

Citibank, 43, 202
    ABCP market emergence in 1983
        and, 86–88
cognitive capture, 52, 186
cognitive capture theory, 62–63
    lack of regulation of shadow
        banking and, 111
commercial paper market, rise of in
    U.S., 80–84
compliance officers, 15

Printed in the United States
By Bookmasters